# Critical Thinking

# Critical Thinking

Tools for Living an Examined Life

*First Edition*

Joshua Lott
*Sacred Heart University*

cognella
SAN DIEGO

Bassim Hamadeh, CEO and Publisher
Michelle Piehl, Senior Project Editor
Susana Christie, Senior Developmental Editor
Casey Hands, Production Editor
Emely Villavicencio, Senior Graphic Designer
Alexa Lucido, Licensing Manager
Natalie Piccotti, Director of Marketing
Kassie Graves, Senior Vice President, Editorial
Jamie Giganti, Director of Academic Publishing



Printed in the United States of America.

cognella® | ACADEMIC PUBLISHING
3970 Sorrento Valley Blvd., Ste. 500, San Diego, CA 92121

*To Mom, for your unconditional love, and to Nalin Ranasinghe,*
*for seeing more in me than anyone else ever did.*

# Brief Contents

# Detailed Contents

# Introduction

## A World without Critical Thinking?

Close your eyes for a moment and do as the late, great John Lennon once suggested—*imagine* a different world. Imagine a world that has no computers, no laptops, no smartphones, no cell phones, and not even any telephones. Imagine a world that has no televisions, no stereos, and certainly nothing that can be played on such devices. Imagine a world without music, literature, art, or any form of recreational entertainment. Imagine a world without automobiles, airplanes, buses, trains, or trucks. Imagine a world devoid of any machinery that aids humanity in the cultivation of the world around them. Imagine a world devoid of any form of medicine. Simply put, imagine that human beings remained forever in an indescribable state of nature without the capacity to narrate or document its existence and the events that took place within it. Such a world is the kind that would exist if humanity never discovered, refined, and augmented its capacity for *critical thinking*. And despite Lennon's insistence, imagining such a world is not so "easy if we try," as no conception of such a world can escape the determinations of modern consciousness. Any such conception will inevitably fall short of capturing with accuracy such a world. In essence, a world without critical thinking amounts to a world not only devoid of the amenities, luxuries, and comforts afforded by modern technology but also a world devoid of humanity in its current form.

So, what is "critical thinking?" The English word "critical" derives from the Greek word *kritikos*, which essentially means related to judging, fit for judging, or skilled in judging. Hence, becoming an efficient critical thinker essentially means learning how to judge correctly. Becoming a suitable judge entails several abilities, including the following:

- Distinguishing truth from falsity, or fact from fiction
- Distinguishing knowledge from opinion
- Abiding by the rules of reason and logic
- Understanding how ideas and beliefs are formed
- Becoming aware of the obstacles to knowledge and true belief
- Understanding scientific reasoning, scientific theories, and progress in science
- Understanding morality and moral reasoning

Courses in critical thinking are taught in some form at nearly every college and university across the globe. Typically, but not always, such courses form part of the curriculum administered by the philosophy faculty. Just as philosophy instructors more frequently than teachers of any other discipline must justify their profession and its place in modern-day education, the teachers of critical thinking must frequently justify the necessity of learning and embracing the subject.

Not only is there practical value to the study of critical thinking and philosophy—given that prospective employers of most businesses, corporations, and institutions desire individuals with a broad liberal education—but the two seem *inevitable*. To paraphrase the Greek philosopher Aristotle, as he famously argued in his *Protrepticus* (*Exhortation to Philosophy*, of which only fragments remain), "Either we ought to [think critically] or we ought not. If we ought, then we ought. But even if we ought not, we must [think critically] to *justify the view* that we ought not to [think critically]." If critical thinking is inevitable, then so is the use of the skills associated with it. Given this elegant argument by Aristotle, it will probably come as no surprise that the Greeks, and later the Romans, initiated the movement toward liberal education in the west. Modern Americans tend to favor mathematics, the natural sciences, technical fields, and business courses because of their distinctively *practical* value. The Greeks, however, emphasized the arts of grammar, logic, and rhetoric—collectively known as the ***Trivium***—for their practical effects. With a firm foundation in the art of persuasive speaking and a grasp of the basic rules of reasoning, one could parlay their skills into successful careers as lawyers, orators, or merchants. The more leisurely arts consisted of geometry, astronomy, music, and art, collectively known as the ***Quadrivium***. In essence, the sciences and mathematics afforded leisurely activities to those so inclined.

Despite the general proclivities of modern Americans, however, many founding fathers championed liberal education in America, especially the third president of the United States, Thomas Jefferson, who argued that liberal education provides citizens with a basic understanding of the function and operations of both their government and their rights, thereby allowing them to avoid tyranny and unjust treatment. The privilege of freedom means that people must learn to think autonomously, but with privilege comes responsibility. As free citizens, it is our responsibility to understand how to think, speak, and write clearly in addition to developing the capacity to distinguish right from wrong and thereby recognize injustice when it occurs. It may be argued that many of the greatest and most heinous crimes against humanity occurred because the individuals instigating them failed to grasp moral absolutes and value the dignity and worth of all humans equally. It is easy to detect the errors and failures of mathematicians and scientists and, thus, easier to correct such deviations from excellence. But failed philosophers with corrupted ideologies and lofty ideals they wish to force onto an uncooperative reality are far more dangerous and, much like cancer, are difficult to discern until they grow beyond control. Education in the *liberal arts* and *humanities* is necessary to allow *humans* to continue to value and enjoy *liberty*. Learning how to think critically is the best way to begin a liberal education!

## What You Will Learn in This Book

This book has chapters devoted to a wide variety of topics and disciplines that contribute to the development of critical thinking. Specifically, it has each of the following:

- A chapter devoted to the life and teachings of Socrates, a proverbial giant in the western intellectual tradition. Of specific importance in the chapter on Socrates are his famous claim that "the unexamined life is not worth living," in addition to the Socratic Method, and his moral teaching that the human soul requires justice, an inner harmony that cannot be achieved without reason.

- Chapters devoted to the primary obstacles to critical thinking since understanding these obstacles is tantamount to avoiding them. The first examines closely four specific fallacies first identified by the English philosopher Francis Bacon as the ***Idols of the Mind***. Bacon held that the mind is structured like a "crooked mirror" and, thus, does not always accurately reflect reality, hence, the *Idols of the Tribe*. In addition, every individual has a "cave" or a "den" of their own, which influences their beliefs, attitudes, values, and judgments, *Idols of the Cave*. Moreover, the use of language can be vague and misleading or can be used to arouse passions that cloud one's judgment, the most troublesome idols of all, which Bacon deems the *Idols of the Marketplace*. Finally, many people hold steadfastly to erroneous and/or defunct teachings, "sophistries and false dogmas," without ever truly thinking about them rationally, *Idols of the Theater*.
- An additional chapter addressing obstacles to critical thinking will allow students to consider several of the most common ***cognitive biases***, psychological propensities that affect objectivity. Forced to make sense of the world, the brain attempts to resolve several problems resulting from sensory overload, lack of meaning, and the need to both make fast decisions and remember important bits of information. The results, however, lead to drastic mistakes and prejudices in thought.
- A chapter that addresses sensation and perception, the difference between knowledge, truth, and belief, and the ways in which beliefs and knowledge develop through both innate abilities and interaction with the world, teaching students to trace the development of their beliefs about the world and to reassess their credibility regardless of how obvious they may seem.
- A chapter that continues the examination of knowledge by carefully considering different theories about what can be known about the external world based on human faculties and limitations in addition to the consensus of modern scientists.
- A chapter that explains general forms of reasoning—deduction and induction—in addition to general concepts in logic and diagramming arguments stated in ordinary language.
- A chapter that explains basic principles in both ***classical logic*** (sometimes called *categorical* or *Aristotelian logic*) and ***modern logic*** (sometimes called *truth-functional* or *symbolic logic*). In this chapter, students will learn how to identify and distinguish valid arguments from invalid arguments as well as how to represent sentences to reveal their underlying logical form.
- A chapter that focuses specifically on two common forms of inductive reasoning—***analogical reasoning*** and ***causal reasoning***. In this chapter, students will learn how to construct and evaluate arguments based on analogies and how to distinguish between different types of causes in addition to learning Mill's Methods—a set of five inductive methods for detecting causal relationships—and fundamental principles of scientific reasoning.
- A chapter that presents and explains the most common ***informal fallacies***, in which students will learn how to identify and avoid errors that occur due to personal attacks, emotional appeals, diversionary tactics, faulty induction, false presumptions, and ambiguity in language.
- Finally, a chapter that explains moral reasoning and theories of morality that may be applied to concrete situations in which one's decisions and actions affect the well-being of others.

## How to Use This Book

Each chapter in this book has the following sections:

- An introductory section usually titled "Preparing to Read Chapter X." Each section presents an overview of the themes of the chapter, a set of terms to look for while reading, and a set of open-ended questions for consideration, questions that do not demand an immediate answer but rather compel the student to think about the importance of the current chapter. Before reading the entire chapter, devote careful thought to these questions.
- The main text of the chapter, which presents and explains the themes of the chapter in detail. Typically, bullet points and boldfaced writing highlight important terms and concepts. Students are strongly advised at least to commit to memory the highlighted terms and concepts.
- A chapter summary that reinforces key concepts and terms, as well as more concisely reinforcing the central narrative of each chapter. It is strongly recommended that students carefully look over the chapter summary before reading the chapter itself, as doing so will present a map of the terrain before the actual journey, so to speak.
- Finally, a set of problems and open-ended questions usually titled, "Exercises for Practice and Application." While students will have to use what they learned in each chapter to complete these problems and questions, they are advised to look over the problems before reading each chapter, becoming acquainted with them and allowing for a cognitive incubation period of sorts before directly addressing them.

Ultimately, however, the goal of this book is to allow students to become more fully human by augmenting and refining their most distinctly human attribute—the ***power of reason***.

# 1

# "The Unexamined Life Is Not Worth Living." The Life and Teachings of Socrates

INTRODUCTION

## Preparing to Read Chapter 1

This chapter explores the life and major teachings of Socrates who, alongside Plato and Aristotle, remains one of the three most famous Greek philosophers. The teachings of Socrates will be contrasted with those of the sophists, who in many ways served as the chief opponents not only of Socrates but also of critical thinking in general. In addition, the inspiration for the mission to which Socrates devoted himself and the ideas of later thinkers from both antiquity and the modern world who manifested a Socratic pedagogy—specifically Plato, Aristotle, and the French thinker, Jean-Jacques Rousseau—will be presented.

## Why Study Socrates Today?

The question of the relevance of thinkers from the ancient world, including that of Socrates, arises for many students. In short, the importance of Socrates in the history of Western thought and the relevance of his teachings for the purposes of contemporary everyday life cannot be underestimated. Here are just a few reasons why:

- The Socratic method is central to critical thinking and problem-solving in a wide variety of disciplines.
- Plato, the most famous of Socrates's students, established the Academy, the world's first university of higher learning. It is entirely possible that without Socrates, higher education would be much different today, if not nonexistent.
- Socrates's intellectual pursuits arose from practical concerns, specifically about how one can live a happy and meaningful life.
- Socrates concerned himself not only with how one's beliefs and actions affect the world and others but also with how they affect oneself.
- Socrates set a near-divine example of courage and integrity that few could imitate, let alone replicate. His strength of character sets a moral standard that many world leaders, government officials, CEOs, and teachers should strive to emulate. In fact, it is not uncommon for historians and intellectuals to compare Socrates to Jesus Christ, Buddha, Gandhi, and Confucius.

Socrates is, without question, one of the first giants of the Western intellectual tradition. Standing on his shoulders, one will see far and wide, learn much, live well, and leave a legacy of goodness enshrined in the very same immortality he achieved.

## AS YOU READ, WATCH FOR THE FOLLOWING TERMS, PHRASES, AND PEOPLE

- The Maxims of the Delphic Oracle
  - Know thyself
  - Do nothing to excess
- Plato's *Apology*
  - "The unexamined life is not worth living"
  - Knowledge of ignorance
  - Care for the soul
  - The invincibility of goodness – No one can harm a just person
    - Justice is good for the soul
    - Injustice is harmful to the soul
  - Virtue is knowledge
  - The autonomy of ethics
- The Socratic Method
  - Dialectic
  - Dialogue
- Protagorean Relativism – "Man is the measure of all things"
  - Alethic Relativism
- Nihilism
- Skepticism
- Subjectivism
- Thrasymachus – "Justice is the will of the stronger"
  - Nietzsche – "Will to power"
- Ethical Relativism
- Anamnesis Thesis – "Learning is recollection"
  - Meno
- Rousseau
  - The natural goodness of humanity
  - *Discourse on the Arts and Sciences*
  - *Emile*

- Education from nature
- Education from others
- Education from things

**KEEP THE FOLLOWING QUESTIONS IN MIND AS YOU READ**

How are the life and teachings of Socrates relevant to today's world?

How are the life and teachings of Socrates relevant to my life?

What does it mean to live an "examined life?"

Why is it important to live an "examined life?"

What is the soul?

How can I be certain that the soul is different than the body?

How are the ideas and mistakes of the sophists relevant to today's world?

How is the legacy of Socrates reflected in the teachings of Plato, Aristotle, and Rousseau?

How can the Socratic method be used to improve modern methods of education?

## "There Is No One Wiser than Socrates." The Life, Mission, and Teachings of Socrates

### The Central Maxims of the Delphic Oracle and the Mission of Socrates

Inscribed on the temple of the Oracle at Delphi were many maxims of which the two most central were,

(1) Know thyself, and

(2) Do all things in moderation.

These maxims are central not only to the life and mission of Socrates but also to the never-ending quest of every human to find happiness and meaning in life. Suppose you ask a therapist, counselor, teacher, professor, priest, pastor, or psychic the oft-asked question "What is the meaning of life?" or the related question "How can I be happy?" and the answer you received matched the two central maxims of the Delphic Oracle word for word. Most would probably dismiss such counsel and leave frustrated. The problem is not that most people would lack the intelligence or the insight to understand that these succinct principles are, indeed, the key to both meaning and happiness, but that few people have the patience and diligence to seriously reflect on and follow such advice. Most people want a quick and easy answer along with a detailed list of step-by-step instructions. Few people wish to figure out the answers to deep mysteries on their own.

The first maxim, "Know thyself," forces the individual to think about what he or she is, to think deeply about the nature of a human person, in fact. If one is to be happy, one must pursue the things that will make a human being happy. Items that please a squirrel, a cat, a dog, or any other nonhuman animal will not suffice. While no one would honestly deny that simple pleasures and comforts are desirable and even necessary, their returns soon diminish. Even a very young child who successfully wins a video game multiple times will eventually become bored with it and wish to move on to something more challenging. It is for similar reasons that our minds and intellects can never truly develop if they are not challenged by rigorous and difficult tasks. Yet, ironically, people are still natural creatures and like other natural objects try to find the path of least resistance. So much easier is it to reach for a popular and entertaining magazine than to dust off *The Complete Works of Shakespeare* or *Plato's Collected Dialogues*! The point: if you wish to be happy and live a full life, then you must first know and understand *what* you are. You must understand what makes you human in addition to possessing an awareness of your own unique abilities, talents, and preferences.

Moreover, the second central maxim, "Do all things in moderation," is tied directly to the first. The English word "moderation" has its equivalent in the Greek σωφροσύνη, or "sophrosyne." While the original Greek term signified a plethora of character traits, the term as it is understood today refers to self-control, refraining from excessive indulgences or behaviors. The second maxim, thus, serves as an admonition to know one's limits and boundaries. Self-knowledge, thus, is a necessary condition for self-control, and both for living a full and happy life. Refuse to take any risks, and you will never reap the benefits of crucial opportunities. Take too many risks without carefully thinking them through, and you will likely lose everything. Never take a pleasant holiday to enjoy the fruits of your labor, and your life becomes a veritable unrelenting and thankless grind that will make you wonder why exactly you labored in the first place. Remain on a permanent vacation in which you indulge in alcohol, recreational drugs, and unhealthy food, and you will likely become a homeless and irretrievable addict within a few months.

Socrates, whose father is rumored to have helped build the temple of the Oracle at Delphi, not only embraced these central maxims but lived them. Even though he lived a humble life as a stone cutter, he served as a soldier in the Peloponnesian Wars and reportedly carried a wounded soldier named Alcibiades to safety. The young man and Socrates became lifelong friends and were rumored to be lovers. Socrates also amassed quite a following of friends and de facto students, as he spent most of his leisure time in the *agora* (marketplace) conversing about deep, theoretical questions.

One of his friends, Chaerephon (whose name literally means "bat boy") became convinced of Socrates's acumen and journeyed to the Delphic Oracle, asking if anyone is wiser than Socrates. **The Oracle answered that no one is wiser than Socrates.** This answer startled Socrates since he did not think himself very wise or intelligent. In fact, among his most famous assertions is his **profession of ignorance**:

- "All I know is that I do not know."

Determined to establish the truth of this claim, Socrates set out to test himself against the most famous and reputable teachers during his time. During these conversations, the interlocutors speaking with Socrates came across looking rather foolish. Eventually, Socrates came to understand the Oracle's assessment of him: at least Socrates knew that he was not wise, whereas others professed to possess true wisdom.

Nonetheless, Socrates became a hero to many, including the youth of Athens. Inspired by Socrates, they applied his conversational tactics on their parents. Hence, not only did Socrates aggravate many powerful people in Athens, but the parents of his youthful coalition as well. Subsequently, the people of Athens brought Socrates to trial on charges of corrupting the youth and impiety (as he began referring to Gods not recognized by the Athenian canon, specifically, a monotheistic God). Despite a legendary eloquent defense, a jury of 500 found Socrates guilty and sentenced him to death by ingestion of hemlock.

- Plato's *Apology* (from the Greek *apologia*, meaning "defense") details the trial of Socrates and the defense he put forth.

Supposedly, Plato attended the trial in person and visited Socrates in prison on the day of his execution. Socrates could very easily have escaped, but he decided to remain in prison and accept his punishment. Even though

Socrates never transcribed any of his teachings, several theses he put forth during his defense and during various other conversations in his lifetime may be attributed to him.

## Socrates's Basic Teachings

Even though he never published any of his ideas, many profound ideas are attributed to Socrates. Principally, he accepted each of the following:

- The unexamined life is not worth living.
- **Dualism**, the position that a human being is both a body and a soul, or both a body and a nonphysical mind.
- **Curatorship of the soul**, the idea that care for and improvement of the soul is the most important goal of life.
- The **autonomy of ethics and morality**, the idea that ethical and moral principles have independent intrinsic value and, thus, are not merely instrumental.
- The primary goal of the soul is to achieve **justice**, understood as inner harmony.
- As the primary goal of the soul, **justice is good for the soul,** while **injustice is bad for the soul**.
- **Virtue is knowledge**, or people only do wrong out of ignorance.

All these teachings are interconnected and, thus, will be addressed together.

First and foremost, Socrates propounded an exhortation to philosophical inquiry expressed by his famous statement, "The unexamined life is not worth living." Imagine buying a car that you never drive or purchasing a household appliance or a tool that you never use so much as once. Most would conclude that your purchase was not worth the expense. Surely, life is far more precious than any car or household appliance. Given that life is precious, it is the responsibility of everyone to make *something* of one's life. Just as one must examine an appliance or tool to understand how to use it, figuring out what to make of one's life requires examining it as well, which in turn demands asking questions about why one exists and what one can contribute, both for one's own well-being and that of others.

In essence, it is the nature of human beings to ask, "Why?" Humans are rational creatures and, thus, are reflective and inquisitive creatures. Awareness of our own existence inevitably leads to questions about its meaning and purpose. The problem is not that there are no answers but that there are too many! To ignore the question "Why?" is to ignore one's humanity and live as a totally different kind of animal.

In connection with his insistence on examining one's life is the Socratic belief in the human soul. Even though he professed to know for certain only his own ignorance, Socrates seemed to hold the position that modern philosophers of the mind refer to as *dualism*. Socrates, and Plato after him, insisted that the soul is more important and in fact more real than the body. The soul comprises the true being and essence of the human person. Plato gave a more detailed account of the soul and its faculties than did Socrates in addition to providing several arguments for the soul's immortality, suggesting that since the soul is nonphysical, it cannot be destroyed. Nonetheless, both thinkers agreed about the immortality of the soul and on the importance of **curatorship of the soul**: care for and improvement of the soul is the most important goal of life. In keeping with the maxim to "know thyself," one must understand that one is more than a merely visible, tangible, and perishable being. Living an examined life means knowing and understanding one's soul.

Since the soul is the essence of the person, what the person needs to be happy basically translates into what the soul needs to be happy. But the question naturally arises as to why Socrates would believe in the soul and in anything more than that which is revealed by the senses while only professing his own ignorance. The answer seems to be that Socrates believed in moral absolutes. Specifically, he maintained the **autonomy of ethics and morality**, the idea that ethical and moral principles have independent intrinsic value and, thus, are not merely instrumental. In other words, the autonomy of ethics and morality is a thesis that implies that everyone ought simply to do the right thing because it is the right thing rather than because one hopes for a reward or fears punishment. The autonomy of ethics and morality and the importance of care for and improvement of the soul converge at the concept of justice. That is, **the primary goal of the soul is to achieve justice**.

While a complete account of the nature of justice cannot be given here, suffice it to say that Socrates understood justice by analogy with physical bodily health. For the body to be healthy, it must be balanced and maintain homeostasis. Likewise, for the soul to be healthy, it must be balanced and in harmony. And the only way for the soul to be healthy and just, the person must live a moral life.

The implications of moral autonomy and the prescription of justice for the soul comprise the remainder of the teachings of Socrates: **the invincibility of goodness** and the thesis that **virtue is knowledge**. To begin with the former, Socrates held that since the most important goal of life is for the soul to achieve justice, he went so far as to claim that *no one can harm a just person*. Specifically, this thesis of the invincibility of goodness applies to the soul, rather than the body. A just person can be harmed physically, but no harm can come to the soul of such a person. That is, if a person is truly good, possessed of great integrity and honor, then no matter how much physical pain one endures, one's mind will remain balanced and at peace. Hence, **justice is good for the soul**, regardless of the circumstances. The corollary of this principle, however, is that **injustice is bad or harmful to the soul** regardless of what one gains by trespassing against others. A famous Socratic claim connected to the invincibility of goodness and its corollaries is the following idea: *it is better to suffer injustice than it is to commit it*. Thus, by harming others, one *harms one's own soul*.

Admittedly, these principles are difficult to digest in their abstract form. A concrete example will be helpful. Combat veterans who return from war often suffer from post-traumatic stress disorder, not only because of the harm they endured but also because of the pain and suffering they doled out to their enemy combatants. Such mental illnesses likely would not be so prevalent if humans were supposed to be comfortable with killing. Though our species became the rulers of the animal kingdom and in fact the planet, the irony is that physically we are comparably weaker than most other species. Nature armed humanity with very little to defend itself. Humans have no thick, protective fur to shield them from the cold, no claws or fangs, no wings with which to fly, and we are considerably smaller than most of our cousins in the animal kingdom. Humans are not supposed to be natural killers and to do so, even in self-defense, conflicts with the inner dictates of our nature.

The criminal element within humanity seems to run contrary to the previous argument, especially when considering the most violent and dangerous of criminals, such as serial murderers and rapists. For example, imagine a man who early in life suffers many humiliating rejections from the women he fancies. Subsequently, he develops a misogynistic attitude and begins fantasizing about harming and killing young women. Such a mentality coupled with the fantasizing itself each constitutes injustices. Through them, the desire to harm women for real becomes increasingly strong and intense, rendering fantasy insufficient. Eventually, the man will have to rape and kill a woman for real. But with that initial act, the urge only grows. The assailant will have to find another victim, then another, and still another, ad infinitum. Does not such a person enjoy killing? Does not such an individual achieve a kind of "peace" with himself? Perhaps this individual is self-actualized since he lives out his fantasies. Surely, he incurs the risk of getting caught and losing his freedom but let us suppose that this man remains undetected until the day of his death.

Has this individual made himself worse? Socrates would answer in the affirmative. Not only does this individual damage himself through his actions, but he is even worse off than his victims. First, besides other murderers and rapists, statistically a remarkably insignificant percentage of the population, very few people consider violent criminals to be happy. If one were happy and at peace with oneself, one would not have to destroy the lives of others. Moreover, in most cases, the experiences of serial killers and rapists, like with many leisurely activities in life, produce diminishing returns. After the first kill, each subsequent kill produces less intense gratification. Just as with drug addictions, nothing compares to that elusive "first high," and each subsequent kill only takes the addict further from the level of wanting the drug to *needing* it. The fun is essentially over when a want becomes a need and a fun, leisurely game becomes a mission.

The freedom such an assailant achieves by evading detection constitutes freedom in name only, as the individual is enslaved and ruled by his appetites. His rage, vengeance, and destructiveness only brought him to the very bottom of the hill, dooming him to the fate of unrequited repetition. Hence, the final Socratic principle to be addressed here: the idea that *virtue is knowledge*. This principle does not necessarily mean that if one simply knows the definition of a virtue such as courage, one then becomes courageous. It should also be distinguished from the notion that if one simply knows and understands the difference between the laws of one's culture and one's own intentions, then one is incapable of doing harm to anyone. This principle is best understood in a negative way, that *people only do wrong out of ignorance*. In essence, this term means that people would only harm others and break the law because they expect to achieve something good from the experience. The undetected serial killer, for example, believed that his course would lead to a much different outcome. Perhaps if he knew all along what would truly make him happy, he would have chosen differently. It brings us directly back to the first maxim of the Delphic Oracle: know thyself! Knowing oneself means knowing and understanding what is best for oneself, knowing one's limitations, and what is dangerous and harmful to oneself so that one can avoid such things.

## The Sophists

Prior to his notoriety, the most famous teachers during the lifetime of Socrates were the **sophists**. Essentially, the sophists and Socrates became public opponents of each other. Plato, in fact, devoted many of his dialogues to conversations between Socrates and famous sophists.

- The most basic teaching of the sophists consisted in an exhortation to live by appearances and pursue practical affairs whereby one could amass wealth and power and live a luxurious life.
- The significance of the sophists is that they are the first teachers on record to receive payment for teaching. Primarily, they taught **rhetoric**, the art of persuasive speaking.

The sophists owe their success largely to their ability to practice what they taught. Many parents hired the sophists to teach their children rhetoric so that they could win court cases or become famous orators, pursuant to the very wealth and comforts promised to those who learned the craft. In many ways, the sophists were the lawyers and motivational speakers of ancient Greece. If someone brought a lawsuit against you, you could hire a sophist to defend you. If a statesman needed to pass a law that would limit the freedom of his citizens, he could hire a sophist to convince them that the law really served their best interests. Even in medicine, the talents of the sophists could be useful. If a doctor had to convince a patient to endure a painful cauterization, he could hire a sophist to persuade the patient for him. The nature of their work demanded that many of the sophists live itinerant lifestyles, traveling to different communities.

The major sophists were prominent between the years of 460 and 380 BCE. The early sophists consisted of the likes of Gorgias, Protagoras, Prodicus, and Hippias. The later sophists consisted of men such as Thrasymachus, Antiphon, and Critias (Plato's uncle). The teachings of Protagoras, Gorgias, and Thrasymachus best capture the central principles of the sophists. Protagoras famously asserted a form of subjective relativism also called **alethic relativism:**

- "Man is the measure of all things," from which it follows that truth is relative to the individual.

Gorgias, also a famous teacher, not only seemed to embrace subjectivism but also **nihilism** and **skepticism**, given his famous three assertions:

1) Nothing exists (nihilism).
2) Even if anything does exist, it cannot be known (skepticism).
3) Even if anything can be known, it cannot be communicated (subjectivism).

In keeping with the relativistic mantra of his predecessors, Thrasymachus embraced a form of moral relativism based on power:

- "Justice is the will of the stronger." In other words, might makes right.

For Thrasymachus, reality is a manifestation of and struggle for power. Those who are strongest overtake the weak and subsequently make the rules. But power equated with physical force and strength is a relative consideration. An individual is only powerful in comparison to someone or something weaker. Any regime, thus, can be overthrown by one that is itself more powerful. The unstable, shifting reality of the world, thus, cannot sustain moral absolutes. The nineteenth-century German philosopher, Friedrich Nietzsche seemed to propound a similar conception of reality, which he described as "**will to power**."

The motivations of these men to embrace these teachings trace back to earlier periods of the history of philosophy. Many thinkers prior to the sophists and Socrates (now known collectively as the pre-Socratics) attempted to discern and explain the basic nature of things and the apparent order of the universe by finding a universal, underlying substance that can account for all beings, an ἀρχή, or *archē*, literally "beginning" or "origin." The term can also mean *foundation*.

The significance of the pre-Socratics is that they were the first thinkers to emphasize empirical experience rather than mythology. Hence, they became the first true scientists of the Western world. The first of these thinkers, Thales, proposed that everything is water. His student, Anaximander, objected that no one element could explain everything and that the nature of the universe is boundless. Synthesizing these two theories, Anaximenes proposed a more "boundless" physical element as the foundation, air. Emphasizing form over matter, the mathematician Pythagoras suggested that everything consists of numbers and ratios. Privy to the idea that reality is in a constant state of change or flux, and that only strife, conflict, or war can cause change, Heraclitus proposed fire as the possible foundational element. The logician, Parmenides of Elea, following his rationalistic inclinations, argued, "Whatever is, is," meaning that being is absolute. Since nothingness cannot be conceived, it is impossible. Moreover, since any process of change would introduce nothingness, change is impossible. It follows that the appearance of change is only an illusion. Zeno of Elea attempted to defend these arguments using several paradoxes, but other more commonsense-minded thinkers resumed empirical inquiry. Empedocles, for instance, suggested that all reality consists of a combination of four basic elements—earth, air, fire, and water. Anaxagoras proposed that all beings originally consisted of one unified reality. However, this reality became separated from itself and, as a result, all things contain the "seeds" (*spermata*) of everything else. The final thinkers of this long tradition are the world's first atomic physicists, Democritus and Leucippus, who maintained that all reality consists, at bottom, of tiny indivisible atoms, constantly shifting and conjoining to form substances.

Ultimately, there appears to be very little, if any, general consensus between these thinkers and no universal procedure for determining which theory is the best. Moreover, there are two central schools of thought, the rationalistic followers of Parmenides and the naturalists inspired by Heraclitus and the atomic physicists. The former argue that change is impossible and, thus, that our commonsense experience is an illusion. The latter, on the other hand, argue that the solid, physical substances that we observe are not what they seem to be and, thus, that our commonsense experience cannot be trusted! These theoretical controversies left little optimism for the efficacy of philosophical inquiry and the discovery of an absolute foundation for reality and morality.

## The Socratic Method

While his exchanges with many of the famous sophists are well-documented, the details of the conversations between them and Socrates cannot here be addressed in full. However, the question that lingers is whether there is in fact a way to ascertain basic, universal principles. Recall that despite his profession of ignorance, Socrates maintained several basic principles. He also insisted that the most effective way to instruct people is through conversation. That is, truth cannot simply be told to students; rather, students must discover it autonomously. The process of conversation that facilitates such an education is **dialectic**.

- Dialectic consists of a process of question and answer between two or more people discussing a specific topic or issue. An individual asks a question that is answered by the interlocutor. The answer, however, raises an additional question that requires a further answer and possibly modifications to the original answer. This process continues until the interlocutors either exhaust the topic fully, reach a satisfactory conclusion, or reach an impasse that resists solution.

The process of dialectic can be illustrated through two people engaged in a **dialogue**. A dialogue can easily be confused with a debate. Debates have the following features:

1) Debates are *adversarial* in that each participant defends an opposing viewpoint on an issue, and typically, there is a winner and a loser.
2) After a debate, the loser usually is expected to relinquish his or her position, having been "proven wrong."

In contrast, dialogues have the following features:

1) Dialogues are *collaborations* in which the two interlocutors attempt to better understand an idea or issue rather than contests in which one tries to defeat an opponent.
2) At the end of a dialogue, no one is expected to relinquish his or her beliefs, but each participant in the process will usually have a deeper and richer understanding of them.[1]

1 See Chapter 1 of Jay Rosenberg, *The Practice of Philosophy: A Handbook for Beginners*, "The Character of Philosophy," pp 4–11 (London: Pearson, 1995).

The pedagogy of Socrates is best understood as a collaboration between friends who are trying to discover universal truth.

## Socratic Dialectic

The Socratic method of dialectic usually occurs in three steps:

- Step 1: Socrates asks a question that his interlocutor answers quickly, efficiently, and with total confidence. In some cases, the interlocutor may simply state a position on a topic or provide a definition for a complex term, such as "justice" or "courage."
- Step 2: Socrates exposes flaws in the interlocutor's answer/position, thus forcing the interlocutor to revise his answer/position.

Typically, this process will continue until the final stage:

- Step 3: The interlocutor either (a) contradicts himself or (b) reaches a theoretical impasse (also known as an *aporia*). In either case, the interlocutor is forced to admit his ignorance on the topic or issue under investigation.

Through this process, Socrates attempts to show his "students" that the knowledge they seek cannot be obtained easily and cannot be simply delivered to them by the teacher. While several dialogues illustrate this process, the most efficient example of it occurs in *Meno*.

## The Recollection Thesis and Socratic Pedagogy in *Meno*

At Tulane, my grad school professor of ancient philosophy, Ronna Burger, once taught me that the key to understanding a dialogue of Plato is embedded within the very first word of the dialogue. The first words of *Meno* are "Tell me." The central question of the dialogue is whether virtue can be taught or rather whether a person can become a good person simply by being told what constitutes a virtuous character. This central question and the conversation surrounding it raises a broader question about the nature of education and whether one can learn simply by being told information. The process of the conversation in the dialogue suggests that genuinely educating a person demands that the teacher allow a student the opportunity to discover truth autonomously. After all, the English word "education" derives from the Latin word "ex-ducere," which literally means "to lead out of." *Meno* displays Socratic education as the process by which the teacher guides the student into developing a more lucid and explicit awareness of universal truths that they already know but only in a vague way.

In their initial conversation, Socrates insists that Meno define virtue since by establishing the nature of virtue they can then know its properties, whether it is *teachable*. After several failed attempts to define virtue, Meno proposes to Socrates the **paradox of inquiry**:

1. If you know what X is, you *would not* ask about it.
2. If you do not know what X is, you *cannot* ask about it.
3. It seems to follow that inquiry about anything is impossible.

Hence, their current conversation about virtue seems doomed to failure.

Socrates, however, proposes a solution that is sometimes called the **anamnesis thesis**:

- **Learning is recollection (remembering).** Taken literally, this thesis implies that everyone lived past lives, during which we acquired knowledge, and when we are reborn into our current life, we recall that knowledge.

Many religions of the world have a similar doctrine of **reincarnation**. Socrates demonstrates this thesis with a young boy, one of the workers on the estate that Meno is visiting. Supposedly, this boy had no previous education in geometry. Socrates, nonetheless, gives him a difficult geometry problem to solve, asking him the length of the sides of a square with an area of 8 feet. The boy hastily suggests 4 feet as the answer, half the area. Of course, this answer is incorrect, as such a square would have an area of 16 feet. The boy then amends his answer, proposing 3 feet as the length of the side. Once, again, he is proven wrong, as such a square would have an area of 9 feet.

At this point, the boy becomes bewildered but has an increased determination to solve the problem. Socrates offers to help by drawing the following picture:

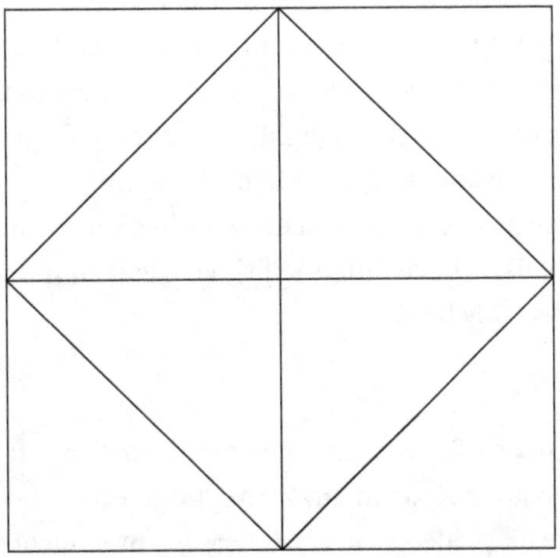

He first draws the square with an area of 16 feet, the blue square, corresponding to the boy's initial answer. He then subdivides the square into four separate squares, delineated by the black lines. He then cuts each smaller square in half, illustrated by the red diagonal lines. Once this picture is complete, the boy instantly recognizes the diagonal line as the side of the 8-foot square, and he is correct. Since each of the four squares has an area of 4 feet (1/4 of 16) and is then cut in half. As half of 4 is 2, and 2 multiplied by 4 is 8, the four diagonal lines comprise the 8-foot square.

The boy seemingly intuited the answer, recognizing it clearly after a series of confident but erroneous answers. Ultimately, only by getting the wrong answer several times did the boy become genuinely invested in solving the problem. Moreover, mathematicians recognize the square root of 8 as an irrational number, not a whole number that an individual would hazard as a guess, especially not a boy with no formal education. Truth is, thus, more complex than any simple lesson that can be conveyed through concrete terms and convenient definitions, even in mathematics in which one is guaranteed a decisive and certain answer.

Socrates suggests that the boy must have known the answer all along, learned from a previous existence. But the lesson to be learned from *Meno* need not literally invoke reincarnation. Rather, the exchange between Socrates and the boy shows the Socratic method in action and demonstrates its effectiveness in engaging students and augmenting their ability to discover truth autonomously, without having simply to be told.

## The Legacy of Socrates: Plato, Aristotle, and Rousseau

Three thinkers who successfully carried the proverbial "torch" of Socrates in the history of the Western intellectual tradition are Plato, Aristotle, and Jean-Jacques Rousseau. It is not a surprise that the first two followed in the footsteps of the Gadfly of Athens, with Plato a student of Socrates and Aristotle a student of Plato, but the inclusion of Rousseau might surprise people. Hopefully, I can clarify my choices.

### Plato

While his mentor believed that conversation is the only way truly to educate one's students rather than forcing them to memorize principles recorded in writing, Plato chose the best of both worlds, writing in dialogue and putting on display the process of dialectic. Plato's dialogues brought to life the Socratic method and illustrated Socrates the man at his very best. Even though all the themes of Plato's philosophy cannot be addressed here, the general consensus among philosophers is that Plato believed that there is a transcendent realm of universal, immaterial, eternal entities, Forms, of which all concrete, physical objects are mere imperfect copies. As knowledge requires truth, and truth demands that belief match reality, genuine knowledge can only be ascertained by acquaintance with the Forms. Plato seemed to embrace the recollection thesis, as Socrates argues in more than one dialogue that we all have prior experience of the Forms in previous lifetimes. Through the process of dialectic, contradictions can be exposed and eliminated leading to achieving genuine knowledge through the Forms. Plato also defended the idea that it is the purpose of the human soul to achieve justice, a virtue achieved when one possesses the cardinal virtues of wisdom, courage, and moderation. For Plato, like his mentor, the primary flaw of humanity is ignorance, as no one would do wrong if everyone knew what was truly best.

### Aristotle

Even though he was Plato's student, Aristotle rejected many of the doctrines traditionally attributed to Plato. As an empiricist and a natural scientist, Aristotle rejected any form of the recollection thesis and staunchly criticized the theory of the Forms. Nonetheless, like his predecessor, Aristotle was a proponent of virtue ethics, and his conception of virtue does not stray too far from that of Plato. For Aristotle, virtue is a trait of character manifested through habitual action and is the mean between two extremes. For example, the virtue of courage is the mean between actions that are totally rash and not well thought out on the one hand and actions that are completely cowardly on the other hand. The Socratic method applies to Aristotle's thought in many ways, but most explicitly in the process through which individuals must find the mean between extremes of action. No one can simply tell a person how to be courageous, for instance. One must expose oneself to situations through which one can gradually develop the character trait, situations in which eventually one simply knows how to act, just as the boy in *Meno* recognized the correct answer when he saw it. Aristotle suggests that happiness is the goal of life but that the only way to achieve happiness is through a life of contemplation, which demands deep, reflective thought. As humans are rational creatures, human happiness demands the augmentation of rationality. I will explain Aristotle's ethics in more detail in a later chapter.

### Jean-Jacques Rousseau

From Plato and Aristotle, quite a leap is taken to Jean-Jacques Rousseau. Rousseau was an eighteenth-century French thinker whose writings on education coincide with the implicit assumptions of Plato and Socrates. While Rousseau's writings are very diverse, the unifying theme in all of his thought is **the principle of natural goodness**:

- People are basically good, and it is through external forces and social institutions alone that they become bad.

Rousseau's principle of natural goodness echoes the famous lyrics of Pink Floyd's "Another Brick in the Wall" since he seems to suggest that if people are simply *left alone*, they would be fine! That is, so long as people are free to do as they please without interference from others, we would essentially all instinctively and naturally function in peaceful, civil ways.

Rousseau's central principle also hearkens to the Platonic-Socratic notion of the invincibility of goodness, the idea that anything inherently good is good for the soul and that anything inherently bad is bad for the soul. Rousseau also seems to embrace the notion that no one would do wrong willingly but only when acting on the specious assumption that harming another person in some way would yield some good. If people are basically good, then they would only seek out things that are good and would have no interest in harming anyone. But Rousseau maintains that modern society corrupts individuals in many ways, primarily by forcing people to develop false, artificial needs and desires that have no built-in natural limits. The worst event that ever happened to human beings was that they became self-aware and left the state of nature for modern civilization, a shift inaugurated when one individual supposedly needed the help of another, paving the way for complex social relations and increasingly complicated needs and desires. In short, people want things that they do not truly need, but they would not desire such luxuries if not for the imposition of society. For instance, no one would desire an everyday item such as coffee were it not introduced by one's culture, promoted, and advertised on a regular basis. And once one tastes it for the first time, it becomes an irresistible need without which one cannot function.

In his first major publication, *Discourse on the Arts and Sciences*, Rousseau wrote an award-winning essay responding to a question posed by the Academy at Dijon: "Has the restoration of the arts and sciences had a purifying effect on morals?" Rousseau's answer was a resounding, "NO!" Rousseau's essay is divided into two parts. In Part I, Rousseau enumerates several examples of cultures that became far more depraved despite achieving sophistication, including the Greeks and the Chinese, but the most prominent example is that of the Roman Empire. Emperors such as Nero, a murderer and a necrophiliac, as well as Caligula, who bestowed consulship on his horse merely to make a point about his authority, testify to the claim that sophistication in the arts and sciences does not alone make people morally reputable. In Part II, though, Rousseau explains why sophistication in the arts and sciences cultivates moral deterioration. In short, academia in Rousseau's time emphasized the achievement of esteem, reward, and glory rather than virtue and truth. Once a position, such as a professorship, is valued within a society, one might seek such a position merely for material reward, thereby disrupting personal integrity. Moreover, a coveted position may be achieved only by an elite few. Those in such positions may, to reinforce their own sense of superiority, oppress and shame others. In turn, those who cannot achieve these positions feel resentment and envy toward those who do. Institutional education, thus, constitutes an education in name only and really impedes both education and happiness.

Rousseau proposes a form of education that facilitates the recovery of *natural spontaneity*, exemplified by the successful student of the Socratic method who intuits truth upon its discovery, as well as by the successful student of Aristotelian virtue theory who discovers the proverbial mean between extremes and adaptively tailors oneself to many different situations. In *Emile*, Rousseau's famous treatise on education in which he raises the titular pupil, Emile, Rousseau distinguishes between three kinds of education:

- **Education from Nature:** The internal development of one's faculties and organs.
- **Education from Others:** The internalization of principles and customs that one learns from one's culture and from various institutions and authority figures.
- **Education from Things:** The use we learn to make of the development of our faculties through our unique, personal experiences of events and things in our environment.

Rousseau would insist that far too much emphasis is placed on education from *others* and not nearly enough on education from nature or from things. Education from others is the most conventional, but it does not necessarily extend a person's intelligence or improve their understanding. It only prepares people to observe and safeguard the values of a community, which are usually determined by those with the power and authority to do so, and as Rousseau argued in his famous essay, such an education can cultivate animosity between people and lead them to seek prestige rather than truth.

Only by first emphasizing an individual's natural development and then allowing that individual to experience his or her world and environment firsthand can the individual cultivate genuine curiosity and creativity analogous to the bewilderment that provokes the desire to seek truth and become a person of integrity and honor. Creativity does not necessarily refer to originality but autonomy in thought and action. Two people may develop the exact same invention, but so long as they did so independently, both are creative. The first creative activity of humans is learning how to walk since doing so forces humans to break free of habitual patterns and figure out how to do something new on their own. Throughout *Emile,* Rousseau applies a long-term variation of the Socratic method, igniting genuine curiosity within the child but also cultivating the child to do only what the tutor wants! That is, the child not only learns the principles of the tutor but learns to recognize and accept them as his own.

Rousseau's pedagogy directs itself not merely at teaching a child information but also at teaching a child to be a genuine person, in connection with the maxims of the Delphic Oracle. In the appendix to his *First Discourse,* Rousseau mentioned those he recognized as true geniuses of his time, one of whom was Francis Bacon (referred to by his Latin name of Verulaum). Chapter 2 devotes itself to an examination of Bacon's Idols of the Mind, the most general obstacles to critical thinking.

## Chapter Summary and Key Points to Remember

Socrates's contributions to culture and intellectual history serve as a foundation for critical thinking. The highlights of the life and teachings of Socrates are the following:

- Socrates espoused a form of epistemic humility, suggesting that true wisdom consists in **knowledge of one's ignorance**, awareness of the fact that no one can know everything.
- **The Delphic Oracle** claimed that no one is wiser than Socrates, who then devoted the rest of his life to testing his intellectual prowess against the most reputable teachers of his day, many of whom were **sophists**.
- The sophists were the first people to accept payment for teaching. The basic mantra of the sophists consists of the following:
    - Since it is impossible to achieve ultimate knowledge of reality, people ought to live by appearances and devote themselves to accumulating wealth and luxury.
    - Primarily, the sophists taught **rhetoric,** the art of persuasive speaking, through which one can amass a great deal of money and fame.
    - Three of the major sophists during Socrates's time were the following:
        - **Protagoras**, who maintained a form of **alethic relativism**, the idea that "man is the measure of all things" or that all truth is subjective.

    - **Gorgias**, a famous teacher of rhetoric who maintained **nihilism** ("Nothing exists."), **skepticism** ("Even if anything does exist it cannot be known."), and **subjectivism.** (Even if anything can be known it cannot be communicated.")
    - **Thrasymachus,** who maintained, "Justice is the will of the stronger," or that *might makes right.*

- Socrates employed a unique method of **dialectic** in which he would cross-examine his interlocutor to expose flaws and contradictions in the person's position.
- One of the best examples of the **Socratic method** occurs in Plato's dialogue *Meno.* Therein, Socrates converses with the titular Meno about whether virtue can be taught. After a rigorous series of exchanges, Meno proposes **the paradox of inquiry**:
    - If you know what X is, you *would not* ask about it.
    - If you do not know what X is, you *cannot* ask about it.
    - It seems to follow that inquiry about anything is impossible.
  - Socrates responds by proposing the **anamnesis/recollection thesis**, the idea that all learning is a form of remembering, comparable to the Eastern conception of reincarnation. Socrates presumably establishes this thesis by demonstrating that a teenage boy with no academic training can solve a difficult geometry problem.
- Socrates amassed a substantial following that included adolescents, who attempted to embarrass their parents as Socrates did famous teachers. Socrates also began to introduce new deities not recognized in the Athenian canon. Hence, he was brought to trial, found guilty, and put to death. Even though Socrates very easily could have escaped, he chose to die with courage and honor.
- While Socrates chose not to record any of his teachings in writing, Plato wrote dialogues, most of which, especially the early ones, feature Socrates as the main character. Traditionally, philosophers agree that the words of Socrates represent the bulk of Plato's teachings. Via his presentation of dialectic through dialogue, Plato seemed to establish that most truths are too complicated to be packed into concrete words.
- Unlike his predecessor, it seemed that Aristotle favored lecturing to his students rather than teaching them through dialogue, although not all historians of philosophy agree. Important points of agreement between Plato and Aristotle are the following:
  - As rational creatures, humans must augment their capacity for thinking and reflection to be happy.
  - To achieve virtue, one must find the mean between extremes of action, which is very difficult and takes many years of practice. It can only be taught by example.
- Jean-Jacques Rousseau was an eighteenth-century French thinker whose writings reflect many of the pedagogical assumptions of both Plato and Socrates.
  - Rousseau's most fundamental principle is that people are basically good and become bad through external forces alone, primarily through social institutions.
  - In his first major publication, *Discourse on the Arts of Sciences* (the *First Discourse*), Rousseau argued that sophisticated education in the arts and sciences not only failed to create people of virtue but in fact produced the exact opposite by emphasizing prestige over virtue and forcing people in resentful and aggressive competitions against each other.

- In his *Emile*, Rousseau illustrates the process of education whereby a child can be raised to live in society without losing his natural spontaneity and creativity. Rousseau distinguished three types of education:
    - <u>Education from Nature:</u> The internal development of our organs and faculties.
    - <u>Education from Others:</u> The internalization of principles and customs that we learn from various authority figures.
    - <u>Education from Things:</u> Our unique experiences of how things affect us.

## Exercises for Application and Reflection

**Instructions:** Use what you learned in this chapter to help you respond to the following questions.

1. Explain why the teachings of Socrates, who lived in ancient Greece, are relevant to today's world.
2. Explain how the two central maxims of the Delphic Oracle apply to everyday life. Specifically, how can adherence to them make one a happier person?
3. Which of Socrates's teachings do you think is the most important? Why?
4. Do you agree with Socrates that it is better to suffer injustice than it is to commit it? That is, do you agree that acts of injustice are in some way harmful to the perpetrator? Explain.
5. Do you agree with Rousseau's fundamental principle that people are basically good? Why or why not?
6. Compare and contrast Socrates with the teachings of any of the following: Jesus Christ, Buddha, Confucius, Gandhi, Martin Luther King Jr.
7. Read Book I of *The Republic*, specifically focusing on Socrates's conversation with Thrasymachus. Explain how Socrates refutes Thrasymachus.
8. Choose any of the following topics and write a hypothetical Socratic dialogue on that topic: the death penalty, global justice and famine relief, climate change, affirmative action and reverse discrimination, gun control, abortion, euthanasia, the rights of nonhuman animals, the effectiveness of public education, cloning.
9. Read Aristophanes's *The Clouds*. Then, write a three- to five-page essay describing how you believe Aristophanes is trying to portray Socrates.
10. Watch *The Twilight Zone* season 5 episode, "The Masks," and write a one- to two-page essay describing how this episode illustrates the Socratic thesis that injustice is harmful to the soul of the perpetrator.

# 2

# Obstacles to Critical Thinking (I)

## The Idols of the Mind

INTRODUCTION

### Preparing to Read Chapter 2

This chapter aims to define and explain the most general obstacles to critical thinking, the four "idols that beset [the minds of human beings]" identified by the English thinker Francis Bacon. In addition, this chapter attempts to establish that human beings are poised to make errors in judgment by their very nature. While there are many theories of human nature, this chapter directly refers to the transcendental, naturalistic, and Aristotelian theories, each of which implies that human beings are inherently fallible. After the exposition of the idols of the mind, this chapter ends by providing a brief description of the stages of learning as outlined by William Perry.

### AS YOU ARE READING, BE SURE TO WATCH FOR THE FOLLOWING TERMS

- Transcendental View of Human Nature
- Naturalistic View of Human Nature
- Aristotelian View of Human Nature
- Thomas Nagel – "The view from nowhere"
- Idols of the Mind
- Idols of the Tribe
    - Anthropomorphic Error
    - Formal Fallacy
    - Informal Fallacy
    - Cognitive Bias
- Idols of the Cave
- Idols of the Marketplace
    - Category Mistake
    - Denotation

    - Connotation
    - Group Polarization Effect
    - Euphemistic Language
- Idols of the Theater
    - Dogmatic
- Perry's Stages of Learning
    - Dualism ("Garden of Eden")
    - Multiplicity ("Anything Goes")
    - Relativism ("Critical Thinking")

**KEEP THE FOLLOWING QUESTIONS IN MIND AS YOU READ**

- Why is it important to have a general understanding of how people think and behave?
- Why does it matter how people develop their beliefs?
- How would it make my life better to understand and avoid errors in my judgments?

## The Political Animal and Theories of Human Nature

Thread through all human affairs, the central maxims of the Delphic Oracle—that all people (1) know themselves and (2) do nothing to excess—deserve continual attention not only in the context of the life, mission, and legacy of Socrates but also for the purposes of overcoming general obstacles to critical thinking. A rudimentary understanding of human nature coupled with the acknowledgment of human limitations serves to regulate an exposition of the various ways that people go astray. History recognizes Aristotle—Plato's most famous student, thus, a student of Socrates by proxy—as the Western world's first polymath. He wrote extensively on virtually every subject known to academia and practically invented some of them, specifically logic. Among those subjects addressed by Aristotle are human nature and ethics. With respect to the latter, Aristotle admonished people to work to achieve a form of moderation in all activities to become virtuous, necessary for ultimate happiness. With respect to the former, Aristotle designated humans not only as possessing a rational soul, but he famously wrote in *The Politics*, "Man is a political animal," or, more generally, a "social animal."[1]

Aristotle seems to give three arguments to establish the social and political nature of human beings.

- **First**, people instinctively gravitate toward other humans.
- **Second**, human beings are the only creatures on the planet who seem to possess sophisticated language, specifically, speech.
- **Third**, in connection with the first argument, just as a whole is greater than the sum of its parts, a community is greater than the sum of its individuals.

1 Aristotle, *The Politics*, 2nd ed., trans. Carnes Lord (Chicago: University of Chicago Press, 2013), Book I, Chapter 2.

With respect to the *first* argument, people desire relationships, intimate and romantic relationships, as well as friendships. Not only do people desire companionship, but all people seem to depend on others at least to some degree. No one is an island. At some point, an individual's survival will demand the help of other people. The availability of food, clothing, shelter, health, tools, and various other items demands the existence of individuals who can provide the services that produce such necessities. People desire both intimate relationships in addition to connections to groups of people greater in number, which expand concomitantly with basic needs. Small groups become tribes. Several tribes become cities. Many cities become a nation, etc. Different kinds of social groups, thus, emerge naturally through the course of human interactions.

With respect to the *second* argument, speech facilitates the development of communities by allowing people more easily to communicate with each other. Since communication between people usually equates to more effective cooperative efforts and the pooling of resources, communication allows for the expansion and continual improvement of the world. Just as knowledge is power and knowledge consists of information, at least in part, any process that allows for the transmission of information will enhance power.

As for the *third* argument, several people who congregate and merely loiter on a street corner do not constitute a genuine group. Several people jointly engaged in the pursuit of a common goal, however, not only constitute a genuine group but also provides each individual member with a purpose. A common goal not only unites people but even precedes the group itself. Just as the fragmentation of a group renders futile the achievement of any common goal, alienation from a group leaves the individual fragmented and incomplete. The goal of an individual life can no more be achieved in isolation than could the pyramids of Egypt build themselves. Aristotle wrote that to live in isolation, an individual must be either a "beast," beneath humanity, or a "God," above humanity.[2]

It is interesting that Aristotle conceived of humanity as neither fully beast nor fully divine but rather as existing on a continuum between the two. The two most popular conceptions of human nature proposed throughout intellectual history place humans at one extreme or the other.

- The **first** may be called the ***religious*** or ***transcendental*** **view**, on which humans are created in the image and likeness of an omnipotent, omniscient, and perfectly just God who places humans in a privileged position, giving them dominion over other animals.
- The **second** may be called the ***naturalistic*** **view**, according to which human beings are the product of several billion years of evolution.

On the first view, despite humanity's primal divinity, perfect union with God, and blissful, leisurely existence, the first humans eventually disobey God's commands, become alienated from each other, experience shame when made aware of their sexuality, and subsequently endure exile, pain, and death as punishment for their disobedience. All future generations of humans bear the curse of the "original sin" of the first humans. Hence, on the religious view, human beings are fallen creatures, thus, fallible.

On the second view, approximately 13.85 billion years ago, an event known as the "big bang" supposedly gave rise to our universe. Roughly ten billion years later, the first living creatures emerged on the planet Earth from a common ancestor. Several billion years later, during an event called the Cambrian explosion, complex, multicellular creatures burst on the scene. After additional hundreds of millions of years of evolution, during which many species of animals went extinct, creatures known as primates emerged. Descending from earlier primates, *Homo Sapiens*, human beings as they are understood today, eventually emerged. Most scientists agree that the mechanism by which

2 Aristotle, *The Politics*, Book I, Chapter 2.

evolution occurs is *natural selection*, a chance process of genetic transmission that favored some organisms over others. Those animals that have traits conducive to survival continue to live, passing on their traits. Those creatures that lack such favorable traits eventually go extinct. Human beings, thus, occupy no special place in creation except that they were simply lucky enough to make it to the top of the food chain. The day will come when Earth's resources are inevitably exhausted, forcing humanity into extinction. Be it tomorrow or several hundred million years from now, luck runs out. On such a view, human beings are animals struggling to survive for as long as they possibly can, thus, once again, fallible.

Whichever conception of human nature one adopts, its proponents must concede that human beings are bound to make errors simply by virtue of the fact that they are human. On the religious view, humans are God's greatest creation and more like Him than any other creature. Nonetheless, they sin, go astray, and suffer for doing so. On the naturalistic view, human beings are naturally selfish creatures who must embrace their egoism so they can survive. On the Aristotelian view, a more modest theory, placing human beings on a continuum between "beasts" and Gods, human beings are still creatures who will inevitably make mistakes. Since humans are not mere "beasts," their behavior cannot be reduced to instinctual drives. Insects such as ants, bees, and spiders cannot be "wrong" in what they do. Animals, whether they are dogs, cats, lions, tigers, or bears (Oh my!), etc., cannot be wrong in their actions. A dog would never be put on trial for biting a person, just as an alligator would never be given a life sentence if it ate a small child. Gods, on the other hand, are totally infallible. Since human beings exist somewhere in between, they are the very sorts of creatures who can and do make all-too-human errors.

The entire human race, universally, is vulnerable to some types of errors. But there are kinds of errors that are unique to individuals. Recall that as social creatures, we are incomplete as individuals. Those who fail to think beyond the scope of an individual point of view are bound to make errors in judgment based on their own, specifically subjective window to the world. No one has, nor can anyone ever really achieve what Thomas Nagel called **"the view from nowhere," a completely detached and purely objective understanding of the world**.

Furthermore, as the only kind of animal that uses speech and complex language, human fallibility inevitably will give rise to errors that occur specifically within the domain of and *because* of speech and language. Language is the process by which information is transmitted from one individual to another, making what is private to the individual public to everyone else. But since no human can possibly be totally and completely objective, language and speech are bound to reflect biased opinions or distorted views of reality. Moreover, words can be dangerous since they can arouse strong emotions and instigate aggressive and violent behaviors.

Finally, not only is the use of language essentially a social activity but also the primary method by which people learn from others. As social creatures, people inevitably fall under the influence of others. Virtually everyone would rather suffer the oppression of a tyrant than live totally isolated from other people burdened with the dread of creating and living in accordance with their own worldview. As comforting as human companionship may seem, it can also produce irreflective dogmatism, blind conformism, and destructive forms of loyalty.

In short, what people are dictates the kinds of errors they can make both in reasoning and judgment. The sixteenth-century English philosopher and scientist, Francis Bacon—who, ironically, heavily criticized the Aristotelian principles that dominated the Middle Ages—outlined four types of fallacies that obscure humanity's understanding of reality, which he called **idols of the mind**.

- The first are universal tendencies for error shared by all humans, which Bacon called **idols of the tribe**.
- The second reflect flaws or capacities for error that emerge from flaws within or unique to the individual, which he called **idols of the cave**.

- Third, Bacon recognized errors caused by the misuse of language, which he called **idols of the marketplace**.
- Finally, Bacon addressed errors that emerge from adherence to false dogmas and teachings, which he called **idols of the theater**.

Understanding these types of fallacies and taking every reasonable precaution to avoid them in everyday life are necessary if one wishes to think critically and respect the legacy left by Socrates. In fact, Bacon's attention to the idols of the mind reflects his attempt to approximate the elusive "view from nowhere," which no doubt inspired Rousseau to name him as one of the great geniuses of the modern world.

## The Idols of the Mind: An Exposition

### Idols of the Tribe

The first type of errors that concerned Bacon, the **idols of the tribe**, refer to tendencies for misjudgment and errors to which all human beings are susceptible. Such errors arise naturally from the basic constitution of people. Bacon believed that the human mind resembled a crooked mirror that can easily produce a false image of reality. He describes idols of the tribe in the following way:

> For man's sense is falsely asserted … to be the standard of things: on the contrary, all the perceptions, both of the senses and the mind, bear reference to man and not to the universe; and the human mind resembles those uneven mirrors, which impart their own properties to different objects … and distort and disfigure them.[3]

The most common errors that constitute idols of the tribe are the following:

- **Anthropomorphic errors**. An idea or image may be described as anthropomorphic if such an image or idea ascribes human attributes to nonhuman things.
- **Errors of sensation and perception**, such as optical and various perceptual illusions.
- **General reasoning errors**, such as both **formal and informal fallacies**.
- **General psychological barriers to objectivity**, such as defense mechanisms and cognitive biases.

Each of these types of errors will be addressed in turn.

### Anthropomorphic Errors

***Anthropomorphic errors*** constitute some of the most basic examples of idols of the tribe. Examples include the gods and goddesses of the world's religions, most of which have human form (although not all, of course, such as in Egyptian mythology). Furthermore, cartoon characters often have the form of nonhuman animals but possess human personality traits and abilities. An anthropomorphic error occurs when human qualities are falsely attributed to nonhuman items. For instance, if one assumes that a fox deliberates about killing and eating a rabbit or a chicken while the fox merely behaves instinctively, one errs in attributing the human capacity for deliberation to the fox. Bacon himself gave examples of such errors when he wrote, "[T]he human understanding, from its peculiar nature, easily supposes a greater degree of order and regularity in things than it really finds."[4] One example of such fictions is the belief that the motions of the planets form perfect circles because human beings find a such a model pleasing to the

3 *Novum Organum*, cited in Will Durant, *The Story of Philosophy* (New York, NY: Simon & Schuster, 2006), 165.
4 Durant, *The Story of Philosophy*, 166.

intellect and suitable to their desires. Moreover, an idea that greatly perturbed Bacon is the belief that everything in nature acts with a purpose or to achieve a goal. Because human beings behave with purpose and intent, it is within their nature to assume that everything else does.

## Errors of Sensation and Perception

Try to remember the last time you placed a straight stick in water. From your perspective, it almost certainly appeared bent. The following common optical illusion deserves consideration as well:

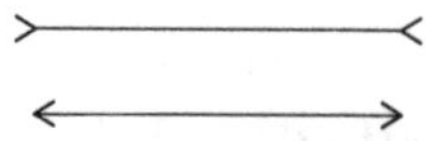

Which line appears to be longer? The top or bottom line? They are both the same length, but the top line probably appears to be longer.[5] If you were to make such a judgment, your error would constitute an idol of the tribe, based entirely on the capacity of your brain to impose on sensory data an order or form that does not reflect reality. Other errors of sensation and perception are more common. It is possible to be so intensely focused and engrossed by a task that it consumes one's attention to the point that one does not notice someone standing beside them. And even when people are not specifically focused on anything, they tend to overlook minute details in their everyday lives. Magic tricks work primarily because the best magicians understand how to distract their audience. Moreover, in his most famous thought experiment, the French philosopher Rene Descartes elaborated on the similarity between dream states and waking life. Often, while dreaming, people believe that they are awake. There exists sufficient similarity between the two states of consciousness to infer the possibility that one's entire life may be a dream! Mistaking one's state of consciousness certainly constitutes an idol of the tribe.

## General Errors of Reasoning

Both formal and informal fallacies exemplify general errors of reasoning. **Formal fallacies** occur when an argument has a faulty structure such that its premises do not entail its conclusion, in which case the argument is *invalid*. For example, consider the following two arguments:

(a) All dogs are mammals.

All Labs are dogs.
Therefore, all Labs are mammals.

(b) All Labs are mammals.

All dogs are mammals.
Therefore, all Labs are dogs.

Notice that in both arguments, all the premises and the conclusion are true. However, only argument (a) is *valid*. That is, only argument (a) has a structure in which the premises, if true, jointly entail that the conclusion is true. For any argument that shares the structure of (b), the premises do not jointly entail the conclusion. Thus, it is possible to produce a *counterexample*, a substitution instance in which the premises are true while the conclusion is false, such as the following:

5 This illusion is sometimes called the Müller-Lyer illusion.

(b*) All dogs are mammals.

All cats are mammals.
Therefore, all dogs are cats.

Chapters 6 and 7 will provide more detailed definitions of validity and invalidity in addition to a concise exposition of valid and invalid argument forms and further explain the connection between truth and validity. For the purposes of the present chapter, it will suffice to say that all human beings are vulnerable to formal fallacies, especially with very complicated arguments.

**Informal fallacies** can occur due to many types of flaws but usually will not involve a flaw in an argument's structure. In most cases, informal fallacies consist of flaws in the reasons that one marshals to support an argument's conclusion. One very common type of informal fallacy is an *abusive ad hominem* (from Latin, "against the man"). Such a fallacy occurs when an individual attacks a person rather than genuinely engaging and critiquing an argument. For example, consider the following argument:

(c) If Brandon dresses poorly, then his advice to eat healthy food should be ignored.

Brandon dresses poorly.
Therefore, Brandon's advice to eat healthy food should be ignored.

Argument (c) has a valid form, *modus ponens*, but simply because a person dresses poorly does not justify ignoring his advice. Chapter 9 will provide an exposition of the following types of informal fallacies: personal attacks, emotional appeals, inferences of weak induction, diversionary tactics, unwarranted presumption, and ambiguity.

## Psychological Barriers to Objectivity

Defense mechanisms and cognitive biases reflect the sorts of errors that Bacon called idols of the tribe. In short, cognitive biases reflect general psychological barriers to objective thought. Since human beings are rational creatures, incongruity between one's accepted beliefs and new, opposing information is the source of mental disharmony called *cognitive dissonance*. To resolve such a conflict, most people tend to deny the opposing information and seek out any information to confirm what they already accept, twisting their experiences to accommodate the prejudices of their prior beliefs and accepted theories, more succinctly described as *confirmation bias*. To illustrate, an individual who discovers evidence that his spouse may be having an affair with his best friend might pretend that such evidence does not exist and seek out his own evidence that confirms that his wife is loyal, thereby resolving the mental discomfort and dread brought about by the very thought of betrayal. As another example, imagine a scenario in which a religious student is exposed to the theory of evolution for the first time. For this individual, the idea that the entire human race is a glorious accident, the product of several billion years of evolution that gradually progressed from simpler to more complex life forms according to a completely impersonal process of natural selection simply is unacceptable! This theory and all its supporting evidence she most certainly would judge to be the work of Satan testing her faith! The following passage demonstrates Bacon's grasp of confirmation bias: "Having first determined the question according to his will, man *then* resorts to experience; and bending her into conformity with his placets, leads her about like a captive in a procession."[6] Ultimately, "what a man would rather were true, he

6 Durant, *The Story of* Philosophy, 166.

more readily believes."[7] The very next chapter will explore several cognitive biases in more detail. The next section addresses **idols of the cave**.

## Idols of the Cave

Since idols of the tribe constitute the most general types of errors in judgment that people make, the other idols listed by Bacon may be described as very broad illustrations of his idols of the tribe, including Bacon's second class of errors, the **idols of the cave**. While idols of the tribe comprise mostly general tendencies shared by all people, *idols of the cave*[8] are errors specific or unique to an individual, typically rooted in individual flaws: "For every one … has a cave or den of his own which refracts and discolors the light of nature."[9] Idols of the cave can be illustrated by the errors in judgment to which a specific individual is prone based on either his or her personal agenda, prejudices, personality, or education. Idols of the cave may also be described as the product of both nature and nurture, where the process of an individual's education or socialization contributes to the sorts of fallacious judgments such an individual might make. More succinctly, idols of the cave may be defined as the error of *universalizing that which is relative to the individual.* Protestants traditionally criticize the authorities of the Catholic Church for universalizing their interpretation of the Bible. In turn, a person raised in a Catholic household may believe that all people should convert to Catholicism, just as people raised in a democratic society most likely will believe that democracy is the best form of government. Additional examples of idols of the cave can be illustrated by errors that arise from personal preferences or agendas. For example, if a young woman has an affinity for surreal art, such as paintings by Dali, Picasso, or Davinci, she may not approve of your home decorations if you included no such paintings.

As a precaution, keep in mind that judgments about religion, models of government, or the aesthetic appeal of a friend's apartment might not be "wrong" in the sense that they contradict reality. But determining the veracity of such judgments demands a far more thorough investigation than individuals prone to idols of the cave are likely to give. Moreover, even if an individual's judgment happens to be correct, it is still entirely possible that their judgment reflects *the flaw of individual prejudice.* To be correct in one's judgment may be a matter of luck and, thus, may not constitute genuine knowledge. The subject of knowledge will be further explored in Chapters 4 and 5.

Before proceeding to explain the remaining idols of the mind, the distinction between idols of the tribe and cave deserves further clarification. Imagine a homicide detective who, throughout his career, witnessed the very worst and most reprehensible acts that human beings can commit. Such a person would most likely believe the worst about people and perhaps be unduly suspicious of everyone with whom he or she came into contact. At the opposite end of the spectrum, a more sheltered person, raised by charitable law-abiding citizens would most assuredly assume the very best about people even when there may be reason to think otherwise. Notice that each of these cases reflect both *general* and *specific* tendencies for error. The general tendency in each case is illustrated by the capacity to be influenced by the world around us and, thus, to construct a model of reality based entirely on personal experience. The specific tendency in each case is illustrated by the *content* of each model. Similar examples can be drawn from the topic of informal fallacies and cognitive biases. Any informal fallacy or cognitive bias reflects an idol of the tribe since all human beings have the tendency for them. However, specific instances of informal fallacies or cognitive biases may reflect idols of the cave or the remaining two, idols of the marketplace and theater.

---

7 Durant, *The Story of* Philosophy, 167.

8 The question will arise as to whether Bacon intended to reference Plato's allegory of the cave when developing his conception of idols of this type. While he most certainly seemed to have Plato in mind, Plato's allegory of the cave is broader and more complex than Bacon's idols of the mind.

9 Durant, *The Story of Philosophy*, 167.

## Idols of the Marketplace

The **idols of the marketplace**, a third source of errors and according to Bacon the most troublesome of all, arise from communication between people. More specifically, idols of the marketplace comprise errors made based on confusion over the meaning of words. In Bacon's own words,

> [Idols of the marketplace arise] from the commerce and association of men with one another. For men converse by means of language; but words are imposed according to the understanding of the crowd; and there arises [from] a bad and inapt formation of words, a wonderful obstruction to the mind.[10]

Why exactly did Bacon label idols of the marketplace as the most troublesome? The most obvious answer seems to be that words and language in general cannot easily be separated from thinking and reasoning. The failure to speak and write with clarity and coherence reflects an inability to think clearly and coherently. Awareness and avoidance of the idols of the marketplace also carry great import because words represent thoughts, beliefs, and ideas. Words comprise a substantial component of language, by which the information held by one person or group of people is transmitted to another. Thus, to a significant extent, language provides a model or a mirror of reality. Miscommunication very easily leads to misinformation. Three variations of idols of the marketplace concern the present text.

- **First**, words do not always adequately match the idea they are intended to convey.
- **Second**, complete statements, claims, messages, and judgments can become confused when transmitted between people (often referred to as the "telephone game").
- **Finally**, words and statements can be used as rhetorical devices to evoke emotional responses from people that obscure their understanding and judgment.

Bacon seemed to be concerned primarily with the *first variation* of idols of the marketplace, specifically with terms used by the academics and the great theoretical thinkers of his time, especially religious authorities. For example, a medieval theologian might talk about God as being "infinite" and as being the "first cause" or the "unmoved mover." However, the meanings of such terms are never made precise, nor are the terms themselves used with any great degree of precision. Given their vagueness, people are left to their own devices to imagine what they might mean. And given that every individual has a "cave or den" of their own, perhaps no two people will agree on the meaning of such terms. Moreover, the individuals who express such words seem to use them only as a mask for their ignorance. Like Plato, who wished to ban the poets from his Republic and admonished people to stay on their guard against the orators of his day, Bacon understood the power of words, especially their tendency to conceal truth, elicit emotions, and persuade people to act against their will. In an earlier dialogue, *Gorgias*, named after the famous sophist who features as a central character, Socrates criticizes the titular character, whose discipline, rhetoric, functions only as a "phantom" or a mask for true justice and wisdom.[11]

Additional instances in which words do not adequately correspond to reality include what philosopher Gilbert Ryle called "**category mistakes**."[12] For instance, consider the word "university." Suppose you visit the campus of a college for a tour. Your tour guide walks you through various buildings. You see several classrooms, offices, and

10 Durant, *The Story of Philosophy*, 168.
11 Note on Plato's *Republic* and *Gorgias*.
12 Gilbert Ryle, *The Concept of Mind* (Chicago: University of Chicago Press, 1949), 16. Ryle seems to coin this term in the context of a criticism of Cartesian dualism, a topic that I address in Chapter 4.

lounges. You learn to distinguish between academic buildings, administrative buildings, and recreational facilities. You walk down several different paths. You see the athletic field and various parking lots. Perhaps you visit the cafeteria at lunchtime. Now suppose that at the end of the tour someone asks the guide, "Where exactly was the *university* on this tour?" Clearly, this person had a different understanding of the term "university" than everyone else. This individual probably believed that the "university" was an individual building, a specific, concrete, indivisible entity. The term itself, however, corresponds to multiple individual realities, including the network of people who study and work at the institution. To assume that the term "university" refers only to one specific building would, in Ryle's terms, constitute a category mistake. And it is this very sort of mistake that Bacon seemed to have in mind when he referred to idols of the marketplace.

The *second variation* of idols of the marketplace are extensions of the first. Messages often become confused when they pass from one person to another. Consider the following statement: "A burglar stole the ham for Christmas dinner." A second person may attempt to relay this message, but it becomes, "The Hamburglar is invited to Christmas dinner." Many disagreements arise because individuals attempt to communicate but only succeed in talking past each other due to the vagueness of terms. Consider words such as "good" and "like." Teachers of English language and composition often chide their students for their misuse of the word "good." For instance, if a student claims that she "did *good* on her exam," the teacher will usually correct her, suggesting instead that she "did *well*." If my friend, Dave says, "I think *The Muppets Christmas Carol* is a good movie," his statement could be interpreted in at least two ways. On the one hand, it could mean that the movie is well-written, well-acted, well-directed, and effectively captures the spirit of the season it is intended to represent. On the other hand, it could simply mean that he enjoyed the movie. Or, of course, it could mean both, that it is a very well-made movie and that he "liked" it. The word "like" can also be vague. "Dave likes *The Muppets Christmas Carol*." "Sally likes Johnny." "Dan likes healthy food." In each of those sentences, the word "likes" has a similar meaning, but no in no two instances is the term used in the *exact* same sense. Enjoying a movie differs from enjoying the company of a person, and both differ from enjoying the benefits of healthy food. The use of vague terms can conceal both the meaning of terms and an individual's beliefs or intentions.

What further complicates matters is that most words have both a concrete meaning and an *implied meaning*. The first is sometimes called *denotation*, the literal definition of a term that one might find in a dictionary. The second is sometimes called *connotation*, which may be positive or negative depending on the feeling evoked by the word in question. Moreover, most words in any language have more than one concrete meaning. For instance, the words "hot" and "cold" can be used in multiple ways. The terms can refer to the literal temperature or can be used metaphorically. In 2008, for example, *The Dark Knight* earned the title of the *hottest* movie of the summer. Many fans of the movie described Heath Ledger's legendary interpretation of the Joker as *hot*, while Jack Nicholson's portrayal of the character in the 1989 film went *cold* years earlier. In the present context, the term "hot" has a positive connotation, meaning that the item so described is popular and well-received at a given point in time, whereas that of "cold" is negative, and suggests that an item is irrelevant at a specific time and place.

The complexity of language also makes people vulnerable to fallacies of ambiguity. The clearest example is *equivocation*, which occurs when an argument employs a term in two different senses. For instance, if one were to predict that *King Kong vs. Godzilla* will be the *hottest* movie of 2021 and, therefore, that it will have a temperature high enough to fry eggs, one commits equivocation in one's use of the term *hot*. Mistaken inferences may also occur due to sentence structure. An example is the fallacy of *amphiboly*. For instance, consider the following sentence: "Standing on a tour boat in the Mississippi river, one can see the Sears Tower." Now, suppose that based on this claim, an individual infers that the tour boat must be enormous if it can hold the Sears Tower! Obviously, such an individual misinterpreted the claim on which his inference is based.

Just as confusion grows with the number of people who transmit a message, individuals can become more extreme in their beliefs based on their exposure to others who hold similar views. Social psychologists refer to this phenomenon as the *group polarization effect*. For instance, if a group of people who have reservations about non-Caucasian races gather and converse about the topic of racial diversity, it is quite possible that they may all come close to embracing a reactionary position, even going so far as to become white supremacists. Since people are social creatures, and since the use of language is a social activity, people are influenced by the opinions and claims of others.

The influence of language over people relates directly to the *third variation* of idols of the marketplace, instances in which words and language evoke strong emotional reactions from people. Many ideas and beliefs are sacred to people, such as religious beliefs. When those beliefs, ideas, or values are threatened, people might respond defensively, becoming aggressive or even violent. People often become embroiled in bitter rivalries even when the subject of debate is comparatively trivial, such as which football or baseball team is the best, or which installment in the seemingly endless *Star Wars* franchise is the best. The demand for retribution against those who refuse to respect and accept more grave ideas, such as one's political and religious beliefs, are exponentially more severe, giving rise to world wars, global persecution, xenophobia, and terrorism. Often, the use of racial invectives and allegations about their use flame the passions of those they are intended to offend. During the infamous O. J. Simpson murder trial, for instance, a key part of Simpson's defense focused on whether the lead detective on the case, Mark Fuhrman, used the dreaded "N-word." An investigation revealed that he did in fact use the word and then perjured himself while on the witness stand, diverting the jury's attention from the very cogent evidence against Simpson and toward the racial prejudices of the LAPD.

One can also twist language to justify one's beliefs and actions or to cultivate one's desired perception of reality. A soldier turned rogue who, convinced of government corruption, plans to destroy a federal building considers himself not a *terrorist* but a true *patriot*. The individuals who perpetrated the 9/11 attacks did not consider themselves *terrorists* but *martyrs* making sacrifices to Allah. In the contemporary world, those who carry out heinous crimes against humanity are not *evil* but just terribly *sick*, suffering from severe mental health issues. Many creative people are called *insane* during their own time but posthumously are appreciated under the more fitting term of *genius*.

In a more mundane context, the use of euphemistic language may be employed to ease emotions, such as with the loss of a loved one. The deceased did not *die* but *passed away*. Words can also be used to incite people to support a cause when they appeal to cherished values and ideas. Cults, for instance, often recruit members by appealing to their sense of vanity, suggesting that people who follow their principles are *special, exceptional*. The same techniques of persuasion are often employed in advertising, in which products are associated with powerful and famous people. Buy the product and you, too, can exemplify such attributes! Such tactics consist of emotional appeals further detailed in Chapter 9.

The avoidance of idols of the marketplace can be immensely instrumental in achieving a clearer understanding of one's beliefs and values, a more objective outlook on reality, and a deeper understanding of others procured through reason rather than blind emotion. In creating his system of logic, Aristotle distinguished three acts of the mind by which a more effective pursuit of each of these goals can be initiated. First is understanding, which consists in part of the clarification of the meaning of individual words. Second is judgment, which consists in clarifying the meaning of specific statements. Third is inference, which consists in the employment of valid forms of reasoning. Chapter 7 further explores Aristotle's acts of the mind and logic in more detail. The discussion of idols of the marketplace leads naturally to the final class of Bacon's fallacies since the inescapable connection between language and thought bears heavily on the ways in which people perceive and understand reality.

## Idols of the Theater

Usually, the perception of reality created by language reinforces biases and prejudices, in addition to cultivating the uncritical and unreflective acceptance of what one is taught. The final category of errors Bacon calls **idols of the theater**, which can be described concisely as mistakes in judgment that arise from worldviews or schools of thought that contain numerous errors and should either be fixed or rendered defunct. Bacon describes them thus:

> Lastly, there are idols which have migrated into men's minds from the various dogmas of philosophers, and also from wrong laws of demonstration. These I call *Idols of the Theatre*, because in my judgment, all the received systems of philosophy are but so many stage-plays, representing worlds of their own creation after an unreal and scenic fashion. ... And in the plays of this philosophic theatre you may observe the same thing which is found in the theatre of the poets,—that stories invented for the stage are more compact and elegant, and more as we would wish them to be than true stories out of history.[13]

The classical Aristotelian/scholastic worldview that dominated the Middle Ages comprised Bacon's primary concern. However, there seem to be two types of general errors that may be classified as idols of the theater.

- First, are beliefs that arise from **adherence to ideas or schools of thought that grossly misrepresent reality**, many of which become discredited and obsolete.
- Second, **intellectual dogmatism**, in which consists the uncritical, unreflective acceptance of principles or ideas one is taught.

As an example of the first sort of error, suppose a person believes that Earth is at the center of the solar system, and all the planets and the sun revolve around it. This belief adheres to the geocentric model of the solar system, which was rejected roughly 500 years ago. Such an error could be deemed an idol of the theater. Some ideas that were popular but are now recognized as "junk science" also fit under this category. For example, psychologists once believed that males with an extra Y chromosome were destined to become violent offenders (XYY syndrome). Geneticists, however, debunked such an idea decades ago.

One might also attempt to create an entirely new, original idea or system of thought that fails to capture reality. Often, scientific hypotheses and theories are modified based on the data collected to test them, as will be further explained in Chapter 8. Marx is credited as the putative father of communism, and his predictions about the inevitability of a future communist utopia receive continual endorsement from his most ardent defenders, according to whom Marx's philosophy simply needs to be implemented *correctly*. Certainly, it will not occur to such thinkers that Marx simply got it wrong. Freud based his psychoanalysis on the assumption of an unconscious that constitutes and accounts for virtually 90 percent of the human psyche. Primarily, Freud based his idea of the unconscious on the fact that people dream, so surely there is some truth to his model of humanity. But he could not endure criticism. Anyone who dared to question his authority he banished from his inner circle. Psychoanalysis underwent numerous modifications since Freud's death. When Darwin initially formulated his theory of evolution, he did not know how traits passed from parent to offspring. Many religious figures claim to possess the truth about ultimate reality for which there is no better alternative, such as L. Ron Hubbard's Scientology, by which many people, both famous and anonymous swear. There is a fine line between a cult and true religion, a line one crosses when one becomes irretrievably split from the world rather than being connected with reality in a deep and rich way.

13 Durant, *The Story of Philosophy*, 168–9.

An error of judgment does not have to emerge from worldviews that are known to be false to constitute an idol of the theater, which leads to the second sort of error, that may be grouped under this category: beliefs that may be true or false but that *emerge from mere dogmatic adherence to any school of thought*. For example, Christianity, a religion with many denominations and literally billions of practitioners, does not constitute a worldview whose doctrines are known to be false, even though its doctrines are, at the very least, debatable. But suppose that a Christian insists that all homosexuals are sinners and will be punished in the afterlife if they do not repent. Suppose also that said Christian holds this belief solely because the Bible says so or solely because their pastor told them so. Such a belief may be called an idol of the theater. The same may be said of those who embrace any school of thought without seriously evaluating that system or deeply considering the reasons for making such an adoption. Many people who believe in God hold such a belief only because they hear "God" referred to incessantly. Many people who prefer a naturalistic worldview embrace an evolutionary theory of human origins primarily because they heard it referred to incessantly.

In short, while the idols of the mind are inextricably embedded in human nature and it may be impossible to avoid them all the time, becoming aware of them and understanding their various manifestations can facilitate their evasion most of the time and compel people to evaluate objectively the viewpoints of oneself and others in addition to navigating the world at large.

## Conclusion: Perry's Stages of Learning and Additional Objectives

While no one can purport to know everything about human nature, at least three facts can be surmised about people: they are rational, social, and fallible. As rational creatures, humans not only can use reason but must do so for the sake of their own well-being and happiness. As social creatures, humans can neither avoid the help nor the influence of others. Finally, as fallible creatures, humans may often be mistaken in their judgments and their actions may precipitate unintended and harmful consequences.

Just as the idols of the mind are embedded in human nature, the capacity to learn unfolds over time through natural stages of development. According to Harvard psychologist William Perry, everyone goes through three stages of learning.

- First is the ***dualistic* stage**, also known as the **"Garden of Eden"** stage.
- Second is the stage of ***multiplicity***, also known as **"Anything Goes."**
- Finally, is the stage of ***relativism***, also known as **"Critical Thinking."**

During the first stage, knowledge is clear, certain, absolute, and determined by authority figures. At this stage, whatever authority figures say is accepted without question, and anyone who disagrees with the authorities must be wrong. However, because authority figures not only disagree with each other but are often shown to be mistaken and, thus, fallible, people will move on to the stage of ***multiplicity***, the "**Anything Goes**" stage. At this stage, since no authority figures agree completely with each other, no one really knows what is true or false, right or wrong, or even how to tell the difference. Hence, all beliefs are of equal value and no one can determine whether one belief makes more sense than another. Notice the similarity between this stage and the Protagorean version of relativism considered in the previous chapter, also called *alethic relativism*. Recall that such a point of view inevitably leads to contradictions, since it allows people to hold opposing beliefs and worldviews that cannot logically coexist and even the doctrine itself seems to be self-referentially inconsistent, for if the doctrine of relativism itself is true, then either not all truth is relative or the doctrine itself is relative and may be denied. Hence, people naturally graduate to the third and final stage, **"Critical Thinking,"** which, ironically, Perry deemed the stage of ***relativism***. Perry's version of relativism, however, suggests that some beliefs or ideas are better than others, not because authorities say so, but because there are cogent reasons to accept such viewpoints. Hence, some viewpoints are better *relative to* others.[14] It is entirely possible that given the entire intellectual history of humankind, there are no "new" ideas or truths to be discovered, in which case it remains the task of educators not to create new ideas but to distinguish the true from the false. The task of the remainder of this text is to provide the tools to do so.

## Chapter Summary and Key Points to Remember

Aristotle maintained that human beings are political animals, meaning that they are inherently social creatures who inevitably rely on and are influenced by each other in ways that extend to beliefs and ideas that are either erroneous or too hastily adopted. Moreover, alternative theories of human nature range between two opposing options—the **transcendental** and **naturalistic** views. The former maintains that humans are created by a divine higher power, could not live up to the standards of this entity, and, hence, fell from grace. As fallen creatures, humans are fallible. The latter understands humans as highly evolved animals caught in the tumultuous throes of the struggle to survive. As mere animals, humans are on a continuum with all others and, thus, are fallible. Either way, to err is human and the most general human errors Bacon called **the idols of the mind:**

- **Idols of the tribe** consist of universal errors committed by all humans. The most common examples are the following:
  - **Anthropomorphic errors**, in which human attributes are misapplied to nonhuman entities
  - Errors of sensation and perception, such as occur with optical illusions
  - General errors of reasoning, such as occur in both **formal** and **informal fallacies**
  - **Cognitive biases**, general psychological obstacles to objective thinking and judgment
- **Idols of the cave** consist of errors that arise from flaws within the individual, either due to individual prejudice, preference, or natural inhibitions.
  - The most common form of idols of the cave occurs when **an individual universalizes that which is subjective**
- **Idols of the marketplace** arise from errors of communication and the misuse of language. The most common forms of idols of the marketplace are the following:
  - The use of words in ways that do not accurately correspond to reality, such as occurs with **category mistakes**
  - Miscommunications and/or errors in the transmission of information, such as occurs with the "telephone game"
  - The use of language deliberately to manipulate an audience psychologically and distort objectivity, such as occurs with emotional appeals

14 A similar explanation of Perry's stages can be found in Chapter 5 of John Chaffee, *Thinking Critically*, "Constructing Knowledge," 12th ed. (Boston: Cengage, 2019), 199–201.

- **Idols of the theater** arise from adherence to false teachings, defunct schools of thought, or from dogmatic, unreflective adherence to what one assimilates.

Understanding the idols of the mind and how they arise can be valuable in becoming an efficient and critical thinker. Equally important is understanding the three stages of learning as outlined by Harvard psychologist William Perry:

- **Dualism** ("Garden of Eden"), in which knowledge is clear, certain, absolute, and determined by authorities
- **Multiplicity** ("Anything Goes"), in which one discovers that authorities often disagree with each other and, thus, that no one knows the truth; hence, all opinions are equal
- **Relativism** ("Critical Thinking"), in which one learns how to evaluate beliefs and opinions using logic, rational investigation, and experimentation

## Exercises for Application and Reflection

**Instructions:** Use what you learned in this chapter to help you respond to the following questions.

1. Which theory of human nature do you think is more plausible, the transcendental, the naturalistic, or neither? If neither, propose your own theory.
2. Why did Aristotle consider humans to be "political animals"? What do his arguments imply about people who prefer to be alone?
3. Explain how Aristotle's conception of humans as political animals directly ties into each of Bacon's idols of the mind.
4. List and explain each of Bacon's idols of the mind. Give a specific example of each.
5. Choose one of the theories of human nature proposed at the beginning of this chapter and explain how it is vulnerable to all of Bacon's idols of the mind.
6. Based on your answer to question 5, explain how your chosen theory can avoid all of Bacon's idols of the mind.
7. Give examples of how you fell victim to each of Bacon's idols of the mind at some point in your life.
8. List and explain Perry's stages of learning. Then, how at each stage it is possible to fall victim to each of Bacon's idols of the mind.

# 3

# Obstacles to Critical Thinking (II)

## Cognitive Biases

INTRODUCTION

### Preparing to Read Chapter 3

Like the idols of the mind, cognitive biases constitute general obstacles to objective thinking. The aims of this chapter are threefold:

- First, it will present and explain general problems that the human brain frequently encounters and must solve to make sense of the world.
- Second, it will present and explain the most common and troublesome cognitive biases that arise from the brain's attempts to make sense of the world.
- Finally, once a cognitive bias is presented and explained, ways to avoid these cognitive biases and approximate a more objective understanding of reality in addition to your beliefs, attitudes, and values will be suggested.

Like the idols of the mind, cognitive biases are instinctive and distinctively human phenomena. And like the idols of the mind, awareness of one's susceptibility to them facilitates avoiding them and limits their development.

**KEEP THE FOLLOWING QUESTIONS IN MIND AS YOU READ**

Why should we be aware of problems the brain tries to solve?

If the human brain filters out important information and constructs meaning, then what does that imply about our knowledge of the external world?

Can we train our brains to remember specific information?

Why is it important to be aware of cognitive biases?

To which cognitive biases covered in this chapter am I most vulnerable and how can I avoid them?

If everyone were more aware of cognitive biases and less susceptible to them, what kind of positive impact would it have on the world?

Are cognitive biases ever beneficial in any way?

**AS YOU READ THIS CHAPTER, WATCH FOR THE FOLLOWING TERMS**

- The Filtering Problem
- The Construction Problem
- The Impulse Problem
- The Memory Problem
- Cognitive Bias
- Cognitive Dissonance
- Confirmation Bias
- Belief Bias
- Hindsight Bias
- Anchoring
    - Dogmatic Anchoring
    - Estimative Anchoring
- Implicit Bias
- Negativity Bias
- Heuristic
    - Availability Heuristic
    - Representativeness Heuristic
    - Affect Bias
- Attribution
    - Fundamental Attribution Error
    - Actor-Observer Bias
    - Self-serving Bias

## Making Sense of the World

Not only did Aristotle argue that humans are naturally social and political creatures but also that on a more basic level humans are rational animals. The line with which he began the *Metaphysics* asserts, "All humans by nature desire to know." Humans naturally desire the acquisition of knowledge and meaning. The world, however, is a very large, confusing, and daunting place, causing fear, anxiety, and generalized discomfort. While Aristotle believed the brain to be nothing more than a cooling system for the blood, contemporary science recognizes the brain as the seat of human consciousness. The brain itself functions as a natural supercomputer and built-in problem solver. The world poses several problems for the brain, and, much like electricity, the brain often takes the "path of least resistance" to solve these problems. As a result of these "solutions," additional problems can arise.

The following comprise the four most basic kinds of problems that the brain must solve on a regular basis:

- The **Filtering Problem:** Our brains have to sort through thousands of bits of sensory information and decide what is important.
  - **BUT:** A LOT of important information gets left out.

For example, imagine that your best friend introduces you to a new acquaintance. You may focus so intently on what this person says that it is entirely possible that seconds after meeting this person you forget his or her name. Moreover, you likely forgot the exact date on which you met this person. It is probable that you cannot give a detailed description of the person's clothing or distinguishing characteristics. Even more likely is that you would not be able to describe the details of the surrounding environment. Such a scenario constitutes an instance of filtering.

- The **Construction Problem:** Lack of meaning is confusing, so we often fill in the gaps and construct meaning.
  - **BUT:** We have tendencies to read meaning into the world that does not really exist, at least not independently.

At some point in everyone's life, they saw a face on the moon or recognized a pattern in the clouds. But it would be very odd to suggest that such patterns exist independently of the mind that recognizes them. After all, it is not as though an artist painted them across the sky. A similar judgment could be made about an insect that traces a pattern in the sand that resembles one of the American presidents, such as George Washington. If the ant had no intention or awareness that its path in the sand resembles George Washington, then is it *really* a picture of the famous inaugural US president? In addition to pattern recognition is pattern projection. Most people tend to believe that the events of the past and present will continue to run their course into the future, that things will never change. Conversely, people may be inclined to believe that after a string of bad luck, one's fortune is simply bound to change, sometimes called the "gambler's fallacy." Any of these instances constitute instances of meaning construction.

- The **Impulse Problem:** Sometimes, we are under pressure to solve problems quickly, and we jump to conclusions.
  - **BUT:** Frequently, decisions made too quickly can be erroneous, self-serving, and unfair.

Making decisions impulsively can expose what psychologists often refer to as the **Overconfidence Effect**, the process by which one systematically overestimates one's own abilities. For example, suppose that you have one hour to load heavy furniture onto a truck and you have no one to help. Since the job must be completed quickly, you are likely to believe that you can lift the furniture on your own. Yet, when you attempt to do so, you probably will not only fail but also injure yourself. A similar phenomenon occurs when people overestimate their knowledge. That is, people often believe they know a lot more than they really do, a phenomenon sometimes called the **illusion of knowledge**. Forcing a person to make a difficult decision quickly is likely to expose such an illusion. If a person's car breaks down, for instance, even if said individual has very limited knowledge of auto mechanics, he may very well attempt to fix the problem and subsequently do further damage.

- The **Faulty Memory Problem:** We have to remember important bits of information.
  - **BUT:** Often, memories can only reinforce errors.

It is impossible to overestimate the importance of memory, especially since how and what people remember can be very selective. People tend to remember most poignantly events that stand out from the norm. Events that are unusually significant or drastic not only are recalled more easily and quickly than others, but they can lend themselves to a person's general disposition and distort one's conception of reality.

For each problem that the brain tries to solve, other problems can arise that distort objectivity. Such problems, those previously described and those that will follow, may be termed **cognitive biases**, psychological tendencies that interfere with objectivity. Any of the four problems that confront the brain may give rise to many different cognitive biases.[1] The remainder of this chapter will survey and explain 13 of the most common cognitive biases.

## Cognitive Biases

### Cognitive Dissonance

In his much-heralded textbook *The Social Animal*, eminent and respected social psychologist Eliot Aaronson invites his audience to imagine a scenario in which a young man named Sam is hypnotized. At the stroke of 4:00, Sam is to don a raincoat and galoshes, grab his umbrella, walk eight blocks to a local grocery store, buy six bottles of bourbon, and then return home. When he reenters his apartment, he will "snap out of it." When Sam regains awareness, his friend, the hypnotist, is present and the two have the following conversation:

"Hey Sam, where have you been?"

"Oh, just down to the store," Sam says.

"What did you buy?"

"Um … um … it seems I bought this bourbon."

"But you don't drink do you?"

"No, but … um … um … I'm going to do a lot of entertaining over the next several weeks and some of my friends do."

"How come you're wearing all your rain gear on such a sunny day?"

"Well … actually the weather is quite changeable this time of year and I didn't want to take any chances."

"But there isn't a cloud in the sky."

"Well, you never can tell."

"By the way, where did you buy the liquor?"

"Oh, heh, heh. Well, um … down at the supermarket."

"How come you went that far?"

"Well, um … um … it was such a nice day, I thought it might be fun to take a long walk."[2]

Aaronson attributes this exchange between Sam and his hypnotist to the universal human instinct for self-justification. People want to justify their actions, no matter how seemingly inexplicable or absurd. People also share

1 For a list of cognitive biases that correspond to these sorts of problems, see Terry Heick, "The Cognitive Bias Codex: A Complete List of 180+ Cognitive Biases," Tech Thought University, October 19, 2020, https://www.teachthought.com/critical-thinking/the-cognitive-bias-codex-a-visual-of-180-cognitive-biases/.

2 Eliot Aaronson, *The Social Animal*, 12th ed. (New York: Worth Publishers, 2018), 57–8.

a general tendency to justify their thoughts, beliefs, attitudes, and values. As rational animals, people experience conflict when detecting any kind of contradiction and, thus, try to eliminate the conflict by eliminating the contradiction. Conflict causes discomfort, and people avoid discomfort just as readily as they avoid physical pain. That is, people want to avoid cognitive dissonance.

- **Cognitive dissonance** is the experience of mental or psychological tension when an individual holds two conflicting or contradictory thoughts, beliefs, attitudes, or ideas. It can also occur when one's actions conflict with their thoughts, beliefs, or values.

Ironically, resolutions to cognitive dissonance usually are irrational. Generally, there are two kinds of responses to mental conflicts of this sort.

- First, an individual may engage in **denial.**

For example, imagine an overweight person who ought to adhere to a strict diet. But this individual has a momentary loss of self-control and indulges himself by consuming an entire pizza. This behavior will cause a conflict in the individual. To resolve this conflict, he may simply pretend that the indiscretion did not happen.

- Second, an individual may **rationalize** the behavior that caused the conflict.

Returning to the previous example, if the man convinces himself that he deserved his momentary indulgence owing to several days of fasting, it would likely assuage the dissonance brought about by his behavior.

Cognitive dissonance can yield additional consequences, the most common of which is a change in one's attitudes or values. For instance, imagine that you pay $12 to see a recently released movie at a theater. Imagine also that you pay an additional $15 for popcorn and soda. Suppose also that you truly did not find the movie very entertaining. Your experience results in a conflict. You spent nearly $30 to see a movie that you did not genuinely enjoy. To eliminate the conflict, thus, you convince yourself that the movie was in fact very entertaining and enjoyable. Contrast your experience with that of a person who did not pay for either his ticket or his refreshments. Such an individual likely will not change his opinion, as he sacrificed less.

Sales representatives, in fact, use tactics that rely on cognitive dissonance. One illustration consists of the "foot-in-the-door" phenomenon, in which an initial minor agreement leads to more significant and demanding agreements in the future. For instance, suppose that an agent selling kitchen supplies allows you to use a sample for 30 days for free. At the end of your free trial, you decide not to make the purchase. However, the sales rep asks you for a "small favor" in which you may keep the supplies but share them with the rest of the neighborhood to acquire more customers. Since you made the initial agreement, you would probably feel conflicted if you refused to help again, so you are likely to agree to the more time-consuming effort.

One can more easily guard against the biases that arise from cognitive dissonance by doing the following:

- Reflecting on the initial reasons for one's specific course of action
- Becoming aware of the phenomenon of cognitive dissonance itself

Taking these two measures will allow one to avoid changing one's attitudes, beliefs, or values, in addition to avoiding rationalizing or denying the experience of any mental conflict. Such processes would involve both situational awareness in addition to an understanding of general psychology and the instinct to resolve mental conflict.

## Confirmation Bias

The names of many cognitive biases serve to facilitate learning and understanding their meaning. Confirmation bias is no exception. Perhaps the most general and common cognitive bias, awareness of it can enhance one's objectivity and self-awareness.

- **Confirmation bias** occurs when an individual seeks out or acknowledges only the evidence or arguments that support one's beliefs and ignores and/or fails to seek out evidence, arguments, or positions to the contrary.

In other words, confirmation bias consists in embracing that which is consonant with one's beliefs, that which *confirms* one's beliefs, and ignoring everything and anything that *disconfirms* one's beliefs. Hence, it is *biased* in favor of that which *confirms* one's worldview.

- The clearest and most common examples of confirmation bias occur in **debates between people who hold opposing points of view**.

Specifically, confirmation bias almost always occurs in the courtroom, especially during trials. In such cases, it is extremely atypical for either side to consider thoroughly or objectively the point of view of the other. The defense attorney's job is to present the strongest, most effective case possible for the client's innocence. In some cases, defense attorneys will attempt to bury evidence that implies their client's guilt and instead construct an alternative scenario to plant reasonable doubt in the minds of the jurors. In many cases, lawyers may not even care if their client truly is innocent or guilty! Conversely, the prosecutor's job is to present the strongest, most cogent case possible for the defendant's guilt. The prosecutor certainly will not seek out evidence that exonerates the defendant, even if such evidence is readily available.

Confirmation bias is common in many academic debates as well, which is ironic since academia champions critical thinking. Nonetheless, suppose that a young student previously raised by a family of Christian fundamentalists is exposed to Darwin's theory of evolution for the first time. It is entirely possible that such a student ignores the theory and all the evidence supporting it, instead clinging to the teachings of the congregation to which they belong, their family, and the Bible. While those who are religiously inclined are often the targets of ridicule, keep in mind that the other side of the debate exhibits confirmation bias as well. Those who favor a secular or naturalistic worldview may too quickly dismiss evidence for the phenomenon of intelligent design, the idea that an intelligent agent, perhaps a God, designed our universe, instead insisting that religious people too eagerly apply an anthropic principle, reading human qualities into non-human reality. Unfortunately, such a pattern of bias is not unique to students, as professional academics, including college professors, may also exhibit such behavior, typically by dismissing arguments that run contrary to their beliefs as "trivial" and "not worth the effort" it takes to refute them, all the while blindly marshaling the very same kind of flawed or dubious arguments that confirm their mantra.

There are myriad other examples of confirmation bias, too many in fact to list here. A few other common instances include the following:

- Too quickly generalizing trends and/or patterns that confirm one's suspicions or beliefs
- Overemphasizing the personal qualities or traits of individuals that confirm your opinions about them
- Relying on biased sources of information
- Self-fulfilling prophecies (such as if an individual with social anxiety interprets their isolation as ostracism from a group)

Confirmation bias can be the result of many factors, including the problems that the brain attempts to solve and the universal human tendency to prove that one's viewpoint is, indeed, the correct one. Few people will truly want to admit when they are wrong. However, the most effective ways to avoid confirmation bias are the following:

- *Keep an open mind.* Try to understand the other side's point of view before dismissing it. This process will include discussing the topic with many people and consulting many sources of information, not only those who agree with you.
- *Focus on the facts.* Instead of trying to prove that YOU are right, focus instead on confirming whether the available facts and evidence support your beliefs or your position on a given topic.
- *Take an active approach to your investigation.* Seek out possible information that could prove your view false.

## Belief Bias

Akin to confirmation bias is **belief bias**. What they have in common is that both occur when one's beliefs or reservations affect their assessment of evidence. The difference, however, is that confirmation bias occurs when an individual seeks out only evidence that supports one's beliefs and ignores all evidence to the contrary. Belief bias, on the other hand, occurs when one makes an error in *evaluating* available evidence. The bias may be defined in the following way:

- **Belief bias** occurs when one's previous or current beliefs affect one's ability to evaluate the strength of evidence or validity of arguments that conflict with those beliefs.

For example, consider the following two arguments:

Argument (A):

1) If Buster is a Lab, then Buster is a dog.
2) Buster is a Lab.
3) Therefore, Buster is a dog.

Argument (B):

1) If *Halloween* is the best horror movie ever made, then John Carpenter is a creative genius!
2) *Halloween* is the best horror movie ever made.
3) Therefore, John Carpenter is a creative genius!

Both arguments A and B are *valid*. They are instances of the argument form *modus ponens:*

If A, then B.

A.

Therefore, B.

Most people will recognize that argument A is valid, as its premises evoke no controversy. The only issue would be determining whether the animal named Buster truly is a Lab! But in the case of argument B, belief bias is more likely to occur, given that the second premise of the argument states a matter of opinion that may vary depending on one's personal taste in movies. If one believed that *The Exorcist* was the best horror movie ever made, for instance, or if one did not specifically like John Carpenter, that same individual might be inclined to judge that argument B is invalid, even though it has the same logical form as argument A.

Returning to the issue of cognitive biases in everyday life, consider again the context of a courtroom. The Apple+ TV series *Defending Jacob* illustrates a remarkably clear case of belief bias. In the show, Jacob Barber, the son of lead prosecutor Andrew Barber, stands accused of murdering his classmate, Ben Rifkin. Jacob had sufficient motive, as Ben frequently bullied Jacob. Jacob also had the perfect opportunity to kill Ben, since Jacob's movements on the morning of the murder placed him at the scene of the crime, on a path through a local park. Jacob also had the means to commit the murder since he possessed a combat knife consistent with the wounds on Ben's body. Moreover, Jacob had some physical contact with Ben, given that the police found one of Jacob's fingerprints on Ben's jacket. Most damning of all, Jacob apparently wrote a story recounting the murder. Nonetheless, Andy Barber remains totally convinced of his son's innocence. Both he and Jacob's lawyer, in fact, judge the case and the evidence against Jacob to be very weak and circumstantial. They, thus, rest assured that a verdict of guilty would be *very* unlikely.

Belief bias can be less obvious in cases where the evidence that one judges is more complex, such as when one estimates complicated statistical or experimental data. Nonetheless, there are several ways to avoid and counter belief bias.

- *Understand Logic.* Become familiar with valid forms of deductive reasoning and learn to distinguish such reasoning from induction. In connection with this proposal, learn how to distinguish factual truth from the strength of reasoning.
- *Understand Evidence.* Learn how to distinguish a strong argument from a weak argument, specifically, by basing your judgment on the evidence that supports the argument in question.
- *Distinguish Your Feelings from the Argument.* Realize that simply because you disagree with an argument's premises or conclusion, disagreement does not imply that your opponent's view is false. The opposing viewpoint might still be true, just as the argument supporting it may still adhere to the rules of valid inferences, and the statistical or experimental evidence supporting it may still be compelling.

## Hindsight Bias

A common aphorism is the expression, "Hindsight is always 20/20," which basically means that it is always easier to understand an event or some sequence of events after the event or events in question happened, just as a picture is much clearer when one stands back and observes it from a broader perspective. Such bias is common in the study of history. Students of the history of the early twentieth century, for instance, puzzle over the reality of the Jewish Holocaust. How could humanity allow such horrible things to happen? How could so many nations stand by and do nothing while it happened? From a contemporary point of view, the resolution to such crimes against humanity is obvious: simply never let it happen in the first place!

Furthermore, the fact that most events do not happen spontaneously but rather develop gradually further complicates matters. For example, many people who suffered abuse in long-term relationships become veritable prisoners within the relationship because the abuse typically unfolds over a long period of time with increasing phases of intensity. Two people meet and experience a mutual attraction to each other. They begin dating and discover that they enjoy each other's company. Then it begins, flashes of explosive, unprovoked anger from one of the two parties, perhaps some slight physical abuse, an aggressive grab, or even a slap across the face. But such incidents are considered anomalies. The aggressor summarily apologizes and assures the victim that "it will never happen again," until of course it does, many times over through incidents that are increasingly violent and debilitating. The victim eventually can take no more and ends the relationship, finally able to understand fully the gravity of the situation and the severity of the damage done. Once liberated from such a relationship, the traumatized individual may wonder how they did not possibly know sooner the nature of the relationship. Such a person may wonder why they could not intuit the true intentions of the perpetrator from the very beginning. After all, many poised, intelligent, and strong people suffer abuse but only see it clearly in hindsight.

**Hindsight bias** can be defined in the following way:

- **Hindsight bias** occurs when one's knowledge of some past event distorts one's memory of the sequence leading up to that event.

More generally, hindsight bias occurs when one overestimates one's knowledge of the past. The most common forms of hindsight bias are the following:

- The belief that one knew all along that some outcome would occur
- The belief that one should have been able to predict some outcome
- The belief that some event was inevitable, unavoidable, or fated to happen

As an illustration, consider the hypothetical scenario of a teenager learning how to drive. Suppose that on his first outing, he collides with another vehicle while making a left turn. When recalling the event, the teenager may protest that the accident was not at all his fault. Given the narrowness of the street and the size of the two vehicles, the collision could not be avoided! The teen's father, however, who rode along in the passenger's seat, claims that he *knew* from the beginning of the drive that his son would cause an accident, as the boy did not grip the steering wheel correctly, drove too fast, and did not turn the wheel soon enough. The driver of the other vehicle involved in the collision, nonetheless, offers a third perspective, suggesting that he should have predicted the accident since the traffic light turned yellow and the car at the opposite side of the intersection seemed primed to make a left turn.

Surely, there are cases where events can be avoided or predicted, but not all possible outcomes can be anticipated. Moreover, sometimes even those events that can be anticipated are difficult to predict. Hindsight bias typically occurs in cases where one claims to have privileged knowledge of an event that either could not be anticipated or at the very least would have been very difficult to predict. Not all instances of hindsight bias are dangerous, but *the past informs the future*. The overconfidence in human memory and knowledge implied by hindsight bias can lead to harsh policies and restrictions on individual freedoms and actions that some authority figure or political administration deems dangerous based on past tragedies. Since harsh words can occasionally incite violent incidents, the day may come when freedom of speech in America is more conservatively regulated. The idea of fatalism, furthermore, when extended to the future and taken to its extreme can lead to hopelessness and despair. For instance, if one believes that traffic accidents are always inevitable, one will never attempt to drive. If the victim of prior abuse decides from the start that a potential suitor will abuse her, she will refuse to participate in a possibly healthy and fulfilling relationship.

Thus, everyone should and can avoid hindsight bias, preferably by doing the following:

- Consider how different outcomes could have happened.
- Consider different decisions you or others could have made to prevent a specific outcome.

Remember that if different outcomes are conceivable, then they are possible. Learn from the past, but do not be a prisoner to it![3]

## Implicit Bias

Like hindsight bias, implicit bias typically arises from distortions of memory:

- **Implicit bias** occurs when one's actions are the effect of attitudes or stereotypes that one learned from various institutions and authority figures or, in some way, those to which the individual had exposure that, in a seemingly unconscious way, influence one's judgment or behavior.

The primary difference between implicit and hindsight bias is that, in the former, one's actions conflict with their publicly affirmed beliefs, attitudes, or values. For example, suppose that there is a professor who claims that he treats all his students fairly and objectively. However, in his classes, his female students always seem to get lower grades than the male students, even though their work is equally adequate. Such a professor seems to be an implicit sexist. Similar examples occur when a professor claims that he has no racial biases or prejudices but, nonetheless, his students of African American, Hispanic, Asian, and Middle Eastern descent all seem to receive lower grades than his white Caucasian students, in which case the professor seems to be an implicit racist.

How can one possibly guard against implicit bias if such a phenomenon is the product of unconscious factors? One can take the following suggestions:

- *Accept* that unconscious factors exist and exert influence over your actions and judgments. While such acceptance can be difficult, self-reflection and possibly psychotherapy can be helpful in exposing and helping one to understand these factors.
- Attempt to *understand why and how* such unconscious motivations came to exist in the first place. Thinking back to one's childhood and education can expose the source of hidden prejudices and biases.
- *Evaluate the consistency* between your actions and your supposed attitudes, beliefs, and values. If inconsistency exists, try to eliminate it in a way that is fair and impartial to everyone regardless of race, sex, or creed.
- In connection with the previous point, keep in mind **the principle of comparative justice**, the idea that those who are similar in morally relevant respects should be treated similarly. If your actions conflict with this principle, they should be corrected.

In short, implicit bias can be countered with *explicit integrity*!

## Negativity Bias

Negativity bias, like the two previous biases, typically arises from faults within one's memory:

- **Negativity bias** occurs when negative experiences exert a greater psychological affect over an individual than equally compelling positive experiences.

For instance, imagine a famous self-made billionaire who also is a very respected humanitarian but who, nonetheless, remains haunted throughout his entire life by an insult levied at him decades earlier by an elementary school classmate. The same phenomenon would likely occur at the level of the public consciousness if it were discovered

3 For more detailed information on confirmation, belief, and hindsight biases, consult Chapter 4 of David Kelly and Debbie Hutchins, *The Art of Reasoning* (New York: Norton & Norton, 2020), 148–68.

that the famous billionaire in the previous example committed a heinous crime. Perhaps he sought out his childhood rival and avenged himself. Such a man would not likely be remembered for his charitable endeavors or for the story of his ascent to the very top of the capitalist empire. He would be remembered for that one horrific crime. As the Joker said in *The Killing Joke*, "All it takes is ONE BAD DAY."[4]

On a smaller scale, negativity bias is common in the lives of most people. For the typical, average, hardworking individual, one negative experience on an otherwise positive and productive day can taint one's assessment of the previous 24 hours. Moreover, usually one specific positive experience will not be enough to brighten sufficiently a day consisting mostly of a series of unfortunate events. However, negativity bias can be avoided:

- *Focus on the positives.* It is said that we should all count our blessings. Usually, any negative experience or event and the feelings of sadness, dread, or anger can be counterbalanced by recounting one's positive experiences and the good things in one's life. Rebounding to the positives in times of crisis can make one cherish them even more.
- *Understand how* the negative experience occurred and how it can be avoided in the future.
- *Avoid exaggerated thinking* by putting the negative experience into perspective. Typically, exaggerated thoughts ("Today is the worst day of my life!" "I will never live this down!" etc.) misrepresent the reality of one's situation.

Just remember that the "power of positive thinking" is empty without the power of *critical* thinking and the resilience to engage in it.

## Anchoring

The bias of anchoring can be understood in two ways: *dogmatic anchoring* and *estimative anchoring.*[5]

- **Dogmatic anchoring** can occur when an individual adopts a principle, belief, custom, or value at an early stage of their life or education that subsequently taints all other beliefs.

Children are often very impressionable. What they learn early in life keeps them grounded in the same way that the literal anchor of a boat keeps it in place. Religious and moral standards lend themselves as the clearest examples of anchors for people. The religion to which one is introduced in one's childhood one will usually continue to practice throughout one's life span. A person raised Catholic may frown upon all those who prefer a different denomination or a different religion altogether. In addition, imagine a person whose parent was a vet and taught her child never to trust anyone who does not have a pet dog. That child then grows up to be someone who judges people based solely on whether they have dogs as pets.

Anchors are not always beliefs learned early in life. They may also consist of ideas that one learns very early in the study of a subject, usually those to which one is first exposed when learning a new subject. For example, consider a freshman in college who takes her first philosophy course, and after her exposure to the position of subjective idealism on the first day of class, she becomes convinced that she does not have a body. Her newly acquired position may become an anchor if she rejects any other position that is inconsistent with it. Beliefs can become anchors in virtually any subject, and such anchors can be the source of many dangerous biases, such as racism or sexism.

---

4 Emphasis mine.

5 Paul Herrick, *Think with Socrates: An Introduction to Critical Thinking* (New York: Oxford University Press, 2015), 126. The book focuses on this form of anchoring in the chapter devoted to cognitive biases.

Notice that this cognitive bias is reminiscent not only of the idols of the mind, specifically, idols of the cave and theater but also of confirmation bias. In both confirmation bias and dogmatic anchoring, an individual's prior and current beliefs influence how one evaluates evidence that conflicts with one's beliefs. However, there are at least two key differences.

- First, dogmatic anchoring concerns beliefs that one adopts either early in life or early in their study of a subject that influence other beliefs and judgments one makes about the beliefs and dispositions of others, whereas confirmation bias occurs when one's beliefs prejudice the *evidence* one chooses to acknowledge or ignore.

For example, a person can be "anchored" to a specific belief but still acknowledge the evidence against it and marshal those arguments in favor of it, such as the philosophy student in the previous example. Moreover, the discipline of apologetics in Christianity constitutes the rational defense of Christian doctrines.

- Second, the beliefs one defends in confirmation bias may not necessarily constitute "anchor" beliefs, although the two biases can sometimes occur together.

For instance, a student writing an essay on global climate change might consult biased sources to defend her position that the phenomenon in question is a hoax, but her position may not dominate all her other beliefs and thought processes. She may, in fact, have friends who believe that the data supporting climate change is legitimate, and she may not think any less of them for their inclinations. However, a Muslim who condemns anyone who is not also a Muslim and refuses to acknowledge the doctrines of any other religion manifests both confirmation bias and dogmatic anchoring.

A different form of anchoring can result in false judgment about quantities.

- **Estimative anchoring** consists of the tendency to make an erroneous judgment about a quantity based on its relation to a specific reference point.

For example, imagine going to a used car lot to purchase a relatively new vehicle. Suppose that you intend to spend no more than $5,000.00. The first car the dealer shows you, however, costs nearly $10,000.00. Eventually, you agree to purchase a vehicle priced at $8,000.00. In comparison to the original vehicle, your current purchase seems like a bargain. Restaurants employ similar strategies. Often, management will place advertisements for very expensive specials near the entrance so that lesser-priced, but still rather expensive, meals seem worth the price.

Both forms of anchoring can be avoided:

- To avoid *dogmatic anchoring*, consider alternative reasons for holding a specific belief or attitude besides the fact that you had exposure to it early in life or early in your education on a specific subject. Timing is not always of the essence in the pursuit of truth.
- To avoid *estimative anchoring*, consider a different anchor, a different reference point, and ask yourself whether you would have changed your course of action if you were not unduly influenced.

Since estimative anchoring applies a *heuristic* function, understanding the concept of a heuristic more generally can help to avoid heuristic anchoring, and it is to *heuristic biases* that we now turn.

## Heuristic Biases

Like electricity, people usually want to take the path of least resistance when solving a problem. A *heuristic* allows people to do just that.

- A **heuristic** is a mental strategy, shortcut, or "rule of thumb" for making a fast decision and solving a problem quickly and efficiently.

Developing solutions to problems quickly can be beneficial, but as revealed by heuristic anchoring, it can also lead to errors in judgment. I will focus on the heuristic errors of **representativeness** and **availability** before devoting some consideration to **affect**.

### Representativeness

The basis of representativeness is thinking in terms of stereotypes.

- A **stereotype** is an exaggerated and overly simplistic conception of the characteristics that members of a group have in common.

Stereotypes can also be described as a failure to see the "trees" through the proverbial "forest," a failure to discern the unique and distinctive attributes that individuals have despite belonging to a group that obscures them. For example, when most people think of birds, they usually imagine a small creature with wings that can fly. But of course, not all birds are especially small, and not all birds can fly. Turkeys can be rather large, and an ostrich is often taller than the average human. Moreover, penguins and dodos have wings but cannot fly. Similar attitudes can prejudice one's assessment of people.[6] A common stereotype of student-athletes is that they have dull personalities, bully those weaker than them, and lack intelligence. Certainly, there are student-athletes who have these attributes, but a significant number, if not most, are very affable, intelligent, and kind. Racial and ethnic minorities often suffer from stereotypes, such as when reactionary Americans judge all people of Middle Eastern descent to be "heathen Muslims" or terrorists, people of Hispanic descent to be "border jumpers," or people of African American descent to be physically strong and athletic but not as intelligent or sophisticated as white Caucasians.

- The **representativeness heuristic** occurs when a judgment is made about an individual based on a stereotype, surface characteristics that members of their associated group tend to share.

A related bias that should not be confused with representativeness is the *halo effect*:

- The **halo effect** occurs when one's overall impression of a person's character influences what one thinks and feels about more specific character traits of that person.

For instance, if you meet someone who is friendly and charming and on that basis judge that he is also intelligent, sophisticated, and wealthy, you fall victim to the halo effect. Stereotyping factors into both biases, and both biases involve making inferences are made in a "top-down" direction. The difference, however, is that the halo effect usually occurs when inferences are made from attributes a person possesses to other possible characteristics, whereas representativeness occurs when one makes inferences about a person's attributes based on some group to which that person belongs.

---

6 See Kelly and Hutchins, *The Art of Reasoning*, 168–9.

## Availability

People remember some events more easily than others, as established in the discussion on negativity bias. Not only are negative events and experiences recalled more easily than positive ones, but those events that are more dramatic than most and deviate starkly from the norm tend to leave a deeper and more indelible impression on one's memory than ordinary, mundane events. Such events that are more easily recalled may be deemed more *available* than others.

- The **availability heuristic** occurs when one erroneously judges that some event happens far more frequently than it truly does or that it is far more likely to happen than is truly probable.

For example, suppose that a couple who have an eight-year-old child allows that child to walk to school each morning. But suppose one morning they read in the newspaper that two children recently were kidnapped in neighboring cities. Persuaded that it is highly probable that their child will be abducted, they decide that the child will take the bus to school. An additional example that, unfortunately, is relevant to contemporary life concerns the frequency at which mass shootings occur. Imagine that a college professor becomes aware that mass shootings happen in schools, colleges, and universities at a more regular rate than in previous decades. Convinced that he may become the victim of such an event, he decides to change professions and become an author instead. In each example, the individuals in question fail to consider the true base rates at which such events really happen and rely on information that is very easy to recall given how it stands out in one's memory.

The availability heuristic is likely to occur whenever judgments are made about events that can be very quickly recalled or that differ drastically from the norm, as in each of the following cases:

- *Catastrophic* or *dramatic incidents*, specifically those highlighted by news and media outlets. People tend to think that plane crashes, earthquakes, terrorist attacks, and violent riots happen at far more regular rates than they really do, often because such events receive the most coverage in the media.
- Dramatic or significant experiences in one's *personal* life. Negativity bias, itself, often aligns with availability since negative experiences usually signify breaks from the norm. Commonly, tragic or unfortunate experiences during one's childhood exert a greater influence over their development and are remembered more keenly than all of the positives, precisely because such events stand out from the norm of an otherwise happy and healthy childhood. The same may be said about a former couple who remember their breakup more poignantly than all the happy months or years they spent together.
- Events, ideas, or situations that are referred to *continually or repetitively*. At the end of the twentieth century, specifically in 1999, many people were paranoid about the "Y2K" problem, in which computers would either collectively cease to function or take over the world, depending on which source you consulted. The true problem, however, consisted in the frequency to which various media outlets referred to it. When the year 2000 came, virtually nothing happened. In our time, climate change and its implications receive similar attention. Typically, the more recent a tragedy or drastic event is, the more attention it will get, which can stamp such incidents onto the memories of most people.

One positive takeaway from understanding the availability heuristic, nonetheless, is that at least tragic, unfortunate events and natural disasters are not nearly common enough to warrant the all-too-common paranoia about them!

## Affect

In short, affect refers to one's feelings, mood, or emotional disposition. Emotions are very powerful and, thus, can lead to biases in judgment.

- **Affect bias** occurs precisely when one's feelings influence one's judgments.

For instance, if a professor is in a good mood, he or she is more likely to evaluate students in a more favorable way. On the other hand, if the same professor is in a particularly bad mood, he or she may evaluate students more harshly.

Emotions can affect one's judgment in other ways, for instance, consider the following two hypothetical sentences:

a) Dwayne "The Rock" Johnson gave $2 million to Oxfam in 2020.

b) Dwayne "The Rock" Johnson gave no money to charity in 2020.

I do not know, personally, whether either statement is true. But if one were to take a poll of random people and ask them which of these two statements is true, each person would likely make a judgment based on their feelings about Dwayne "The Rock" Johnson. If a person likes Johnson or generally has a positive appraisal of Johnson, said person would likely judge (a) to be true, whereas a person who hates Johnson would most likely judge that (b) is the true statement.

How can heuristic biases be avoided? One might take the following strategies:

- To avoid *representative bias*, avoid stereotypes. Separate the individual from the group to which he or she belongs. Try to reserve judgments about individuals until learning more about that individual.
- To avoid the *availability heuristic*, take the time and effort to seek out information beyond what you can readily remember. Obtain legitimately strong and cogent statistical studies on the matter in question and make decisions based on the true background rates at which events happen.
- To avoid *affect bias*, try to take the perspective of a person with a different attitude or mood. Doing so can help to weigh the pros and cons of a decision objectively.

In short, remember that heuristic biases occur because people too often attempt to make decisions quickly. It can be beneficial to move quickly, but it is better to move *efficiently*.

## Attribution Biases[7]

Psychologists use the term "*attribution*" to describe how people explain and interpret behaviors and actions, in addition to evaluating performances at specific tasks, both our own and those of others. Generally, there are two kinds of factors involved when making attributions:

- **Internal factors**, which refer to specific personality traits, desires, goals, and abilities of the individual.
- **External factors**, which refer to the environment or the circumstances surrounding an individual's actions.

For example, suppose that an athlete attempts to bench press 300 pounds for the first time and fails. His coach might ask, "To what do you attribute your failed attempt?" If the athlete attributes his failure to *internal* factors, he might respond, "I'm just simply not strong enough yet. I have to do more work building up to that weight." If the

7 For more on attribution biases, see Kelly and Hutchins, *The Art of Reasoning*, 180–4.

athlete attributes his failure to *external* factors, he might respond, "It's not my fault! I had a fight with my girlfriend last night, and I'm under a lot of stress studying for finals!"

In many cases, whether one's behavior is due to external or internal factors is a matter of interpretation, but usually both factors contribute significantly. Nonetheless, *attribution bias* can occur quite often:

- **Attribution bias** occurs when one's own behavior or the behavior of others is explained in terms of the wrong factors.

There are many variations of attribution bias. The three most common are the following:

- **Fundamental Attribution Error:** The tendency to explain a person's behavior in terms of personal (internal) factors and ignore situational (external) factors. For example, I judge the person who cut me off as a jerk and an unsafe driver, but unbeknownst to me, he had to rush his sick wife to the hospital. Or when a woman judges that a man's behavior is indicative of a generous personality, even though he is only trying to curry favor with her so that she will sleep with him.
- **Actor-Observer Bias:** The tendency to ignore internal factors and overemphasize external factors when judging one's own actions. (In other words, the fundamental attribution error tends to occur when we judge others, but the opposite tends to happen when we judge ourselves.) For example, he failed the test because he is a bad student, but I failed the test because my dad made me help him with yard work the night before.
- **Self-Serving Bias:** Attributing our successes to our personal traits, such as ability, and our failures to external circumstances. Whereas actor-observer bias is more of a cognitive shortcut, the goal of self-serving bias is to preserve one's self-esteem.

There are other attribution biases, but these are the most common. To counter attribution bias, one can do the following:

- Try to consider how another person's environment, situation, or other external factors could have provoked or at least contributed to their behavior.
- Be aware of your dominant personality traits and try to consider how they could have contributed to your actions.
- Consider how other people would act in similar circumstances.

In short, avoid attribution bias by understanding why or how you developed your point of view and by trying to understand situations from the point of view of others.

## Chapter Summary and Key Points to Remember

The human brain tries to solve several problems of cognition and perception, specifically, the following four:

- **The Filtering Problem:** The brain is constantly bombarded with information, and as a result, a lot is filtered out, including important information.
- **The Construction Problem:** Meaning is often unclear, so the brain fills in gaps and constructs meaning, which may not accurately reflect reality.

- **The Impulse Problem:** Often, decisions have to be made quickly, but making fast decisions can be counterproductive.
- **The Faulty Memory Problem:** We have to remember important bits of information but often what is remembered reinforces biases and prejudices.
- **Cognitive biases** are psychological tendencies that interfere with objectivity.
- **Cognitive dissonance** is the experience of discomfort either when one holds two conflicting beliefs or ideas; one's actions conflict with one's attitudes, beliefs, or values; or when one holds two contradictory beliefs or ideas. The resolution to such conflict usually takes nonrational means.
- **Confirmation bias** is the tendency to acknowledge and gather only the evidence that already supports one's beliefs while ignoring all evidence to the contrary.
- **Belief bias** is the tendency to evaluate the strength or validity of an argument based on whether that argument supports or conflicts with one's beliefs.
- **Hindsight bias** occurs when one's knowledge of an event or of an outcome of an event distorts one's memory of those events, usually leading one to believe that such events could not be avoided or should have been predicted.
- **Negativity bias** occurs when negative experiences exert a greater psychological affect over an individual than equally compelling positive experiences.
- **Implicit bias** occurs when one's actions are the effect of attitudes or stereotypes that, in an almost unconscious way, influence one's behaviors, judgments, or decisions.
- The bias of **anchoring** can be understood in two ways:
  - **Dogmatic anchoring** occurs when the first information one learns about a subject taints everything else one learns, or when beliefs and values learned early in one's life tend to influence one's judgments about other beliefs.
  - **Estimative anchoring** occurs when one mistakenly estimates a quantity based on how near or far it is from some arbitrarily chosen reference point.
- A **heuristic** is a procedure or strategy for solving a problem or getting an answer quickly. It can result in several kinds of biases.
  - **Representativeness bias** occurs when one makes judgments or decisions based on stereotypes of a group and overlooks the differences between individuals in that group.
  - **Availability bias** occurs when one judges the likelihood of an event based on how easily one can remember instances of such an event.
  - **Affect bias** occurs when one's mood or emotional disposition influences one's behaviors, judgments, or decisions.
- **Attribution** refers to the way in which we interpret the behavior of ourselves and others. One's behavior may be the result of **internal factors**, such as personality, goals, intentions, or abilities, or **external factors**, such as one's environment, situation, or circumstances. **Attribution bias** occurs when one explains or interprets the behavior of oneself or another based on the wrong factors. The most common kinds of attribution bias are the following:
  - **Fundamental attribution error**, which typically occurs when one mistakenly explains another's behavior in terms of internal factors when external factors are the more likely explanation.
  - **Actor-observer bias**, which occurs when one explains one's own behavior in terms of external factors but emphasizes internal factors when explaining the behavior of others.

- **Self-serving bias**, which occurs when one judges one's successes to be the result of internal factors but emphasizes external factors when explaining one's failures.

- Cognitive biases can and should be avoided. There are several ways to avoid each bias, but one can avoid all of them by following **three simple rules**:

1) **Emphasize Facts.** Pursue truth rather than pride, ego, or comfort.
2) **Understand Logic.** Judge arguments based on their validity, soundness, strength, or cogency rather than on whether they align with your beliefs.
3) **Take the Perspectives of Others.** Try to see things from a different point of view, specifically, from the vantage point of the person with whom you have a dispute or a conflict.

## Exercises for Application and Reflection

**Instructions:** Use what you learned in this chapter to help you respond to the following questions.

**Section I – Reflections:**

1. Explain how a different cognitive bias can emerge from each of the different problems that the brain tries to solve.
2. Explain how each problem that the brain tries to solve can lead to the same cognitive bias.
3. Explain how each idol of the mind from Chapter 2 can produce a *different* cognitive bias.
4. Explain how each idol of the mind from Chapter 2 can produce the *same* cognitive bias.

**Section II – Applications:** Do any of the following scenarios indicate a cognitive bias? If so, name the cognitive bias. Otherwise, simply write, "No bias."

1. Alan and Sandy meet with a real estate agent to discuss buying a house. They explain that their budget is no more than $350,000.00. The agent, however, first shows them a house listed at $650,000.00. Alan and Sandy eventually agree to purchase a house listed at $450,000.00.
2. When Henry allowed Maci to sit in on his class, he thought that there would be sufficient withdrawals to add her. After the add/drop period ended, however, there was no space to add Maci, and he had to dismiss her. Reflecting on the incident, Henry told himself that he "should have known all along" that there would be no space for a new student.
3. While walking through the cemetery, Gregg discovers what appears to be an antique ring. He places it on his finger and spins it around. Remarkably, he learns that when the ring is turned inward toward the palm of his hand, it makes him invisible! Not sure what to do with his newfound ability, Gregg wanders around town. He eventually makes his way to a local bank and decides to hide inside until after closing and steal a significant sum of money. Later, he feels guilty, as he never broke a law before. But he decides that since the bank's money is insured, he need not worry about it.
4. James is convinced that the behavior of his cat, General, predicts the weather. He cites as evidence the three times that his cat spun around in circles for an hour just before a violent thunderstorm. However, he ignores the ten times that nothing unusual happened after General's strange behavior.
5. Frank reads a newspaper article detailing a violent melee that took place in a local restaurant. Even though Frank wanted to take his wife out for her birthday, he decides that it would probably be much wiser for them to spend the evening at home, given the likelihood that something similar could happen and spoil their evening.

6. Katrina learns that Ryan is a fan of professional wrestling. She knows that generally pro wrestling fans are immature, naive, uneducated, and considered to be less "valuable" than the rest of the public at large. Hence, she reasons that Ryan is not worth meeting in person, unaware that he holds a PhD, teaches at several colleges and universities, is respected by all who know him, and is comparably more financially stable than most people.
7. After their first date, Haley judges Blake to be a very compassionate, strong, and charming man, with a great sense of humor. However, Blake only wanted to curry favor with her so that she would be more willing to sleep with him.
8. When Jack failed his logic midterm, he rationalized his poor performance by blaming Myron for overworking him and stressing him out the day before. However, Matt did poorly as well, but Jack suggested that Matt just simply does not understand the subject and will perform poorly on any logic exam no matter how much he studies.
9. Because Dave is a fan of Godzilla, he judges the following argument to be invalid: If there is a movie called *Godzilla vs. Kong*, then Kong will win. There is a movie called *Godzilla vs. Kong*. Thus, Kong will win! However, the argument has the form modus ponens. Thus, it is valid.
10. Katherine took her first philosophy course with Professor Grady, who is a staunch atheist. She, thus, became very skeptical about any philosophical position that endorsed theism or had any aspect of spiritualism.
11. When John earned his black belt in Kenpo, he was very proud of himself and celebrated the fact that he was a very proficient martial artist. However, when he lost in the first round of the "Battle of Baltimore," he reasoned that it was only because he was distracted by the crowd.
12. Because Jeff is in a good mood, he decides that Brian, who bullies younger students, would make a decent camp counselor.
13. When Walter failed his logic midterm, he decided that he simply was not adequately prepared and that he needed to study more carefully.
14. Professor Edgeler claims that he treats all his students fairly, yet his African American and female students always seem to get lower grades, even though their work is equally adequate to that of his white male students.
15. John's childhood was mostly happy, as he received lots of presents from his generous aunt and uncle, had a stable home, and got to take fun vacations every year. However, what stands out most to him is the time he received detention in school and was punished severely by his parents.

# 4

# Foundations of Knowledge

## Truth, Justification, Sense-Perception, and the External World

INTRODUCTION

### Preparing to Read Chapter 4

The Socratic profession of ignorance coupled with the prevalence of the idols of the mind and cognitive biases force the admission that many of our commonsense beliefs are erroneous, unwarranted, or distorted by human instincts and desires. Simply understanding the sources of error and obstacles to genuine knowledge is the most important step to thinking critically but will neither in itself produce knowledge nor prevent us from succumbing to them altogether. Ask any randomly selected person to provide a list of beliefs that he or she *knows with absolute certainty,* and it is very likely that said individual will provide a list of affirmations believed to be true based solely on the testimony of others or the frequency with which they are heard. Everybody "knows" that the sun is the center of the solar system. Everybody "knows" there are seven additional planets in our solar system. Everybody "knows" that light travels at 186,000 miles per second. But out of all those who claim to "know" these facts, very few assent to them based on evidence or firsthand experience. Most believe them based on what they hear repeated frequently. But which among our beliefs truly constitutes knowledge? Can we tell the difference? If so, how? The aim of this chapter is to present and explain possible answers to three related questions:

1) What is knowledge?
2) How is knowledge acquired?
3) What can we know about the external world?[1]

### AS YOU ARE READING, BE SURE TO WATCH FOR THE FOLLOWING TERMS

- Fact
- Opinion

1 These three questions form the basis of the anthology by Louis Pojman, *The Theory of Knowledge: Classical and Contemporary Readings* (Belmont, CA: Wadsworth Cengage Learning, 2003).

- Belief
- True Belief
- The Traditional Model of Knowledge
- Alethic Relativism
- The Correspondence Theory of Truth
- The Coherence Theory of Truth
- Justification
- Testimony
- The "Gettier" Problem
- Undefeated Justification
- Empiricism
- Sensation versus Perception
- Proper Objects of Sense-Perception
- Common Objects of Sense-Perception
- Incidental Objects of Sense-Perception
- Simple versus Complex Ideas
- The Resemblance Thesis
    - Primary versus Secondary Qualities
- Einstein and the Special Theory of Relativity
- The Heisenberg Uncertainty Principle
    - The "Observer Effect"
- The Law of Induction
- Rationalism
- The "Laws of Thought"
    - The Law of Identity
    - The Law of Noncontradiction
    - The Law of Excluded Middle
    - The Principle of Sufficient Reason
- Skepticism
- Realism
    - Direct versus Indirect
- Idealism
    - Subjective
    - Phenomenalism

**KEEP THE FOLLOWING QUESTIONS IN MIND AS YOU READ**

- Which of my beliefs can I know, for sure, are true?
- Why is it important to know the difference between knowledge, true belief, and mere opinion?
- How did I obtain most of my beliefs?
- Are the sources of my beliefs reliable?
- Does the information I am reading give me any good reason for revising my current belief system or being more conservative about the claims that I accept as true?

# What Is Knowledge?

## The Traditional Model of Knowledge

Understanding *knowledge* requires distinguishing it from the following: facts, thoughts, beliefs, and true beliefs.

- A **fact** is whatever happens to be the case about reality, regardless of whatever anyone believes, knows, or has reason for believing.
- A **thought** is an assertion or mental proposition that can have a truth value.
- A **belief** is a thought that an individual affirms or to which an individual gives assent.
- A **true belief** is a belief that corresponds to a fact or reality.[2]

There are facts that can be observed, such as the fact that most birds can fly, the fact that snow is white, and the fact that some apples are green. But there are some matters of fact that cannot be readily observed or even known. For instance, exactly how many stars there are in the entire universe is a *matter of fact*, but only part of the universe is observable. In addition, whether God or anything resembling a God exists is a matter of fact, and people can argue for or against the existence of God, but no one truly knows whether such a being exists. The same can be said about the existence of alien life forms or about what exactly happens after death. There are also matters of facts that only specific individuals know, for example, the number of strokes it takes for a woman to brush her hair back or the number of times a man moves his toothbrush when brushing his teeth.

Thoughts are part of the content of one's consciousness and can have a **truth value**, meaning that they can be judged to be true or false. Consider each of the following:

- (A) "Horse"
- (B) "Cat"
- (C) "There is a horse in my backyard."
- (D) "There is a cat on my welcome mat."

Both (C) and (D) constitute *thoughts*. At the moment, there is neither a horse in my backyard nor a cat on my welcome mat. Hence, both (C) and (D) are false. Both (A) and (B) are terms that can be neither true nor false.

2 David Morrow, *Giving Reasons: An Extremely Short Introduction to Critical Thinking* (Indianapolis, IN: Hackett Publishing, Inc., 2017). The book provides an incredibly clear and concise introduction to epistemology in Chapters 1 and 2. His answers to the question, "What is knowledge?" are like mine in some respects. See pages 1–4.

Thoughts may be entertained without being affirmed. For instance, I can entertain the thought "The sun is a giant ball of ice." If I merely entertain the thought, it is not a *belief* unless I assent to or affirm it. If I were to affirm such a thought, I would have a *false belief*. If the thought I affirmed happened to correctly describe the sun, I would have a *true belief*. Not all true beliefs, however, constitute knowledge. Some beliefs simply happen to be true. For example, suppose that I believe that at 3:57 p.m. (Eastern Standard Time) on April 17, 2021, President Biden is eating lasagna in the White House kitchen. Perhaps I spontaneously conjured up this thought and assent to it, but it just happens to be the case that President Biden is engaged in the activity the thought describes. My true belief in this case is not *knowledge* since I do not have very good reasons for assenting to the thought in question. I have no evidence for it, nor did I take it on anyone's authority. It is simply a belief of mine that happens to match a fact about reality.

Traditionally, a person, S, knows some proposition or some complete thought, P, if and only if,[3]

1) P is true.

2) S believes that P.

3) S is justified in believing that P.

Condition (1) demands the truth of and justification for P. Defining truth is the aim of the next section followed by a discussion of justification.

## Understanding Truth and Justification

Truth is a property that some beliefs have but that others lack. Without people to affirm or deny thoughts, there is a sense in which truth would not exist. There would still be facts, but facts could not be affirmed or known. For instance, the age of the universe and of Earth are matters of fact. But if intelligent beings never evolved, there would be no one to discern, ascertain, and affirm or deny such facts.

In the preceding paragraphs, I made implicit references to the *correspondence theory* of truth:

- The **correspondence theory of truth** maintains that a belief is true when it matches a fact about reality.

While this theory of truth seems intuitively commonsensical, people often disagree about facts. And, as acknowledged in the previous section, some facts cannot be known. Hence, many people are inclined to adopt a *relativistic* theory of truth based on the opinions of individuals. This position is sometimes called **individual alethic relativism**.[4] The English word "alethic" derives from the Greek word ἀλήθεια (aletheia), which literally means "dis-closedness" or "un-coveredness," connoting truth. The doctrine can be defined in the following way:

- **Individual alethic relativism** (hereafter IAR) holds that truth is relative to the individual. Essentially, whatever an individual believes is true is true for that individual.

This theory is appealing because everybody wants to be right all the time! Everybody would love to be able to create truth simply through the power of belief. Everyone would love to be infallible. However, this relativistic theory is severely flawed and most assuredly false.

---

3 This theory is often attributed to Plato based on a theory of knowledge proposed in one of his later dialogues, *Theatetus*.

4 See Paul Herrick, *Think with Socrates: An Introduction to Critical Thinking* (New York: Oxford University Press, 2015), 136–43. Specifically, see Chapter 5 for his discussion of relativism.

In the first place, IAR implies that truth is purely a matter of what an individual happens to think and, hence, that all truth is relative. IAR implies that no belief is objectively true, that no beliefs match independently objective facts about reality. Thus, if anyone affirms this theory, it raises a dilemma:

- On the one hand, to affirm this theory is to affirm that it is true *regardless of what anyone thinks*, that it is objectively true. But if IAR is objectively true, then it is false since the theory maintains that there are no objectively true beliefs!
- On the other hand, a proponent of IAR might acknowledge that the theory itself has no objective validity, that some people just happen to think that IAR is true. But in that case, the theory can be dismissed as merely a matter of opinion.

An additional problem for IAR is that if this theory is correct, then *no one can ever be wrong in one's beliefs!* If a person believes that Earth is flat, then that person is right. If a person believes that there is a pot of gold at the end of every rainbow, then that person is correct. Moreover, two people can hold completely contradictory beliefs and neither person can consistently criticize the other. But as the preceding chapters revealed, no one is infallible. People often hold false beliefs, and typically there are methods for their adjudication. There is, thus, no solid basis for IAR.

A problem, however, remains for the correspondence theory of truth: sometimes there are beliefs whose correspondence to reality cannot be determined. For example, suppose that I tell you that there is currently a purple elephant tap dancing in the street in front of Buckingham palace. Suppose that you are not at that moment in a position to verify whether my statement is true. But there may be other ways that you can make a judgment about this belief, which leads to the **coherence theory of truth**.

- The **coherence theory of truth** holds that truth is a property that a system of beliefs has when those beliefs are consistent with each other.

Through coherence, one can employ a test to determine whether there truly is a purple elephant tap dancing in front of Buckingham palace. One can simply compare this claim to other beliefs that one already accepts as true. If it is inconsistent with those beliefs, then it can be dismissed as false. For instance, if you believe that no elephants are purpose, that elephants do not tap dance, and that elephants would not be permitted on the street in front of Buckingham palace, then you can reject my claim as false.

Coherence, by itself, however, cannot always provide a firm foundation for truth since there are many beliefs consistent with each other that do not correspond to reality. Many works of fiction create imaginary worlds that operate according to consistent laws that differ from those in our own world, for instance. Thus, it is wise to use both correspondence and coherence as criteria for evaluating beliefs.

- Correspondence is a default criterion since beliefs must match the facts of reality to be true.
- But when a belief's relation to reality cannot be established, it can be tested for consistency with beliefs that one already accepts as true. If it is inconsistent with any, the belief in question may be rejected.

Tom Morris uses a helpful analogy to illuminate the concept of truth, suggesting that truth is comparable to an anchor that keeps beliefs grounded in reality.[5] The anchor analogy reflects correspondence. However, if a belief has no anchor, then it can be hitched to some other belief that is anchored to reality. The "hitching" analogy reflects coherence.

5 See Tom Morris, *Philosophy for Dummies* (New York: Wiley Publishing, Inc., 1999), 47. Specifically see Chapter 4.

In addition to being true, a belief must be *justified* if it is to constitute knowledge. There are many ways that a belief may be justified, but they are all variations of two very general methods.[6]

- First, beliefs can be justified by **experience** or empirical, demonstrable evidence. There are three basic ways of justifying a belief based on experience:

  a) *Sense-perception*, in which one observes some fact or facts directly. For instance, you are justified in believing that John Q. murdered Jane Roe because you witnessed the murder yourself. Or you are justified in believing that hydrochloric acid and sodium hydroxide combine to form basic saltwater because you did the experiment yourself.

  b) *Testimony*, in which one's belief is based on what is told by a reliable witness. For instance, you are on the jury of John Q.'s trial, and you believe that he murdered Jane Roe because a witness testifies that he saw the murder happen. Or you believe aliens exist because a television show interviews a man who claims that aliens abducted him.

  c) *Authority*, a form of testimony in which the witness has specialized knowledge or expertise on a subject. For example, you believe that you are healthy because your physician completed an examination and told you so. Or you believe that aliens do not exist because a respected cosmologist examined the possible evidence for such creatures and found it to be very weak.

- Second, beliefs can be justified rationally, through **reason** and logic. There are essentially two principal methods by which reason can justify a belief:

  d) The belief may be justified as a matter of *definition* or the *laws of logic*. For example, I am justified in believing that gold is a yellow metal, or that water is a clear liquid substance, or that a triangle is a closed, three-sided geometric figure. Why may I accept these beliefs? Because they purely and simply state definitions. I may also believe purely mathematical truths, such as that 7 + 5 = 12 or that the area of a circle is calculated by multiplying Pi (3.14) times the square of the circle's radius. I may also affirm purely logical laws, such as the law of identity, that every statement implies itself and that everything is identical with itself.

  e) The belief may be an *inference* based on available evidence. This process may simply mean that one has strong reasons for holding a belief. This method of justification through reason typically consists of a combination of reason and experience. To illustrate, suppose that a librarian is murdered on the college campus where I teach. Suppose also that the available evidence is a silver pendant, small shoe prints, and a piece of beige cloth in the hand of the victim. Next, suppose that I discover that a student of mine, Sally Jones, had a pendant matching the item found in the library, missing since the night of the murder; has a speck of blood on her shoes, which matches the prints left at the crime scene; and has a torn beige T-shirt. Based on this evidence, I infer that Sally probably is the prime suspect in the murder.

As this last scenario establishes, experience and reason usually work together, just as correspondence and coherence can collaborate in establishing truth. The two major foundations of justification tie into the major theories of

6 For a similar account of justification, see Morrow, *Giving Reasons*, 10–17.

how knowledge is acquired, but before addressing the origins of knowledge, a challenge to the traditional model of knowledge must be addressed.[7]

### The Gettier Problem

The **"Gettier" problem** is named after Edmund Gettier.[8] Essentially, the "problem" he identified is that the traditional model of knowledge is incomplete. An individual may possess a belief that is both true and justified but the belief in question may not constitute knowledge. For instance, consider the following scenario:

> While driving down a country road, John Smith passes by a farm and observes what looks like a sheep in the field. As he drives away, he thinks to himself, "I just passed by a sheep." But, unbeknownst to Mr. Smith, the item he observed was merely a rock. Nonetheless, behind the rock hid a sheep out of sight, emerging into view only after Mr. Smith drove away.

In the scenario, Mr. Smith had a justified true belief, "I just passed by a sheep," but it was only a matter of luck that his belief was in fact true. Hence, one can reasonably say that Mr. Smith did not *know* that he passed by a sheep.

The literature responding to the Gettier problem is enormously vast, profound, complex, and difficult. Not all of it can be considered here, not merely because of the sheer amount of it but also because much of it is extremely esoteric.[9] What I propose, thus, is a simple interim solution: *add a fourth condition.* A subject, S, may be said to know some proposition, P, just in case:

1) P is true.
2) S believes that P.
3) S is justified in believing that P.
4) It is not a matter of luck that P is true.

That is, if one has a justified true belief and one's justification is *undefeated*, one may be said to possess knowledge.

## How Do We Acquire Knowledge?

Many thinkers advanced a wide variety of theories to explain knowledge acquisition. But ultimately, all theories are variations of two basic positions:

- The first is **empiricism**, proponents of which maintain that (a) all knowledge derives from experience and (b) only forms of experience such as observation can extend knowledge in important ways.

7 The topic of justification in epistemology is far more complex than what I can present in this chapter. For introductory readings on the topic, see Parts V and VI of Pojman's *The Theory of Knowledge*, "Theories of Justification (I): Foundationalism and Coherentism," 157–256, and "Theories of Justification (II): Externalism and Internalism," 257–366, respectively. For an overview of these theories, see Herrick, *Think with Socrates*, 167–83, 184–98.

8 See Gettier, Edmund. "Is Justified True Belief Knowledge?" in *The Theory of Knowledge: Classical and Contemporary Readings*, 2nd ed., ed. Louis Pojman (Boston, MA: Cengage, 2003), 121–3. While his examples differ from mine, they illustrate the same sort of problem.

9 If the "Gettier" problem interests you, Pojman's anthology *The Theory of Knowledge* contains several major readings introducing the major literature on the topic. Specifically, see Part IV, "The Analysis of Knowledge," 121–55, which contains Gettier's original article in addition to responses from Feldman, Goldman, and Lehrer and Paxton.

- The second is **rationalism**, proponents of which maintain that (a) at least some knowledge is innate (inborn) or a priori (not derived from experience) and (b) reasoning and logic alone can extend knowledge in significant ways.

Each position will be examined in turn.

## Empiricism

There are three major appeals of empiricism:

- First, it is a very *commonsense-based* position that most people intuitively accept.
- Second, empiricism appeals to modern scientists and scientific endeavors.
- Third, people across the globe tend to hold vastly different worldviews. If everyone were born with the same knowledge, there would not be such *widespread disagreement*.[10]

I will address each appeal individually.

*First*, the belief that people learn from experience is nearly a universally held, instinctive belief. Moreover, if a child is dropped off in the wilderness and left alone for the duration of its life, IF the child survives, it will not learn the fundamental principles that separate humanity from all nonhuman creatures, such as language, culture, mathematics, literature, morality, religion, art, and science. The seventeenth-century thinker, John Locke famously professed that human beings, at birth, are "blank slates" or "empty tablets" that can only be filled by experience.[11]

*Second*, scientists are responsible for many technological, medical, and intellectual achievements. Modern life would be vastly different and arguably far less desirable if not for the work of scientists. But the primary method by which scientists work consists of constructing experiments to test hypotheses created with the intent of explaining *observable* phenomena. Experiments, moreover, depend on making and recording precise observations that extend our knowledge of the world.

*Finally*, there often appears to be far more dispute and dissension in the world than there is cooperation and agreement. Disagreements are especially more common and more difficult to resolve when the disagreement concerns a matter that cannot appeal to experience. For example, most religious beliefs—whether the doctrines belong to Judaism, Christianity, Islam, Hinduism, Buddhism, Confucianism, Taoism, Sikhism, or any of the mythologies of the world—make references to spiritual entities that are invisible, such as Gods, angels, and demons. They also make references to events that seem to violate established naturalistic regularities that come to constitute laws of nature, such as the Christian doctrines concerning Jesus Christ—his virgin birth, the incarnation of God in his nature, his various miracles (feeding thousands with two fish and five loaves of bread, changing water into wine, healing the blind, walking on water, etc.), and his eventual resurrection from the dead. Such ideas strain credulity primarily because they contradict experience. Even those events that constitute the history of a religion supposedly happened hundreds or even thousands of years ago and, thus, cannot be observed and verified by any living person today. The best that we can do is trust the authority of those who testify to them, in which case the credibility of the person giving the testimony is in question and can only be resolved by appeals to experience. Everything else is left to interpretation, hence why so many religions have different denominations.

The idea that knowledge derives from experience is appealing, but "experience" is a vague term. What exactly does it involve? Moreover, what is the difference between sensation and perception? As for the first question, the

10 Locke also makes this negative argument in his presentation.

11 John Locke, *Essay Concerning Human Understanding*, rev. ed. (New York: Oxford University Press, 1979), II.I.2.

most primal form of experience consists of external sensation, the reception of external stimuli using the five senses of sight, hearing, taste, smell, and touch. Each specific sense can receive specific types of external stimuli. Aristotle subdivides the possible objects of external sensation in the following way.

- **Proper objects** of external sense consist of objects that a particular sense alone can receive. For instance, only sight can receive color. Only hearing can receive sound. Only taste can receive flavors. Only smell can receive odors and aromas. Only touch can receive textures (roughness/smoothness) and temperatures (hot/cold).
- **Common objects** of external sense consist of objects that can be received by multiple senses. These include objects such as shape, size, and location. For example, the shape of an object can be discerned either through sight or through touch. The same is true for how large or small an object is or close or far an object is with respect to you.
- **Incidental objects** of external sense constitute entire objects that are sensed. Any total object of sense constitutes an incidental object, a bird, a dog, a cat, a horse, a car, a bus, a house, etc.

These distinctions imply another, one made explicit by Locke—the difference between *simple* and *complex ideas*.[12] Moreover, Locke explains that experience, in general, includes more than merely sensation but also the processes of *introspection and reflection*, through which one becomes aware of the operations within one's own mind.[13]

- **Simple ideas** are the smallest units of sense experience. There are four general kinds of simple ideas:
    - Those received through *one sense* (same as the proper objects of external sense)
    - Those received through *more than one sense* (same as the common objects of external sense)
    - Those received through *introspection/reflection alone*. Under this category, Locke includes ideas of thinking and willing
    - Those received through both *sensation* and *introspection/reflection*. Under this category, Locke includes ideas such as pleasure, pain, and existence
- **Complex ideas** arise from the operations of the mind. For example, an apple, even though it is an object of ordinary, everyday experience, constitutes a *complex idea* because it combines multiple simple ideas, such as the color of the apple, the shape, weight, and size of the apple, the scent of the apple, and the taste of the apple. In addition. Locke lists ideas of substances, modes, and relations as types of complex ideas.

As an empiricist, Locke held that our conception of the external world is constructed from the ground up by our various experiences, a process that, in part, accounts for the distinction between sensation and perception:

- Whereas sensation consists of the passive reception of external stimuli, **perception** consists of *actively* constructing sense-data in a meaningful and intelligible way.

Chaffee suggests that the processes of perception involve selection, organization, and interpretation, each of which implies an active process.[14] For example, consider the following optical illusion:

---

12 Locke refers to everything in the mind as an "idea," regardless of whether it is a simple object of sensory apprehension, a complex sensory object, or a thought.
13 Locke, *Essay*, II.I.4.
14 See John Chaffee, *Thinking Critically*, 12th ed. (Boston: Cengage, 2019), 142.

When looking at this drawing, most people will see one of two images: either a young woman looking away from them or an old woman looking toward them.[15] Whichever image one sees is a matter of *perception,* whereas the colors, lines, shapes, and specks all constitute sensations.

The danger inherent in perception and in the Lockean conception of the acquisition of knowledge is that much of what people claim to know with certainty is constructed by the mind. One's perceptions are not always accurate and can become fixed, in which one is forced to understand objects in a specific way. For instance, looking at a blurred image, you will likely struggle to interpret the image, using context clues and shapes to understand it. However, once the image is cleared, you will likely not be able to "unsee" the image if it were distorted once more. Beliefs and expectations, too, can influence perception. If you expect an object to look a specific way, it can appear in such a way to you. If you expect an event to happen, it may seem as though such an event is happening to you, even if others dispute it, as often is the case with people suffering from paranoia.

In short, it seems as though the world often conforms to the dictates of the mind, as implied by the discussion of the idols of the mind and cognitive biases, which can collaborate in the distortion of perception, which leads directly to the problems with the idea that our knowledge is formed from our experiences, contributing to the limitations of empiricism. Generally, empiricism suffers from three major shortcomings:

- First, our senses can and often do deceive us.
- Second, matter frequently changes, along with our understanding of it.
- Third, there seem to exist universally held beliefs and principles that do not derive directly from experience.

Each of these problems will be addressed in turn.

15 This optical illusion is sometimes called the "Boring" illusion, named after psychologist, Edwin Boring.

With respect to the *first* problem, consider numerous examples of optical illusions, such as a straight stick appearing bent when placed in water. Furthermore, as the philosopher Rene Descartes famously pointed out, often our dreams seem so vividly real that one might believe one is awake while one is asleep. On other occasions, one may simultaneously experience different temperatures. For instance, suppose that there are three buckets of water, one cold, one hot, one lukewarm. Stick your right hand in the hot bucket, your left hand in the cold, and then place both in the lukewarm bucket. You will likely feel two different temperatures, despite the temperature of the water being the same.

As for the *second* problem, scientists devote their lives to studying different types of physical matter and the laws that govern the behavior of matter. If knowledge is built from experience and experience derives from external objects, then it must at least be possible to form universal, necessary, and categorical beliefs about external objects. Physical matter supposedly comprises the external objects of sense experience. But if matter is unstable, then it is unlikely that any clear and coherent conception of it can be formulated, hence, why scientific theories, laws, and our understanding of them, frequently undergo changes throughout history in what Thomas Kuhn refers to as *paradigm shifts*.[16]

One example of a major twentieth-century paradigm shift occurred due to the implications of Einstein's work on the special theory of relativity, in which he established that speed of motion can vary from different perspectives. One of his thought experiments consisted of a train moving east with a passenger standing directly in the middle of one of the cars and an observer watching from the outside. Suppose that two lights flash on at both ends of the car. From the perspective of the passenger, both lights flash on simultaneously. But from the observer's point of view, it will appear as though one light flashes on before the other, the light closer to the direction in which the train is moving. As a related example, consider two passengers in a car on the same train who are tossing a frisbee back and forth. Imagine also that once again there is an observer outside the train. From this bystander's perspective, it will appear as though the frisbee moves at two different speeds. When tossed toward the east by the first passenger, it will appear to move at the same speed as the train. But when tossed toward the west by the second passenger, it will appear to move more slowly. Hence, speed of motion seems to vary based on perspective.

An additional example comes from quantum physics, specifically, from the work of German theoretical physicist, Werner Heisenberg, the *uncertainty principle*. This principle is a mathematical law that governs the behavior of subatomic particles, such as photons (light particles). The principle is formulated in the following way: $\mathbf{\Delta\chi\Delta p \geq \hbar/2}$. In short, the principle suggests that the more one knows about a particle's position, the less one knows about the particle's momentum or force. In connection with the uncertainty principle is the "observer effect." Basically, if an experiment is set up to study light as a particle, a single-slit experiment, then light will behave as a particle. If an experiment is set up to study light as a wave, a double-slit experiment, then light will behave as a wave. Thus, the behavior of light and, more generally, the behavior of subatomic particles, which supposedly constitute the basis of matter, varies with the activity of the observer. Analogous to the observer effect is the Boring illusion (the picture that can appear to be either an old or young woman). What one perceives when observing the picture arises substantially from *what the observer chooses to see* and *how the observer chooses to see it*. An observer, therefore, is never merely a passive bystander but a part of the world process.

Finally, with respect to the *third* problem, it is very closely related to the first two. People hold many ideas and beliefs that seem to have no direct basis in experience. For example, consider what logicians call *the problem of induction*, which itself stems from the law of induction:

- **The law of induction**, in its most concise formulation, states that the future will resemble the past.

16 See Thomas Kuhn, *The Structure of Scientific Revolutions*, 4th ed. (Chicago: University of Chicago Press, 2012).

While the general idea indicated by this "law" can be formulated based on one's past experiences (i.e., "The sun will continue to rise because it always has," or "Antibiotics will continue to cure bacterial infections because they always have."), the main problem becomes obvious when closely inspected:

- **The problem of induction** is the idea that regularities and patterns based on past events may cease to occur at some future time.

Essentially, it is impossible for people to have any *experience* of the future (unless, of course, they are clairvoyant or psychic, each of which is controversial!). How then can the law of induction even be formulated? How can it be justified? One can attempt to justify the law of induction by arguing that the law must be true since it always proved to be true in the past. But such reasoning is circular since it uses inductive reasoning to justify the law! The law itself seems to be a principle that people just naturally accept a priori, without any reference to experience, perhaps as a principle that is necessary to give order to our experiences.

The eighteenth-century thinker David Hume, perhaps the most radical of the empiricists during his time, made similar criticisms about inductive reasoning himself. He also argued that similar criticisms can be made about causal relations. Hume insisted that all ideas must trace back to a single sense-impression, just as a photograph is a *copy* of the real object or event it captures. However, if I believe that some event, A, causes another event, B, said belief does not copy any single impression. Typically, one draws the conclusion "A causes B" because of the constant conjunction of A and B, whereby whenever A happens, B shortly follows. What one does not truly *see* is the cause itself. Thus, no one really has any idea of a cause in the sense that Hume intended, from which it would follow that no one has any idea of laws of nature that serve as the basis of natural science either!

Hume made similar arguments about other commonplace beliefs, such as the belief in a permanent self that remains identical across time, the permanence of external objects, and even the very existence of an external world. Hume proposed that such beliefs arise based on the psychological propensity of the human mind to associate events and experiences that resemble each other and occur close together in time, *the law of association.* But this proposal gives rise to a further problem: *How exactly does the law of association arise?* Not only do people universally seem to believe in causal laws and in the permanent existence of an external world, but they all seem to operate according to the law of association as well.

Even more damning for empiricism is that human thinking goes beyond the boundaries of mere cognition. People ask reflective and speculative questions that could not very easily arise from simple experiences. For instance, from human reflection arise questions about the reason for the existence of everything and the ultimate meaning of life itself. *Why* do such questions arise if all knowledge merely derives from simple experience? *How* can such questions arise if the mind merely forms associations between simple sense-impressions? Based on the principles of empiricism, one could only create very simple connections between events, such as "If I touch the fire, I will burn my hand," or "If I jump in the water, I will get wet." One would very likely never ask why or how fire or water came to exist in the first place, primarily because one would not be able to consider the possibility of any variation between experience and reality. Given these problems with empiricism, perhaps rationalism is a more appealing theory.

## Rationalism

Whereas empiricists favor observation and science, rationalists favor reasoning, logic, and mathematics. Traditionally, rationalists draw a distinction between two kinds of knowledge: *inferior* and *superior,* where the latter refers to knowledge based in sense-perception and observation while the former consists of truths of reason that are absolute and certain. One of the most famous rationalists in history, Rene Descartes, maintained that mathematics and logic are superior to the natural sciences because only his chosen disciplines can provide indubitable truth and certainty.

As previously indicated, the basic principles of rationalism can be read as the antitheses of the principles embraced by empiricists. Recall that all rationalists maintain that (a) *at least some knowledge is* a priori (not derived from experience and possibly innate) and that (b) *thinking alone can extend human knowledge in significant, nontrivial ways*. Taking these items in reverse, I will start by pointing out that the second principle is supported by the fact that people can often figure out the solutions to complex problems without having to be told explicitly. Think back to the Socratic method, specifically, Socrates's interaction with the slave. The slave had no education in geometry yet could figure out the solution to a complex geometry problem.

Moreover, experience is not necessary to sustain or extend one's knowledge. For instance, imagine that a person is confined to a dark room with no access to the external world. Suppose that this individual is deprived of the use of all five of his or her external senses. Such an individual could still, theoretically, think. Such a person could still form original ideas. Merely the absence of external objects to stimulate one's senses would neither deprive one of one's current knowledge nor would it necessarily prevent one from forming new ideas.

To establish the first of the rationalists' principles, however, one would have to discover universally shared ideas, beliefs, or principles that all, or at least most, people have in common but do not derive from experience or observation. Typically, rationalists will appeal to the following as universally held a priori principles:

- Principles of Logic
- Principles of Mathematics
- Statements of Definition
- Moral Principles

The first three are less controversial than the fourth, and they were partially addressed earlier, so we can begin with them.

As previously indicated, people tend to share patterns of reasoning and inferential processes in common, such as the principle of induction, the ability to make causal inferences, and the capacity to ask deep, reflective, speculative questions that imply that the mind is not merely a "blank slate" at birth. Additional ideas that people seem to share are commonly referred to as the **first principles of logic**,[17] which are the following:

a) The **law of noncontradiction** states that it is impossible for something both to be and not be at the same time and in the same respect. (For example, no tennis ball can be simultaneously green all over and yellow all over at the same time.)

b) The **law of the excluded** middle states that between being and nonbeing there is no middle ground. (For instance, the statement, "There is a frog on the desk," cannot be both true and false at the same time.)

c) The **law of identity** states that each thing is what it is and no other thing. (To illustrate, for anyone to utter the phrase, "I am not me," is self-contradictory.)

d) The **principle of sufficient reason** states that everything has a cause or an explanation for why it exists.

17 These specific formulations of the first principles of logic are given by D.Q. McInerny, *Being Logical: A Guide to Good Thinking* (New York: Random House, 2005), 26–8.

The first three are sometimes called the "laws of thought." Such principles can not only be understood without observation or experience but the very ability to have coherent and meaningful experiences seems to demand them.

In addition, the laws of mathematics, such as arithmetic, can be understood without any direct reference to experience. Equations that involve numbers do not depend for their truth on physical concrete objects. Moreover, such equations apply to a wide variety of concrete circumstances. The equation "$7 + 5 = 12$" is true whether it applies to rocks, concrete blocks, trees, birds, dogs, cats, buildings, mountains, or any other objects. The same may be said about the laws of geometry and trigonometry. The ancient Pythagoreans insisted that mathematical forms and ratios are the foundation for physical, concrete realities that are essentially unintelligible otherwise. Not only do physical objects conform to mathematical patterns but entire physical systems rely on the ordered and balanced harmony that emerges from the laws of mathematics, such as the health of the human body which demands homeostasis, as well as the patterns of the revolutions of the planets. If numbers and the laws governing them can be known a priori then so can everything else!

With respect to statements of definition, such statements can be known just as soon as the terms are known. For instance, the statement "A triangle is a three-sided figure" is understood immediately once the terms are understood. The same may be said about statements such as "A bachelor is an unmarried adult male," and "Gold is a yellow metal." The denial of such terms results in a violation of the law of contradiction, just as would the denial of mathematical laws.

In addition to logic, mathematics, and definitions, rationalists appeal to moral principles as examples of a priori truths. Many famous thinkers endorsed the idea that morality is not merely a priori but innate. Confucius, for instance, held that all people are born with a moral imperative he called the "Decree of Heaven" inscribed within them. A student of Confucius, Mengzi (known also by his Latin name, Mencius), endorsed the idea that people are basically good and identified four "seeds of the human heart": compassion, which grows into benevolence; shame, which grows into dutifulness; courtesy, which grows into observance of the rites; and moral sense, which grows into wisdom. Mencius attempted to prove that everyone has an innate moral sense by suggesting that anyone who witnessed a child drowning would instinctively dive into the water and attempt to save the child, translating into an instinct for altruism, putting the interest and well-being of others ahead of one's own.[18]

Perhaps the most famous example of a thinker professing that there are innate moral principles comes from Thomas Jefferson, whose first line of the Declaration of Independence reads, "We hold these truths to be self-evident, that all men are created equal, that they are endowed by their creator with certain inalienable rights, and that among them are life, liberty, and the pursuit of happiness." That Jefferson tellingly used the terms "self-evident" and "inalienable" indicates that the "truths" are known a priori and that they are inseparable from the individual, embedded within human nature.

One final example is the eighteenth-century German philosopher Immanuel Kant, who famously wrote in the *Critique of Practical Reason* that in addition to the "starry heavens above," the moral law within" fills the mind with awe., "Kant argued that moral principles can be determined a priori via the use of reason and that morality is *inescapable* for humanity, meaning that humanity cannot help but encounter moral principles and moral reasoning. While more will be said about Kant's moral philosophy in a later chapter, for the time being, notice the similarities between the ideas of Kant, Confucius, Mencius, and Thomas Jefferson, each of whom agrees about moral principles being known a priori.

So, there appears to be evidence for a priori knowledge. But such a claim does not establish rationalism itself as superior to empiricism. Generally, rationalism suffers from the following limitations:

---

18 See David L. Haberman, "Confucianism: The Way of the Sages," in *Twelve Theories of Human Nature,* eds. Leslie Stevenson, David L. Haberman, and Peter Matthews Wright (New York: Oxford University Press, 2013), 30.

- First, people frequently make errors in reasoning, mathematics, and in moral decisions.
- Second, innate and/or a priori concepts seem empty without experience and observation.

Beginning with the first problem, children do not seem to be born knowing arithmetic, algebra, geometry, trigonometry, calculus, probability, or statistics. Typically, learning such disciplines takes years of rigorous instruction and practice. And during that time, many mistakes are made by students. Fewer errors are made in performing simple calculations, but the more complex problems become, the greater the chance for error. If the principles of mathematics are innate, then why must they be learned? One might argue that such principles are not innate, that people are not born with them, but that they can simply be known without any references to specific observations. For instance, equations such as "2 + 3 = 5," and "8 × 9 = 72" can be understood without referring to any specific concrete objects. Fine. But in that case, why do so many children require the use of visual aids in learning how to add, subtract, multiply, and divide? Moreover, even if the principles of such disciplines are not innate but known a priori, then why can errors in calculation be made so frequently and without the individual noticing?

The same problem applies to reasoning in logic. Formal fallacies frequently occur in the construction of arguments, especially when arguments are long and complex. An example of a formal fallacy occurs in categorical logic when the middle term is not distributed:

All P are M.

All S are M.

Therefore, all S are P.

Substituting the term "Dogs" for P, "Cats" for S, and "Mammals" for M reveals that such an argument form is invalid.

The construction of proofs in logic and in mathematics is also problematic. Often students struggle not only to prove the validity of arguments using inference rules, but they struggle to even grasp the very concept of a proof! And some proofs in mathematics are so complex that mathematicians take years to complete them. If the principles of such disciplines are wholly a priori and testify to knowledge not derived from experience, then why are they so difficult? Should not at least teaching them be so much easier?

Furthermore, the propensity for moral failure is no secret to anyone. Most children do not seem to be basically good. The process of parenting, socializing, and educating children so that they will be cooperative and upstanding citizens is a long, laborious struggle that is not always successful. Moreover, even the best people can often struggle to "do the right thing" in a specific situation, in which part of the struggle consists in figuring out just *what* exactly constitutes the right course of action. If the "decree of heaven" or the "moral law within" are self-evident truths, then why do so many people fail to act in the right way so often? One can appeal to the Socratic argument that such actions occur because of ignorance, the belief that doing the wrong thing will yield some good. But such an answer only serves to undercut the rationalists' position since it implies that people do not have an innate moral sense.

Descartes gave an interesting answer to the problem of why errors are so common in reasoning and in judgment. He suggested that when one has a clear and distinct idea, one cannot be wrong in one's judgment about that idea. However, one when hastily makes a judgment before one's intellect can form a clear and distinct perception, one can be wrong.[19] For example, if one quickly glances at a painting, one might not see it entirely and, hence, will not judge it properly. One might believe that it is a picture of a horse when really it is a donkey. However, when one takes the time to form a clear and distinct perception of the painting, one will judge the picture accurately. The same process

19 See *Meditations on First Philosophy* in Donald Cress (Tr.), 3rd Ed., (Indianapolis, IN: Hackett Publishing Co., 1993).

applies to logic, mathematics, and even making moral decisions. When confronted with a problem in either of these disciplines, one should take the time to deliberate about a strategy to solve the problem.

Descartes's suggestion, however, leads to the second problem, which forces us to consider the concomitant principle of rationalism that reasoning or thinking alone can extend knowledge in important ways. What exactly does that mean? How can an individual extend one's knowledge only through thinking? This process seems analogous to satisfying one's thirst simply by knowing how to drink water, or by satisfying one's hunger simply by knowing how to eat. Even if some ideas and principles are innate, they seem worthless unless they can be applied to experience. For example, the principle of induction is useful only if one has previous experiences on which to base one's predictions about the future. Hence, following the procedure Descartes proposed requires that one has experience with some object about which to make judgments. Even the laws of logic are empty and trivial if they do not apply to observations and experience. The law of noncontradiction is worthless without the conceiving of some concrete, existent object, as is the law of identity. And the principle of sufficient reason may as well be gibberish if no item of experience exists to be explained! I reiterate that the principles of arithmetic are best understood if one applies them to concrete objects, while geometry would be impossible if one could not at least imagine shapes and figures in some space.

While this discussion could either continue into more treacherous, philosophically esoteric territory or end aporetically, I propose another interim solution: *rationalistic empiricism*. The impasse between the two theories runs parallel to that between correspondence and coherence, thus, can be ameliorated by a similar solution. The position can be outlined in the following way:

- **Rationalistic empiricism** is the position that knowledge is acquired through the process of

  a) forming ideas based on and matching them to sense-perceptions and observations of facts,

  b) formulating words and coherent thoughts based on ideas that can be verified through facts of sense-perception and observations,

  c) ensuring that one's thoughts conform to the rules of logic and are consistent with those thoughts that correspond to reality, and

  d) revising one's thoughts and one's belief system as new evidence becomes available.

While this position is simplistic, it allows for the collaboration of reason and experience in the development of knowledge.

## What Can We Know about the External World?

This section will address several answers to the question, "What can we know about the external world?" Specifically, the following will be considered along with their associated flaws:

- **Direct Realism:** The position that we experience the external world exactly as it is.
- **Indirect Realism:** The position that we only direct experience our own ideas and sense-perceptions, which are only representations of the external world.

- **Subjective Idealism:** The position that all sensible objects are merely ideas and, thus, that the physical world does not exist.
- **Phenomenalism:** The position that only sense-data are truly real.
- **Skepticism (Global Epistemic Skepticism):** The position that all knowledge is impossible, regardless of the topic or subject.

## Direct Realism

Direct realism is sometimes called "commonsense realism" or "naive realism," as it is the most intuitive, universally accepted position on the question of external knowledge. All people are born with the capacity for external sensations, made possible by vastly complex physiological tissues and organs, specifically the nervous system and the sense organs themselves. What is the point of such things if one cannot use them to navigate the external world? The eighteenth-century philosopher, Thomas Reid gave one of the most famous defenses of direct realism based primarily on its instinctive and universal appeal, despite opinions to the contrary:

> When we see the sun, or moon, we have no doubt that the very objects which we immediately see are very far distant from us, and from one another. We have not the least doubt that this is the sun and moon which God created some thousands of years ago, and which have continued to perform their revolutions in the heavens ever since. But how are we astonished when the philosopher informs us that we are mistaken in all this ... [and that] the objects we perceive are only ideas in our own minds.[20]

Reid insisted that those "uninstructed in philosophy" would be profoundly astonished by any who doubt the veracity of the senses as it runs contrary to natural instincts and, thus, concludes,

> It is therefore acknowledged by this philosopher to be a natural instinct or prepossession, a universal and primary opinion of all men, a primary instinct of nature, that the objects which we immediately perceive by our senses are not images in our minds, but external objects, and that their existence is independent of us and our perception.[21]

However, as established in previous chapters and in the previous discussions of both rationalism and empiricism, people so often make the wrong judgments about their sense-perceptions, and sense-perception frequently does not match external reality. Moreover, modern science teaches that, at bottom, physical objects consist of atoms and subatomic particles, such as protons, neutrons, and electrons, which certainly cannot be seen, felt or touched with raw sense organs. Thus, despite Reid's faith in the natural instincts of humanity, alternatives to direct realism deserve consideration.

## Indirect Realism

Indirect realism is the position that no external object is perceived directly, exactly as it is, in and of itself, but that all people ever directly experience are ideas and sense-perceptions within their own minds, which are largely representations of external objects. Hence, the theory is also sometimes called "representationalism." Early proponents

20 Thomas Reid, "A Common-Sense Defense of Direct Realism," in *The Theory of Knowledge: Classical and Contemporary Readings*, 2nd ed., ed. Louise P. Pojman (Boston: Cengage, 2003), 108–9.
21 Reid, "A Common-Sense Defense," 109.

of this theory included Descartes and Locke. Locke specifically distinguished between two kinds of sensible qualities—*primary* and *secondary*:

- **Primary qualities** consist of sensible qualities within an object itself. Such qualities include an object's shape, size, weight, height, width, length, and location in space.
- **Secondary qualities** consist of sensible qualities within the mind of the perceiver alone. Such qualities include colors, sounds, odors and aromas, flavors, temperatures, textures, and pain.

Locke understands a *quality* as a power within an object to produce a sensation in the mind. His distinction is encapsulated by what is often called the *resemblance thesis*:

- **Locke's resemblance thesis** states that primary qualities resemble physical objects, whereas secondary qualities do not.

Locke's thesis implies that the external world and the objects in it are, in themselves, much different than they appear to the mind. While the external world contains matter and solid objects that, for the most part, match our sense-perceptions, it does not contain colors, sounds, tastes, smells, or feelings associated with the sense of touch. Consider the age-old question, "If a tree falls in a forest, will it make a sound?" The answer, of course, is that there is a sound only if there is a person close enough to hear it.

Locke gives several arguments for his distinction, but the following two are his strongest.

- The argument from pain and nausea.
- The argument from the absence of color in the dark.

To address the first argument, imagine that your friend quickly jabs you with a pin. You would likely feel a sudden sensation of pain. But there is nothing resembling "pain" in the pin. A similar argument can be made with respect to pleasure. Imagine your favorite food. The taste or flavor of the food exists only in your mind, as nothing resembling the taste exists within the food. The same can be said about the germs and viruses that cause illness. As for the second argument, try to observe a supposedly colored object in the dark. Once the light is turned off, the color disappears, but the shape and size of the object remain the same. It is reasonable to conclude that the shapes of different surfaces reflect light differently, thus, causing the idea of color in the mind. Also, recall the examples of the three buckets of water presented in the previous section. Since each hand feels a different temperature, it is not at all likely that one directly feels the water itself.[22] In addition to the implication that no one can truly experience the external world, a further consequence of Locke's arguments is that all a person's sense-perceptions and ideas are private to the individual and that it is entirely possible that no two people have identical ideas or sense-perceptions of the external world.

In accordance with Locke's philosophical contributions to epistemology and evidence available from modern physics, the twentieth-century thinker Bertrand Russell also defended representationalism. Consider what humanity learned about stars, for instance. Many are so far away that by the time the light reaches the eyes of observers on Earth, the star itself has burned out and, thus, no longer exists in physical space! In that case, one cannot possibly see the star. Moreover, light itself is not fully understood by contemporary physicists given that it seems to be able to exist either as a collection of particles or in the form of waves. The position of indirect realism seems more amenable

22 Both Parts I and II of Locke's *Essay* address these arguments.

to modern science, especially in the present context since it resolves the conundrum of what exactly one perceives when one sees "light." One simply sees a representation in the mind. Russell echoes this sentiment: "To say that you see a star when you see the light that has come from it is no more correct than to say you see New Zealand when you see a New Zealander in London."[23] Russell makes his position clear in the following passage:

> The point that concerns us is that a man's percepts are private to himself: what I see, no one else sees; what I hear, no one else hears; what I touch, no one else touches, and so on. True, others hear and see something very like what I hear and see, if they are suitably placed; but there are always differences. Sounds are less loud at a distance; objects change their visual appearance according to the laws of perspective. Therefore, it is impossible for two persons at the same time to have exactly identical percepts.[24]

Even though no two individuals have exactly identical perceptions, there are enough similarities to infer the existence of external objects outside of the mind. Locke maintained that primary qualities are the same for all observers, while secondary qualities can vary depending on one's point of view or the conditions of perception. But what if the primary qualities vary with perception as well? What are the implications? *Subjective idealism* seems to be the primary implication.

## Subjective Idealism

*Idealism* is the position that reality is structured with the features of a mind, while *subjectivism* can loosely be defined as the position that one is trapped within one's mind. Conjoining these two ideas, *subjective idealism* can be defined in the following way:

- **Subjective idealism** is the position that all sensible qualities are ideas, and ideas are mind mind-dependent; thus, all that exists are minds and the ideas perceived by them, from which it follows that *there is no physical world*.

The eighteenth-century thinker, Bishop George Berkeley is the most famous representative of subjective idealism. Like Locke, Berkeley accepted the main principles of empiricism and agreed that we can perceive only our own sense-perceptions and ideas. However, unlike Locke, he insisted that "Esse ist percipi," or "To be is to be perceived." That is, everything that exists depends for its existence on perception, which implies that everything that exists is either a mind or a perception within a mind. Berkeley suggests that prior to any education with philosophy, most people would affirm the existence of external physical objects and that we can have direct experience of those objects. Locke would agree with the first claim but would deny the second. Berkeley can affirm a modified form of the first claim, there are sensible objects, but they are nonphysical. Ultimately, as a religious thinker, Berkeley concluded that everything exists in the mind of God.

Berkeley's *master argument* for idealism, sometimes called the **argument from illusion**, may be reconstructed in the following way to establish that all sensible qualities are ideas:

1) The real properties of an external object cannot change without the occurrence of a change in the object itself.
2) The sensible qualities of an object that I perceive can change without the occurrence of a change in the object itself.

23 Bertrand Russell, "A Defense of Representationalism," in *The Theory of Knowledge: Classical and Contemporary Readings*, 2nd ed., ed. Louise P. Pojman (Boston: Cengage, 2003), 117.
24 Russell, "A Defense," 117.

3) Either the sensible qualities I perceive are real properties of external objects or they are only ideas.
4) The sensible qualities I perceive are not real properties of external objects.
5) Therefore, the sensible qualities I perceive are only ideas.[25]

Berkeley's argument can be understood, in part, as a critique of Locke's distinction and the main rationale for his denial of physical objects. Locke maintained that the primary qualities of objects do not vary with perception, hence why they reflect properties of the actual objects themselves. So why does Berkeley affirm premise (4) in his argument? Why does Berkeley believe that sensible qualities are not real properties of external objects? There are two main reasons:

- First, all sensible qualities can vary with perception, even Locke's primary qualities.
- Second, ideas can only resemble other ideas, not physical objects.

Beginning with the first reason, consider shape, an example of a primary quality. Often the shape of an object can vary with perception. From a specific angle, for instance, a perfectly round object may look like an oval. The same may be said about the size of an object. From a distance, a large object, such as a building or a car may seem small enough to fit between one's fingers. Moreover, Einstein's theory of relativity implied that properties long believed by physicists to be absolute (such as time and speed of motion) can vary with a frame of reference. If any sensible quality can vary with perception, then it seems to follow that all sensible qualities are ideas.

The second reason consists of a more direct attack on Locke's resemblance thesis. No idea can resemble an external object. For instance, the idea of a sandwich cannot satisfy one's hunger. The idea of a glass of water cannot quench one's thirst. Furthermore, what would it mean to say that the idea of a cubed object resembles the cube? It seems extremely unorthodox to refer to an idea as having a shape. Are there also large ideas? Small ideas? Ideas with volume? Surely not.

Berkeley argued that the very concept of an object existing independently of perception is inconceivable. For instance, try to imagine a common natural object such as a tree, isolated and alone in an open field. True, you can imagine the tree without an observer in your hypothetical scenario, but the scenario itself is still *an object of your perception*, on which the tree depends. But what about us? If everything depends for its existence on a mind to perceive it, then what makes it possible for human minds to exist? Moreover, if there is no physical world and, thus, no physical objects, then from where do human perceptions originate? After all, Berkeley is an empiricist, which means he must account for how our ideas come to us from the experience, primarily, the external world.

Essentially, Berkeley's answer to all of the above is God. For Berkeley, all our ideas come directly from God. For our existence, we depend on the mind of God to perceive us. The sensible world, moreover, exists within the mind of God. For instance, the furniture in a classroom is not physical in any sense but, nonetheless is sensible and continues to exist when no people are around because the mind of God sustains them. The only exception to Berkeley's principles is God Himself, who can exist independently of any mind.

Berkeley's idealism is not very well adapted to the contemporary world. It has two major weaknesses:

- First, Berkeley seems arbitrarily to invoke God as a foundation for knowledge.
- Second, Berkeley's arguments do not establish that physical objects do not exist.

25 This reconstruction is given by Garrett Thomson, *Bacon to Kant: An Introduction to Modern Philosophy* (Long Grove, IL: Waveland Press, Inc., 2012) 204–6.

As a bishop, Berkeley could consistently invoke God to support his theory. But he only did so after arguing himself into a corner, so to speak. His appeal to God seems incredibly ad hoc and, even though he does provide arguments to justify this appeal, his arguments are derivative of his predecessors, such as Descartes and Spinoza; hence, they suffer the same flaws.[26] But more importantly, by appealing to God, he inadvertently subverts his own principle, that to be is to be perceived. If such a principle does not apply to God, then why does it apply to everything else? Only because one cannot conceive of an object in itself does not mean that such things do not exist. And anyone's ability to know that things cannot exist in themselves is predicated on their ability to have direct experience of them!

Finally, only because all sensible qualities vary with human perception does not mean that the objects that allegedly have the attributes perceived do not exist in themselves. One might as well argue that because an object has never been observed it does not exist. But to do so would amount to an argument from ignorance. In short, Berkeley fails to establish the fourth premise of his argument. At best, all that he may conclude is that our ideas of objects differ from the actual objects we experience. Perhaps he can reject the resemblance thesis, but not the existence of the physical world.

## Phenomenalism

The flaws in Berkeley's version of idealism lead naturally to the consideration of an alternative, *phenomenalism*. **Phenomenalists** would affirm each of the following:

- First, the only genuinely real items are sense-data.
- Second, we only have direct experience of our sense-perceptions, with no direct experience of anything beyond them. (We are, thus, trapped within our own consciousness.)
- Third, everything other than sense-perceptions, including matter and the external world, are logical fictions.

In other words, *nothing truly exists except sensations and the minds that perceive them and nothing can be experienced except the sense-data within one's mind*. Proponents of this position are typically empiricists and agree with Berkeley that we only experience our own sense-perceptions. However, this position differs from Berkeley's in at least two ways:

- Phenomenalists do not deny the existence of matter but rather argue that matter cannot be proven from observations.
- Phenomenalists will not necessarily argue that everything exists in the mind of God, although some will likely believe in God.

Phenomenalism traces back to the radical empiricism of David Hume, who insisted that all perceptions in the mind are either sense-impressions or direct copies of those impressions, ideas, all of which can exist independently of each other. The mind for Hume is a "bundle of perceptions." A twentieth-century thinker, Walter Stace endorsed phenomenalism by hearkening back to Hume's empiricism, suggesting that descriptions of the physical world—of atoms, stars, causal laws, and forces—only describe sensations and perceptions: "The only reason we have for believing

26 First, there is a *causal argument*, suggesting that only God can be the cause of our ideas since they cannot come from ourselves, from matter, or from other ideas. And given their consistency, the being that produces them must be benevolent and all-powerful, hence God. Second is his *continuity argument* that God is necessary to sustain the being of everything, specifically the being of sensible objects when no human observes them. For details, See Thomson, *Bacon to Kant: An Introduction to Modern Philosophy* (Long Grove, IL: Waveland Press, Inc., 2012), 219–21.

in the law of causation is that we observe certain regularities or sequences. We observe that, in certain conditions, A is always followed by B. We call A the cause, B the effect."[27] In a later passage, Stace writes,

> Suppose there is an observed sequence A – B – C ... seen by observer X. ... What right has he, and what reason has he, to assert the cause of A – B – C ... which he can never observe, behind the perceived world? He has no right, because the law of causation on which he is relying has never been observed to operate outside the series of perceptions, and he can have, therefore, no evidence that it does so.[28]

While phenomenalism is simpler than Berkeley's theory and indirect realism, it is not without flaws. Specifically, phenomenalism suffers from several flaws. As they are self-explanatory, I shall simply list them as follows:

- It cannot account for the independence of the external world and external objects or the fact that there is a difference between things as they are and objects of experience.
- It cannot account for the permanence of objects. In fact, its conception of physical matter is worthless since its proponents insist that such objects are only constructed by the mind.
- It cannot provide an adequate account of cause-effect relations, primarily because it cannot provide an adequate account of physical matter.
- It can lead to solipsism (the belief that "I'm the only person in the world.")[29]

Additional problems for phenomenalism include the following:

- The Shades of Color Paradox
- The Spotted Object Paradox[30]

The "shades of color" paradox can be explained in the following way. Suppose that there are three shades of red that vary very slightly, R1, R2, and R3. Suppose that R1 and R2 vary so slightly that they are indistinguishable. Suppose also that R2 and R3 are indistinguishable. However, we can distinguish between R1 and R3. If the only real items are simple sense-data, then each of these colors should be distinguishable.

The "spotted object" paradox asks us to imagine some object or animal with spots. Suppose that one cannot count the number of spots on the object. One is led to the conclusion that the number of spots is indeterminate. But surely, there is a precise, exact number of spots on the object in question. If the assumptions of phenomenalism are true, then anyone with the idea of the "spotted object" should know the number of spots on the object.

A further implication of phenomenalism is that taking the position seriously forces its proponent to admit that one's mind is not truly real but only a logical fiction, since one's mind is not a directly experienced sense-datum. But since one must presuppose, at least, that one has a mind in order to have experience, perhaps phenomenalism cannot be formulated coherently.

---

27 See Walter Stace, "Science and the Physical World: A Defense of Phenomenalism," in *The Theory of Knowledge: Classical and Contemporary Readings*, 2nd ed., ed. Louise P. Pojman (Boston: Cengage, 2003), 97.

28 Stace, "Science," 97.

29 C. J. Whitley makes these criticisms in his analysis of phenomenalism. See C. J. Whitley, "Phenomenalism: Its Grounds and Difficulties," in *The Theory of Knowledge: Classical and Contemporary Readings*, 2nd ed., ed. Louise P. Pojman (Boston: Cengage, 2003), 100–7.

30 Pojman himself raises these criticisms of phenomenalism. See page 74 of *The Theory of Knowledge*, "Introduction to Part III: Perception: Our Knowledge of the External World." (Boston: Cengage, 2003).

In addition, if phenomenalism can lead to solipsism, does it also lead to skepticism? The two positions are not identical but given the difficulty of answering the question of knowledge of the external world, skepticism should be directly addressed.

## Skepticism

This section specifically addresses a form of skepticism called *global epistemic skepticism:*

- **Global epistemic skepticism** (hereafter, GES) is the position that knowledge of any subject is impossible.[31]

Given the flaws of every position addressed thus far, perhaps it is simply impossible to know anything about the external world, especially since it seems that there can be no direct experience of it. While GES goes beyond the question of knowledge of the external world and challenges knowledge in general, the major appeal of the position lies in the fallibility of the senses and the difficulty in acquiring knowledge of the external world as well as one's own circumstances. A common scenario of proponents of GES involves the possibility that one's brain is installed in a vat of nutrients and, thus, that one cannot know for certain that one has a body.

While some forms of skepticism may be impossible to refute, GES faces two serious problems:

- First, GES has absurd implications, which means it should be rejected.
- Second, GES seems to contradict itself.

With respect to the first problem, if GES were true, then we would have to reject many beliefs supported by evidence and the consensus of authorities, such as the existence of atoms, the model of the solar system, and the theory of evolution. Even though many thinkers argue that one cannot experience the external world directly, they still accept many basic assumptions, such as their own existence, the laws of reasoning, mathematics, and the ability to communicate with others. Moreover, if GES were true, it would follow that no one could ever correct oneself or improve intellectually.

As for the second problem, how can a skeptic formulate the position of skepticism without embracing some basic principles, specifically those of logic? Moreover, how can one be a skeptic and trust that the language one uses is reliable? It is virtually impossible to avoid some assumptions. Thus, skepticism seems to raise the same sort of dilemma as relativism:

- Either nothing can be known except skepticism, in which case something can be known, or
- Skepticism (GES) itself is not justified.

I propose that GES is not justified, although given the fallibility of the senses, it is wise to practice epistemic moderation and remain open to correction on the possibility that one's beliefs are mistaken. This mentality results in a limited but more plausible form of skepticism.

## The Verdict?

The assumption that people have direct experience of the external world is, indeed, universal and natural. But it seems falsified not only by the fact that people constantly make errors in judgment but by the fact that sense-perceptions

31 See Herrick, *Think with Socrates*, 153–63. He acknowledges, as I briefly do, that there are different forms of skepticism, but most of them are far less problematic than GES.

often differ from the objects of perception. Subjective idealism has implications that strain credulity and conflict even more severely with common sense than skepticism. Phenomenalism is basically subjective idealism without God and seems to force on its proponent the conclusion that one's very being is only a logical fiction. As for skepticism, were it taken seriously, one could not function, as one would have to surrender many practical assumptions necessary for life.

Thus far, indirect realism seems to be the strongest position, but it requires presuppositions that are impossible to prove since if no one can experience external objects directly, no one can ever be sure that such objects differ from the ideas one experiences directly. And as Thomas Reid pointed out, even if all thinkers agree that ideas are merely objects in the mind, none of them seem to agree about the nature of ideas. If all that anyone ever experiences directly are one's ideas, then all people should know them best. But there is widespread disagreement about the nature of ideas. Consider the following:

- Some believe that ideas are merely images in the mind.
- Rationalists believe that some ideas are innate.
- Empiricists believe that ideas derive directly from experience.
- Some believe that there are abstract ideas.
- Some believe all ideas are particular and concrete.[32]

In short, indirect realism rests on many unproven assumptions that do not reflect any privileged knowledge about how the mind works and, to an extent, depend on the admission that there is direct experience of external objects. One final observation of Reid testifies to this assumption. For instance, consider the argument that physical items diminish with distance. In doing so, one invokes the laws of Euclidean geometry, which not only are universal and necessary but only apply to objects in space.[33]

While I will not propose a new theory here, any theory that proposes to answer the question of our knowledge of the external world must make the following concessions:

- Physical matter cannot be disproven, even if all that comprise the physical world are subatomic particles.
- The *external* world should not be conflated with the *physical* world.
- Humans DO experience external objects in some way.
- Humanity's experience of the external world is fallible, imperfect, given the nature and limited range of the sense organs.
- If the contributions of contemporary scientists are fully embraced, then the way in which objects are experienced differ from their actual physical constitution.
- Given the limited range of the senses and the capacity of the mind for abstraction, in addition to reasoning and forming concepts, it seems that the mind is different from any bodily organ.

This position preserves the universal and natural belief that one senses the external world and its objects balanced against the fallibility of one's senses. Even though people often make mistakes, they are still capable of correcting

32 In Pojman, *The Theory of Knowledge* (Boston: Cengage, 2003), 113.
33 Pojman, *The Theory of Knowledge*, (Boston: Cengage, 2003), 113. See also his remarks on page 114.

those mistakes, which would not be possible if not for the existence of real, external objects and the capacity to interact with them directly through the sense organs. Just like human beings, the faculty of sense is perfectly imperfect.

## Chapter Summary and Key Points to Remember

The aim of this chapter was to present answers to three questions:

- What is knowledge?
- How do we acquire knowledge?
- What can we know about the external world?

### What Is Knowledge?

The traditional model of knowledge holds that some subject, S, knows some claim or proposition, P, just in case:

1) P is true.
2) S believes that P.
3) S is justified in believing that P.

The two predominant theories of truth are *correspondence* and *coherence*.

- The **correspondence theory** of truth holds that a belief is true just in case it matches a fact.
    - The main problem with this theory is that there are some beliefs that cannot be verified through correspondence.
- The **coherence theory** of truth holds that truth is a property of entire belief systems which obtains when all the beliefs are consistent with each other.
    - The main problem with this theory is that many belief systems are internally consistent but inconsistent with other belief systems.
- Each theory can collaborate. With correspondence as a basis, those theories that cannot be verified through sense experience can be anchored to those beliefs that one already accepts as true.

Beliefs can be justified in the following ways:

- By sense-perception
- By testimony, both general testimony and expert authority
- By reasoning, in one of two ways:
    - The idea or claim in question is a matter of logic, mathematics, or definition
    - One infers an idea or belief from evidence

The **"Gettier" problem** challenges the traditional model of knowledge by suggesting that it is incomplete.

- For instance, there are scenarios in which one has a true belief that is justified, but it is only a matter of luck that the belief in question is true, such as in the example of the sheep given earlier in the chapter.

- As an interim solution to the "Gettier" problem, one can add a fourth condition to the traditional model of knowledge, that S knows that P just in case:

  1) P is true.
  2) S believes that P.
  3) S is justified in believing that P.
  4) It is not a matter of luck that P is true.

## How Do We Acquire Knowledge?

There are basically two positions on how knowledge is acquired: *rationalism* and *empiricism*.

- **Rationalists** generally accept the following principles:
  - At least some of our knowledge is innate and/or a priori.
  - We can extend our knowledge in significant, nontrivial ways through thinking alone.
  - The strengths of rationalism are the following:
    - It accounts for innate and or a priori knowledge of logic, mathematics, and morality.
    - Innate concepts of logic and mathematics are universal and necessary and more certain than ideas that derive from observations.
    - It is possible to extend and sustain one's current knowledge without experience or observation, as a person locked in a room can still think, and the removal of a sensory object does not deprive an individual of the memory of that object. Moreover, people can develop solutions to complex problems without having to be told directly.
  - The weaknesses of rationalism are:
    - Even if there are innate and/or a priori concepts, they are empty without reference to experience.
    - People often make errors in reasoning and in making moral decisions.
    - If the principles of logic, mathematics, and morality are innate, why do people have to be taught such subjects? And why is it so difficult to teach these subjects?
- **Empiricists** generally accept the following principles:
  - None of our knowledge is innate or a priori; all knowledge derives from experience.
  - Only experience and observations can extend our knowledge in important ways.
  - The strengths of empiricism are the following:
    - First, its principles are intuitively and naturally acceptable to most people. They are common beliefs of ordinary life.
      - While **sensation** consists of the reception of data through external stimuli, **perception** consists of the active process of interpreting and organizing that data.
      - Aristotle distinguished three objects of sense-perception: *proper objects*, received through one sense only, *common objects*, received through multiple senses, and *incidental objects*, the total object sensed in any one experience.
      - A famous empiricist, Locke, distinguished between *simple ideas*, the most basic and irreducible units of sense, and *complex ideas*, which are built from simple ideas.

    - Locke acknowledged that we can only directly perceive our own ideas and suggested that our knowledge of the external world is constructed from the ground up.
  - Second, it appeals to science and scientific thinkers.
  - Third, there is widespread disagreement among people that cannot be accounted for by rationalists.
- The weaknesses of empiricism are the following:
  - The senses often deceive us.
  - Matter constantly changes along with our knowledge of it.
  - There seem to be beliefs that are commonly held but do not derive from experience.
    - For example, **the principle of induction** suggests that the future will resemble the past. While such a principle consists of a broad generalization from experience, we can have no experience of the future and, thus, the principle cannot derive from experience alone. Moreover, any attempt to justify the principle is bound to be circular, since it would invoke the principle.

The author suggested a **combination of both rationalism and empiricism** that can support and temper each other, just as the correspondence and coherence theories of truth.

## What Can We Know about the External World?

There are five basic positions that attempt to answer this question:

- **Direct Realism:** The position that we perceive external objects directly; while this position is intuitive and naturally held by most people, our senses are often deceptive and we often perceive objects differently than they are.
  - Locke distinguished between an object's **primary qualities**, sensible properties that accurately reflect external, physical objects, and **secondary qualities**, sensible properties that exist only within the mind of the individual perceiving them, hence Locke's **resemblance thesis**: primary qualities resemble external objects, whereas secondary qualities do not.
- **Indirect Realism:** The position that we can only directly perceive our own ideas and perceptions within our own minds, which are representations of external objections. While this position is quite strong, it clashes with commonsense beliefs and assumes that we can know the difference between our own ideas and external objects, implying some direct experience of them.
- **Subjective Idealism:** The position that all sensible qualities are merely ideas and, thus, that physical objects (matter) do not exist. From this position, it follows that all that exists are minds and the sensible objects perceived by them.
  - The most famous historical proponent of this theory is the eighteenth-century thinker Bishop George Berkeley. Like Locke, he accepted the principles of empiricism, but unlike Locke, he denied that our ideas can resemble physical objects, as ideas can only resemble other ideas. Moreover, even the primary qualities to which Locke referred can vary depending on one's point of view. For Berkeley, all of our ideas come directly from God, and we all depend for our existence on the mind of God to sustain us and other sensible objects that are perceived by no one.
  - The main problem with this position is that it invokes God arbitrarily and does not prove that ALL sensible objects are merely ideas, but only that there is likely a difference between our sense-perceptions and external objects, which is no different than indirect realism.

- **Phenomenalism:** The position that the only real beings are individual sense-data. While this position is simpler than Berkeley's and more appealing to contemporary naturalists, it is difficult to formulate coherently, cannot account for the continued existence of physical objects, the permanence of matter, or the distinction between appearance and reality, and may lead to solipsism. It also raises paradoxes of perception, such as the problems of distinguishing between similar shades of color and precisely enumerating the spots on an object of sense-perception.
- **Skepticism**, more specifically, **GES:** The position that knowledge of anything, regardless of the topic, is impossible, and that includes knowledge of the external world, especially when one considers the problems raised by direct realism. The main problems with skepticism are that it seems self-contradictory, since justifying any position requires some assumptions and it leads to counterintuitive consequences, forcing us to admit that no one knows commonly accepted facts, such as that Earth is round, the sun is the center of the solar system, and that atoms exist.

## Exercises for Reflection and Application

**Instructions:** Use what you learned in this chapter to help you respond to the following questions.

1. Give an example of each of the following: (a) a fact, (b) an opinion or complete thought that you hold but do not know is true, and (c) a fact that you know is true. Then, explain how you are justified in believing your fact.
2. Give an example of each of the following: (a) a fact that everybody knows, (b) a fact that only you know, (c) a matter of fact that nobody knows with certainty, and (d) your answer to (c) and how you justified your answer.
3. Choose one of the following questions. Provide an answer and then explain whether your answer is derived in some way from a form of experience, reasoning, or a combination of both:
   a. Does God exist?
   b. If you do not believe in a God, do you believe in some other transcendent reality or being?
   c. Is there an afterlife?
   d. Are human beings currently living in a simulation?
   e. Do aliens exist?
   f. Did humans really evolve from earlier primates?
   g. Did dinosaurs really exist?
   h. Did Jesus Christ really exist? If so, did he rise from the dead?
4. Consider the Gettier problem. One of Gettier's assumptions is *justificational closure*:
   - **Justificational closure** is the idea that if a subject, S, is justified in believing some proposition, P, and P entails some other proposition, Q, then S is justified in believing that Q.

For example, if Josh is justified in believing that Bridget has a dog named Duchess, and the belief "Bridget has a dog named Duchess" entails that "Bridget has a pet," then Josh is justified in believing that "Bridget has a pet." Can you think of any of your justified beliefs whose implications you are *not* justified in holding? That is suppose you are justified in believing that P, and P entails Q, but that you are not justified in believing that Q. Explain why or why not.

5. It is often said that many stories in mythology and fiction literature are *true* even though they are not factual. For example, the story of how the Olympic Gods overthrew the Titans is not a *factual* story, but it is a *true* story. Is there a way to reconcile this conception of truth with both the correspondence and coherence theories of truth? Explain and give an example.
6. Explain how any cognitive bias can influence an error of sense-perception.
7. Do you prefer rationalism or empiricism? Defend your answer!
8. Do either rationalism or empiricism address any of Bacon's Idols of the Mind? Does either theory commit any of the Idols of the Mind? Explain and give specific examples.
9. Explain which of the following positions you think is the strongest and why: direct realism, indirect realism, subjective idealism, phenomenalism, skepticism, or mitigated realism.
10. Write a Socratic dialogue between a hypothetical rationalist and empiricist in which each character attempts to answer the three questions addressed in this chapter.

### *Image Credit*

IMG 4.1: Source: https://commons.wikimedia.org/wiki/File:My_Wife_and_My_Mother-in-Law.jpg.

# 5

# Logic (I)

## Arguments, Inferences, and Diagramming Techniques

INTRODUCTION

### Preparing to Read Chapter 5

In ordinary, everyday discourse people frequently use the word "argument." Often, if two or more people are shouting at each other, they might be described as "arguing" with each other. The same may be said about two people engaged in a debate or a heated conversation. In other cases, if an individual presents a dissenting opinion or a statement of disagreement, one might describe the individual in such cases as "arguing" with those who accept the majority's point of view or giving an "argument." In each of these hypothetical scenarios, the terms "argument" and "arguing" are used very loosely. Learning the precise and specific meaning of the term "argument" within the context of logic as well as learning to distinguish arguments from other kinds of passages is tantamount to critical thinking. Just as every word whose definition you do not know can be used against you, any argument that cannot be understood clearly or whose connections cannot be distinctly established can be used against you as well. Remember, that is how the sophists and some of the most ruthless dictators in history acquired power: through speech that generated action through emotion rather than reason. This chapter has the following aims:

- To present and explain the precise definition of the term "argument"
- To distinguish arguments from other kinds of passages
- To present and explain how to identify the connections between the statements of an argument
- To present and explain several techniques for diagramming arguments
- To distinguish between deductive and inductive inferences

### AS YOU READ, LOOK FOR THE FOLLOWING TERMS

- Argument
- Noninferential Passages
- Explanations
- Conditional Statements
    - Necessary versus Sufficient Conditions

- Argument Diagram
- Linked Diagram
- Convergent Diagram
- Dependent versus Independent Premises
- Divergent Diagram
- Serial Diagram
- Diagram of an Extended Argument
- Deduction
    - Valid versus Invalid
    - Sound versus Unsound
- Induction
    - Inductively Strong versus Inductively Weak
    - Cogent versus Uncogent

**KEEP THE FOLLOWING QUESTIONS IN MIND AS YOU READ**

- Why should I know how to recognize arguments and distinguish them from nonarguments?
- Why is it important to know how to diagram arguments?
- Why is it important to know the difference between deduction and induction?
- Why is it important to know whether a deductive argument is valid?
- Why is it important to know whether a deductive argument is sound?
- Why is it important to know whether an inductive argument is strong?
- Why is it important to know whether an inductive argument is cogent?

## (I) Arguments and Nonarguments

An **argument** may be defined in the following way:

- An inferential set of statements, some of which are *premises* and one of which is the *conclusion*.

In an argument, premises are given to support or derive a conclusion. Hence, the author of any argument attempts to prove or establish some claim, typically a point of contention that stands in need of defense. Of course, not all passages constitute arguments. Consider each of the following passages:

a) There are no unicorns!

b) Stop!

c) In Book II of *The Republic*, Glaucon refers to the fable of the ring of Gyges, in which the titular Gyges, a shepherd in Lydia, finds a ring that can render himself invisible. Gyges used the ring to seduce the queen, kill the king, and usurp the throne. Glaucon uses this fable to argue that anyone with the power of invisibility would behave unjustly for their own benefit.

d) Here's a nickel's worth of advice: stay off my lawn!

e) In my opinion, life as we know it will end within the next 50 years.

f) Natural selection is supposedly the mechanism by which evolution occurred. In principle, natural selection is the idea that there is a struggle for existence between different species of organisms competing for natural resources that cannot sustain the entire population. Those species that are fit will survive and pass on their traits while those that are not will go extinct.

g) If you ate a carrot, then you ate a vegetable.

h) They should stop making movies in the *Saw* franchise because those films perpetuate tasteless and gratuitous violence, have overly convoluted plots with contrived story lines and predictable twists, and very few people will pay to watch them anymore.

Only one of these passages constitutes an argument. Passage (a) is a simple declarative statement. Passage (b) is a command. Passage (c) is an expository passage that merely reports the content of a book and summarizes information. Passage (d) constitutes a warning and/or a piece of advice. Passage (e) merely states an opinion. Each of these five passages may be classified as **noninferential**. Passage (f) constitutes an **explanation**. Typically, an explanation contains two parts:

- An *explanandum*, an object, event, phenomenon, term, statement, or group of statements to be explained.
- An *explanans*, the statement or group of statements that provide the explanation.

In passage (f), the explanans is natural selection, whereas the explanandum is the definition given of the term. Like passages (a)–(e), passage (f) also is noninferential. Typically, an explanation can function as part of an argument, but in and of itself does not constitute an argument. Passage (g) simply consists of a **conditional statement**:

- A **conditional statement** takes the form of a hypothetical "If …, then …" sentence consisting of an **antecedent** (the "if" part of the statement) and a **consequent** (the "then" part of the statement).

Generally, conditional statements are inferential but do not, in themselves, constitute arguments. There are three types of conditions:

- **Necessary conditions:** A is a necessary condition for B just in case B cannot be obtained without A. Typically, such conditions are designated by the term "only if." For example, "You will pass the course *only if* you attend each session." In this sentence, attending each session is introduced as a necessary condition for passing but students will have to do more to pass the course than simply attend, such as passing every exam and completing all mandatory assignments.
- **Sufficient conditions:** A is a sufficient condition for B just in case A in and of itself is enough to produce B. Usually, such conditions are designated by the term "if." For instance, "If you earn an average of 95, then you will pass the course." In and of itself, earning an average of 95 will enable a student to pass but a student can pass with less than an average of 95.
- **Necessary and sufficient conditions:** A is both necessary and sufficient for B just in case A is required for and enough in itself to produce B. Such conditions are typically introduced by the expression "if and only if" or "just in case." For example, "You will pass this course if and only if you earn a final average of 60 or higher." Earning an average of 60 or higher is required to pass a course and itself will enable a student to pass.

Conditional statements, like explanations, may often constitute part of an argument's inferential process.

Only passage (h) constitutes a clear example of an argument, as only (h) consists of a set of statements, including premises given in support of a conclusion. Usually, one can distinguish an argument from a nonargument by identifying indicator words. Since arguments have both premises and a conclusion, it is extremely helpful to look for both premise and conclusion indicator words. The following consist of several of the most common **conclusion indicator** words:

- Therefore, accordingly, entails that, we may conclude that, thus, hence, it proves that, it shows that, it must be that, it follows that, consequently, in conclusion, for this reason, for these reasons, implies that, we may infer, so, as a result.

The following consist of several of the most common **premise indicator** words:

- Since, as indicated by, as shown by, because, for, the fact that, may be inferred from, it follows from, as, given that, seeing that, assuming that, for the reason that, owing to.

Look back at passage (h). It does not appear to have any conclusion indicator words, but it does have a premise indicator, "because," suggesting that the author stated the argument's conclusion first and then the reasons supporting that conclusion.

In addition to the availability of and ability to recognize indicator words, it is also illuminating to understand different kinds of inferences and to develop the ability to visually represent the underlying structure of an argument. Each of the following sections elaborates on these two topics.

## (II) Deduction and Induction

All passages that qualify as arguments are inferential. In general, an **inference** may be defined in the following way:

- An **inference** is a logical step that leads from one statement, claim, or proposition to another statement, claim, or proposition.

The two most basic inferential processes are **deduction** and **induction**.

- **Deduction** is a form of reasoning in which a statement or group of statements, if true, guarantee the truth of another statement or group of statements.
- **Induction** is a form of reasoning in which a statement or group of statements, if true, make another statement or group of statements probably or likely to be true.

Each form of reasoning constitutes a different form of argument. That is, deductive reasoning usually constitutes a deductive argument, whereas inductive reasoning usually constitutes an inductive argument.

### (A) Deductive Arguments

When an author constructs an argument, he or she always intends to prove or support a claim or point. Such a claim or point may be called the argument's conclusion. The reasons given in support of the conclusion may be called premises. If the author constructs a deductive argument, the premises put forth are supposed to guarantee the truth of the argument's conclusion. Such efforts, however, are not always successful. When the author succeeds, the argument may be called **valid**. When the author fails, the argument is called **invalid**.

- A deductive argument is **valid** just in case *the argument's premises jointly entail its conclusion*. In other words, a deductive argument is valid just in case *its conclusion is true whenever its premises are true*. Or a deductive argument is valid just in case *it is impossible for its premises to be true and its conclusion false, simultaneously*.
- A deductive argument is **invalid** just in case *the argument's premises do not jointly entail its conclusion*. In other words, a deductive argument is invalid just in case *it is possible for its premises to be true while its conclusion is false, simultaneously*.

For example, consider argument (1):

All dogs are mammals.

All Labs are dogs.

Therefore, all Labs are mammals.

Argument (1) is deductive and valid. If its premises are true, then there is no conceivable way that its conclusion can be false. In addition, the premises of argument (1) are, in fact, true and, thus, it is **sound**.

- A deductive argument is called **sound** when it is both *valid* and has *all true premises*.
- A deductive argument is **unsound** when it is either *invalid* or has *at least one false premise*.

Whether a deductive argument is valid is purely a matter of the argument's *form*, or structure. An argument lacking the correct structure cannot not yield its conclusion. However, the validity of a deductive argument does not depend on the truth of an argument's premises. Consider the form of argument (1):

All M are P.

All S are M.

Therefore, all S are P.

Any argument with this form is necessarily valid. An argument of this form may have *false premises* and still be valid. For example, consider argument (2):

All goats are cats.

All calico are goats.

Therefore, all calico are cats.

Argument (2) has a true conclusion but false premises, rendering it unsound. However, *if* its premises were true, the argument's conclusion would necessarily follow. An argument of this form may also be valid if it has *false premises and a false conclusion*. For example, consider argument (3):

All lambs are turtles.

All dogs are lambs.

Therefore, all dogs are turtles.

Once again, this argument is unsound, as both of its premises are false. However, once again, the argument is valid, since *if* its premises are true, then its conclusion must be true. Valid deductive arguments may have false premises and a true conclusion or false premises and a false conclusion but *never true premises and a false conclusion.*

The premises of an invalid deductive argument do not entail its conclusion. In other words, when a deductive argument is invalid it is possible for *its premises to be true while its conclusion is false.* Consider argument (4):

All dogs are mammals.

All Labs are mammals.

Therefore, all Labs are dogs.

Notice that the premises and conclusion of argument (4) are true. However, the premises do not *imply* the conclusion. Argument (4) represents a common formal fallacy in categorical logic called *undistributed middle,* further explained in Chapter 6. Recall that validity depends primarily on an argument's form. If a deductive argument is not structured properly, then a **counterexample** will prove its invalidity.

- A **counterexample** is a substitution instance of a deductive argument proving that the premises of the argument can be true while its conclusion is false.

A counterexample will have the same form of the argument but different terms, terms that will make the premises true and the conclusion false. Argument (4) has the following form:

All P are M.

All S are M.

Therefore, all S are P.

Substituting "cats" for "P," "dogs" for "S," and keeping "mammals" for "M" yields a suitable counterexample illustrated by argument (5):

All cats are mammals.

All dogs are mammals.

Therefore, all dogs are cats.

There are many valid and invalid deductive argument forms, the most common of which will be explored further in Chapter 6. Next, inductive reasoning must be addressed.

## (B) Inductive Arguments

Deductive arguments are either valid or invalid, sound or unsound. The same terms, however, do not apply to inductive arguments. When an author constructs an inductive argument, the premises put forth in such an argument never *guarantee* the truth of its conclusion but rather only suggest that the conclusion is *probably* true. Thus, it is always possible that the premises of an inductive argument are true while its conclusion is false. So, inductive arguments are classified as either **strong** or **weak**, **cogent** or **uncogent**.

- An inductive argument is **strong** just in case its premises make its conclusion likely to be true.
- An inductive argument is **weak** just in case its premises do not make its conclusion likely to be true.
- An inductive argument is **cogent** just in case it is strong and has all true premises.
- An inductive argument is **uncogent** just in case it is either weak or has at least one false premise.

For example, consider argument (5):

Seventy-five percent of New England college students are Catholic.

Jane Roe is a New England college student.

Therefore, probably, Jane Roe is Catholic.

This argument is inductively strong. Suppose, however, that the number in the first premise is 40 percent instead of 75 percent. In that case, the argument would be weak. Whether the argument is cogent depends on the accuracy of the premises and the statistical data. The strength of an inductive argument can be very difficult to determine, especially when quantitative data is not available to evaluate the argument. And even though statistical data can be used to support an inductive argument, the methods for acquiring and interpreting such data can be extremely complicated. In short, evaluating inductive arguments usually requires more than only logic. While later chapters will explore inductive reasoning in greater depth, as a rule of thumb, one must always avoid *hasty generalizations*, jumping to conclusions without sufficient observations.

In addition, the strength of any inductive argument can change based on new information that comes to light. For example, consider argument (6):

The classroom computer will not project to the screen.

Therefore, probably, the projector is broken.

Suppose that the instructor in the classroom were to connect another device to the projector, such as a laptop, and the second device also will not project to the screen. That would strengthen argument (6), supplying further evidence for the broken projector. However, suppose that when the instructor connects the laptop or perhaps some other device, such as the doc cam, and the second device projects to the screen, it would weaken argument (6), providing a reason to reassess the conclusion and look for other possible explanations for the malfunction.

Each of the following constitutes a form of inductive reasoning:

- **Statistical Reasoning.** Inferences are drawn based on statistical data, as in argument (5). Probability calculations and theories also play a significant role in inductive reasoning. Chapter 7 will more closely examine statistical reasoning in addition to theories of probability.
- **Analogical Reasoning.** Inferences are drawn based on analogies, similarities between objects. This form of reasoning is also more closely addressed in Chapter 7.
- **Causal Reasoning.** Attempts to establish causal relationships between different phenomena. Specifically, Mill's Methods help to identify causal relationships and will be examined in Chapter 8.

- **Scientific Reasoning.** Hypotheses are formulated to explain surprising or unexpected phenomena and then experiments are conducted to test those hypotheses. Scientific reasoning will also be more closely addressed in Chapter 8.
- **Legal Reasoning.** Often, cases disputed in court will make appeals to precedent, forms of analogical reasoning. Statistical, empirical, and experimental data are also used in many court cases.
- **Moral Reasoning.** Ethical argumentation can be both deductive and inductive, but cases in which theories are applied to practical issues may be inductive. Chapter 10 will address moral reasoning in more detail.

The arguments presented in this section so far are relatively simple. They consist of no more than two premises, and the forms of the arguments are clearly exposed. However, authors do not typically present arguments in such simple ways. Usually, arguments are long, complex, and convoluted. In those cases, it is helpful to have techniques that can visually represent the underlying structure of an argument. In other words, it is helpful if one can construct an accurate *diagram* of an argument.

## (III) Argument Diagramming

An **argument diagram** may be defined in the following way:

- An **argument diagram** is a visual representation of the underlying structure of an argument.

For example, consider argument (7):

- You did not clean the house, so you may not go to the party.

Argument (7) is very simple, consisting of one premise and the conclusion. In any diagram, the statements are represented by numbers and the connections between the statements are represented by arrows and braces. Hence, to diagram argument (7), we can begin by numbering the statements:

- (1) You did not clean the house, so (2) you may not go to the party.

Moreover, in any diagram, the argument's conclusion will be at the very bottom, as all the other statements support or lead to the conclusion either directly or indirectly. Hence, it is always helpful to identify the conclusion before building the rest of the diagram, just as a construction crew must have the plans for a building in place before constructing it. To identify the conclusion of an argument, look for the appropriate indicator words. In argument (7), just before (2), the word "so" appears. The word "so" is a conclusion indicator, suggesting that (2) is the conclusion of argument (7). The final diagram of argument (7) would be the following:

Granted, argument (7) is the simplest kind of argument diagram that can be given. Nonetheless, following the steps in the process of diagramming argument (7) can produce accurate diagrams for most arguments.

Diagramming an argument correctly will usually depend on the kinds of premises in the argument. Premises can be either **dependent** or **independent**.

- Premises are **dependent** if either (a) the truth-value of one affects the truth-value of another, or (b) the premises must collaborate to produce a conclusion.
- Premises are **independent** if either (a) the truth-value of one does not affect the truth-value of another, or (b) each premise, by itself, can produce a conclusion.

The truth-value of a statement is whether the statement is true or false. Premises are typically dependent if their values are affected by each other. In other words, suppose that there are two premises, A and B. Premise A and B depend on each other if the falsity of one makes the other false. For example, imagine that premises A and B are the following:

(A) Sandy ate an apple.

(B) Sandy ate fruit.

If B is false, then A is false. And even though A may be false while B is true, one certainly cannot infer B based on the falsity of A. Premises may also be dependent in cases where each is necessary to yield a conclusion, where neither premise by itself can do so. For example, consider argument (8):

- (1) There are no red foxes in Trumbull, Connecticut. (2) There is a red fox in the backyard of the Devlin home on 328 Virginia Street. Thus, (3) the Devlin home on 328 Virginia Street must not be in Trumbull, Connecticut.

In argument (8), both (1) and (2) are necessary to yield the conclusion, (3). Without the information given in (1), one cannot conclude from (2) alone that the address is not in Trumbull. Moreover, without knowing that there is a fox in the backyard of the address given in (2), one cannot conclude from (1) alone that the address is not in Trumbull. The diagram of argument (8) would be **linked** and would have the following form:

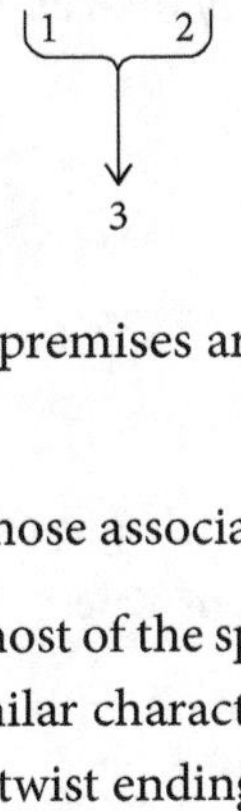


- A **linked diagram** is one in which all the premises are dependent. The connection between dependent premises is represented by braces.

To illustrate another example of an argument whose associated diagram is linked, consider argument (9):

- (1) The 2001 slasher movie *Valentine* keeps most of the spirit of the novel by Tom Savage on which it is based since (2) the movie has the same title, (3) similar characters, (4) the same story line, (5) a killer with the same backstory and motivation, and (6) the same twist ending.

Argument (9) seems to present its conclusion first and then give reasons for the conclusion, as the premise indicator "since" appears after (1), suggesting that reasons are about to be given in support of (1). Moreover, the best diagram for argument (9) would be linked, as the conclusion claims that the novel on which the movie is based captures "most" of the spirit of the novel. Hence, statements (2)–(6) are most likely working together to generate the conclusion. For instance, if the novel only had similar characters, but nothing else, it would not have *most* of the spirit of the original novel. Moreover, the truth-values of some of the premises seem to affect the others. Consider statements (4)–(6). If (4) is false—that is, if the movie had a different story line than the novel—then it is unlikely that the main antagonist of the story would have the same backstory and motivation. Moreover, if the storyline changes, then the twist ending would probably change as well. Argument (9) should, thus, be diagrammed in the following way:

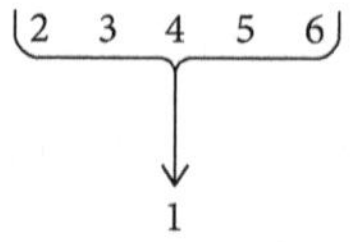


Any purely linked diagram will resemble the diagram of argument (9).

In addition to linked diagrams, some arguments may contain premises that are totally independent, in which each premise by itself can produce the argument's conclusion. In such cases, the argument is best represented through a **convergent diagram**:

- A **convergent diagram** represents an argument consisting entirely of independent premises.

For example, consider argument (10):

- (1) Ethan should not be allowed to have a pet dog because (2) he never cleans his room, (3) never washes the dishes, (4) never takes out the garbage, and (5) cannot manage his money properly.

As did the author of argument (9), the author of argument (10) presented the conclusion first and gave the reasons later, as the premise indicator "because" follows (1). The truth-values of (2)–(4) do not seem to affect each other. It is possible that Ethan could clean his room, for instance, but never complete any of the other tasks mentioned. Moreover, it is possible that he does everything on the list except clean his room. In addition, if Ethan failed to complete any one of these tasks, it may be marshaled as evidence of irresponsibility and, thus, suggest that he cannot properly care for a dog, a much heavier responsibility than any other task listed in argument (10). This argument is best represented by the following diagram:

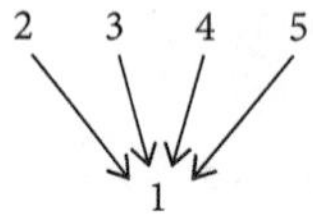


Any purely convergent diagram will resemble the diagram of argument (10).

A third type of argument diagram is the **divergent** type.

- A **divergent diagram** represents an argument with a single premise from which multiple independent conclusions can be inferred.

A divergent diagram is basically a convergent diagram turned upside down. Consider argument (11) as an example:

- (1) John Carpenter recently said that *Halloween Kills* is the ultimate slasher film. Therefore, (2) the movie will make more money than any other in the *Halloween* franchise, (3) the fans will love the movie, (4) Jason Blum will surely commission several more movies in the coming years, and (5) the movie will probably win an award.

The first statement is clearly a premise but everything that follows appears to be a separate conclusion, given that the most common conclusion indicator, "Therefore," appears before they are stated. Moreover, statements (2)–(5) do not appear to constitute a series of implications. Statement (2) does not necessarily entail (3), as a movie can be liked by fans even if it does not make a substantial amount of money; from (3), (4) does not seem to follow, as fans can enjoy a film in a long-running series, but the series may still end without another installment; and certainly, (5) does not follow from (2), (3), or (4). Furthermore, the truth-values of statements (2)–(5) do not seem to affect each other. Even if the movie does not make more money than any other in the franchise, fans may still love the movie, Blum may commission more, and the movie might win an award. And even if the movie makes more money than the other films in the franchise, fans may dislike it, no more installments may be made, and the movie may not win an award. In short, any of (2)–(5) may be true while the others are false. The best diagram for argument (11) is the following:

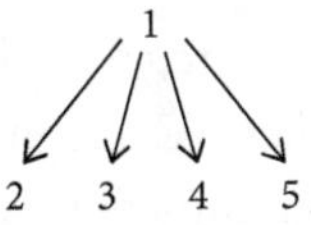


Any purely divergent diagram will resemble the diagram of argument (11).

A fourth type of diagram is called **serial**:

- A **serial diagram** represents an argument in which one statement implies a second, the second implies a third, and so on, until reaching a final statement, the conclusion. This explanation describes a *pure serial diagram.*
- A *second* kind of serial diagram may represent a sequence of statements in which the conclusion of a prior argument functions as a premise in a later argument. This type of serial diagram may be called *extended* or *mixed.*

A *pure* serial diagram may also be called a "chain reaction" diagram, as the diagram resembles a sequence in which an initial event triggers a series of similar events until reaching the end of the "chain." Consider argument (12) as an example:

- (1) Alice recently changed her major from biology to philosophy. So, (2) now she will only take courses that do not have any practical value. Thus, (3) when she graduates, she will not be able to find a suitable, high-paying job. Hence, (4) she will not be able to pay for all her expenses. It follows that (5) after she graduates, Alice will inevitably become homeless after several months.

After (1), every statement in argument (12) appears to be an implication from the previous statement until reaching its conclusion, (5). The best diagram for argument (12) is the following:

A pure serial diagram will look like the diagram of argument (12).

An *extended* or *mixed* serial diagram is so-called because it will usually combine the serial diagramming technique with the linked diagramming technique, representing multiple arguments. For example, consider argument (13):

- (1) No philosophers are dogmatic and (2) Josh Lott is a philosopher. So, (3) Josh Lott is not dogmatic. Moreover, (4) people who are dogmatic are impatient. Therefore, (5) Josh Lott is a patient man.

Premises (1) and (2) seem to link up to generate (3). The word "and" suggests that (1) and (2) are conjoined, while the word "so," a conclusion indicator, appears just before statement (3), which uses terms from both premises (1) and (2). Furthermore, one cannot yield "Josh Lott is not dogmatic" from premise (1) alone. Next, the argument's conclusion, (5) uses terms from both statements (3) and (4). It does not follow from (3) alone that "Josh Lott is not impatient" without some connection established between dogmatism and impatience. Hence, (3) and (4) seem to link up to produce (5). Argument (13) is best diagrammed in the following way:

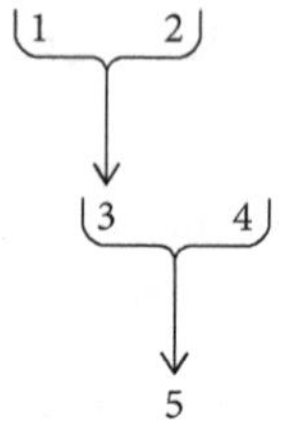


Unfortunately, many arguments are not simple and require more than only one diagramming technique. Some arguments, in fact, may combine all four of the previously addressed diagramming techniques. Consider argument (14) as an example of a complex argument that requires all four diagramming techniques:

- (1) There most certainly is a God, as (2) our universe exhibits evidence of intelligent design, given that (3) the universal constants that govern the forces of gravity and electromagnetism in addition to the principles necessary to give rise to intelligent, complex life are too finely tuned to have occurred by blind chance, and (4) there is no discernible principle or law that can produce such synchronicity. In addition, (5) even the simplest of organisms that can be observed only at the microscopic level exhibit irreducible complexity, suggesting that (6) they could only be constructed by an intelligent being rather than developing gradually through a chance process of evolution. And if there is a God, (7) there most assuredly is an afterlife, and (8) there are also universal moral absolutes. If there is an afterlife, then (9) human beings will continue to exist after their physical death. And if there are universal moral absolutes, (10) then good will prevail over evil through the cosmic justice of God. Thus, (11) in the afterlife, all human beings, both good and evil, will face ultimate justice through a final judgment from God.

This argument is an example of a proof that might be given by a theologian or by a philosopher specializing in philosophy of religion. It is very complex. While statement (1) is not the main conclusion of the argument, it seems to serve as an intermediate conclusion, leading to statements (7)–(11). So, statements (2)–(6) all support (1) in some way. The primary support for (1) seems to come from (2), and (3)–(6), in turn, support (2). The word "and" seems to conjoin (3) and (4), suggesting that they are linked. Moreover, the truth-values of (3) and (4) seem to affect each other since if there were no fine-tuning, then the observable universe could arise from blind chance. Statements (5) and (6) seem to lend support to (2) independently of (3) and (4) given the transitional phrase "In addition." However, (5) and (6) are not independent of each other since immediately after (5), the word "suggests" appears, indicating that (6) follows from (5). Next, statement (1) seems to imply statements (7) and (8), which appear to be independent. Then, (7) implies (9), while (8) implies (10). Statements (9) and (10) then seem to link up to produce the argument's final conclusion, (11), given that (11) contains terms from both (9) and (10).

As an alternative to the complicated discussion of the previous paragraph, one can diagram a complex argument (or any argument) by applying the **NICE Method (N – I – C – E)**:

- **N:** *Number* the statements.
- **I:** *Identify* the *main conclusion* of the argument in addition to any intermediate conclusions.
- **C:** *Cut out* the *content of the statements* and preserve only the *transitional terms* and *indicator words.*
- **E:** *Establish the connections* between the statements based on the transitional terms and indicator words.

Applying the N-I-C-E method to argument (14) yields the following:

- Argument (1), as (2) given that (3) and (4). In addition, (5), suggesting that (6). If (1), then (7) and (8). If (7), then (9). If (8), then (10). Thus, (11).

This reconstruction makes the work much lighter! The best diagram for argument (14) is the following:

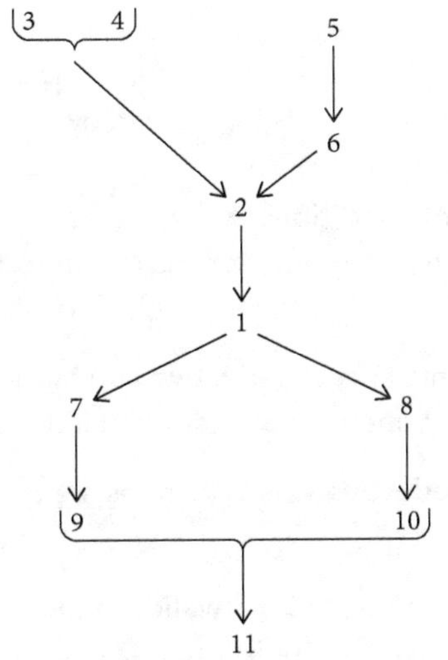


Notice that the diagram for argument (14) applies EVERY diagramming technique covered in this chapter.

The ability to identify arguments and distinguish them from nonargumentative passages lends itself as a crucial critical thinking skill that allows people to evaluate the positions of others and separate those that can defend their beliefs from those who merely state unwarranted opinions. Since most passages are complex and most arguments will not reflect standard logical forms, the ability to diagram arguments correctly allows for the recognition of connections between the claims one makes and the reasons for them, which itself is the basis for challenging those reasons and finding a more solid basis for one's beliefs. In addition, the ability to distinguish between deduction and induction, to identify valid forms of deductive inference and distinguish them from invalid forms, to identify strong inductive reasoning and distinguish them from weak forms are equally if not more important. Chapter 6 emphasizes different forms of deductive reasoning, while Chapters 7 and 8 focus on different forms of inductive reasoning.

## Chapter Summary and Key Points to Remember

- An **argument** is an inferential set of statements, some of which are *premises* and one of which is the *conclusion*.
- Arguments must be distinguished from the following kinds of passages:
    - Simple declarative statements
    - Warnings
    - Pieces of advice
    - Statements of opinion without reasons for them
    - Expository passages
    - Explanations
    - Conditional statements ("If … then …" statements), wherein "If" designates the *antecedent* and "Then" designates the *consequent*
    - Depending on the intentions of an author, a conditional statement may be part of an argument or reflect an argument contained within a single sentence. There are three kinds of conditions:
        - **Necessary conditions,** which are required to generate a result but may not alone be enough to produce a result; usually introduced by the expression "Only if …," i.e., "You will pass only if you attend class."
        - **Sufficient conditions,** which are enough in themselves to generate a result but may not be required to produce a result, usually introduced by the expression "If …," i.e., "If you earn a final average of 95, you will pass the course."
        - **Necessary** and **sufficient conditions,** which are both required to generate a result and alone are enough to produce the result in question; usually introduced by the expressions "If and only if" or "Just in case," i.e., "You will pass if and only if you have a final average of 63 or higher."
- There are two general types of inferences: **deductive** and **inductive**. These two forms of reasoning correspond to two general kinds of arguments, deductive and inductive.
    - An inference/argument is **deductive** when premises are given that supposedly guarantee the truth of a conclusion or consequent.
        - Deductive arguments may be **valid** or **invalid**, **sound** or **unsound**.
        - A deductive argument is **valid** when its premises jointly entail the conclusion; that is, when the premises are true, the conclusion is true.
        - A deductive argument is **invalid** when the premises do not entail the conclusion; that is, it is possible for the premises to be true while the conclusion is false.
        - When an argument is invalid, it is possible to provide a **counterexample**, which is a substitution instance that has the same form of an argument but uses terms that show that the premises can be true while the conclusion is false.
        - A deductive argument is **sound** when it is both *valid* and has *all true premises.*
        - A deductive argument is **unsound** if either it is *invalid* or has *at least one false premise.*
    - An inference/argument is **inductive** when premises are given that supposedly make a conclusion or consequence probable or likely to be true.

- Inductive arguments may be either **strong** or **weak**, **cogent** or **uncogent**.
- An inductive argument is **strong** when its premises make its conclusion likely to be true.
- An inductive argument is **weak** when its premises do not make its conclusion likely to be true.
- An inductive argument is **cogent** when it is *strong* and has *all true premises.*
- An inductive argument is **uncogent** if it is either *weak* or has *at least one false premise.*
- Forms of inductive reasoning include statistical reasoning, analogical reasoning, causal and scientific reasoning, legal reasoning, and moral reasoning.

- Most arguments that occur in ordinary language are long, complex, and do not reflect standard logical forms. Hence, the ability to diagram arguments is an invaluable skill.
- An **argument diagram** is a visual representation of the structure of argument using numbers to represent statements and arrows and braces to represent connections between the premises and the conclusion.
- There are four basic kinds of argument diagrams:
    - **Linked diagrams**, which consist entirely of **dependent premises** working together to support a conclusion.
        - Premises are **dependent** when either the truth-value of one affects the truth-value of another (that is, if one is true the other is true, while if one is false the other is false) or neither premise by itself can generate the conclusion in question.
        - Premises are **independent** when the truth-value of one does not affect the truth-value of the other and each premise by itself can produce the conclusion in question.
    - **Convergent diagrams,** which consist entirely of independent premises supporting a conclusion.
    - **Divergent diagrams,** which consist of a single premise from which multiple independent conclusions can be drawn.
    - **Serial diagrams,** of which there are two kinds:
        - **Pure serial diagrams,** in which each premise leads to another until stopping at a conclusion.
        - **Extended** or **mixed serial diagrams**, which usually combine the linked diagramming style with the serial style such that the conclusion of one argument serves as the premise in another.
        - For longer, more complex arguments, two or more of these diagramming techniques will often have to be combined. In those cases, and in any case for that matter, it is advisable to use the **N-I-C-E Method**:
            - **N:** *Number* the statements.
            - **I:** *Identify* the *main conclusion* in addition to any *intermediate conclusions.*
            - **C:** *Cut out* the *content of statements,* preserving only the transitional phrases and indicator words.
            - **E:** *Establish connections* between the statements based on transitional phrases and indicator words.

## Exercises for Application and Reflection

**Instructions:** Use what you learned in this chapter to solve each of the following sets of problems and/or to answer the questions in each of the following sections.

I. **Argument Recognition:** Determine which of the following passages are arguments. If a passage is an argument, identify the conclusion.

1. You should buy your new HD television at *Best Buy* since you said that you wanted the biggest HD television you could get at the lowest price. *Target* has 60-inch HD televisions for $500, and *Walmart* has 60-inch televisions for $450, but *Best Buy* is selling 70-inch HD televisions for $425.
2. *Best Buy* has 50-inch HD televisions for sale starting at $225 and *Target's* 50-inch HD televisions are on sale starting at $250.
3. My physician told me that if I lift weights on a regular basis, I should mix in some cardiovascular activity as well, such as running on the treadmill or working out on the elliptical at the end of my workout. He also suggested adding vegetables and supplements to my diet.
4. Cardiovascular exercises strengthen the heart, increase endurance, lower cholesterol, contribute to weight loss, and reduce stress. Thus, there is no good reason why anyone should not perform some cardiovascular exercises each week.
5. Each of the world's religions describes a transcendent realm beyond the physical world that serves as a basis for morality. Therefore, the study of religion encourages deep reflective thinking, provides people with a moral compass, and gives humanity hope for a better world after death.
6. The 1998 dark comedy *8 Heads in a Duffel Bag* stars Joe Pesci in a familiar role as a contract killer for the mob tasked with delivering the titular duffel bag filled with human heads to a crime boss known as "Big Sep." Along the way, he accidentally switches bags with a college student, Charlie (portrayed by Andy Comeau) who plans to take a vacation with his girlfriend Laurie (Kristy Swanson) and her parents Richard and Annette Bennett (portrayed by George Hamilton and Dyan Cannon). Pesci's character must go on a desperate hunt to retrieve the lost bag before he loses his head, literally! Upon its release, the movie was critically panned and grossed very little money, although it attempted to provide a vehicle for some lesser-known actors and comedians alongside Pesci himself, who coasts through the film merely acting like diluted versions of his characters from previous films such as *Goodfellas* and *Casino*.
7. Ted Pickford's underrated young adult horror trilogy from the early '90s, *Scared to Death*—featuring the fictional character, Bobby Wimmer, a complex antihero obsessed with first terrifying and then killing each member of the elite group of youths known collectively as "The Five" who tormented him and ruined his life six years earlier—should be required reading for all middle school children. First, it is an engaging thriller that emphasizes suspense and character development rather than cheap scares or high body counts and ignores overtly supernatural phenomena, remaining more grounded in reality than the books in R. L. Stine's more popular *Fear Street* series. As such, it will encourage all students—including those who are not especially studious—to read carefully. Moreover, it provides insight into the psychology of both predators and their potential victims, which can help young people to identify potential similar real-life dangers and take precautions against them. Finally, it lends itself as an interesting cautionary tale against both the dangerous consequences of bullying and the futility of seeking revenge against one's oppressors. On the one hand, the reckless and irresponsible actions of "The Five" ruined a child's life and helped to create a veritable psychopath with little respect, if any, for the life of anyone. On the other hand, Wimmer's revenge campaign leaves his life empty, forces him to kill his one true friend, and ultimately harms more innocent people than his primary targets.
8. I think that it is utterly absurd that they keep making new installments in horror movie series such as *Saw* and *Halloween*. There are currently nine installments in the *Saw* series and a tenth is in the

making as we speak. And there are currently 12 installments in the *Halloween* series with a 13th coming out next year! Are they ever going to stop?

9. Showtime's hit series *Dexter* arguably had the worst final season in the history of television. The primary story line was totally contrived, requiring far too incredulous a suspension of disbelief and forcing the audience to ignore significant events of the previous season that would have a more profound impact in reality. Moreover, the entire experience of watching the final season was frustrating given that it deliberately ignored the story line that fans hoped for and anticipated for seven years to focus on an idea far less compelling, a bland villain, and a recurring romantic interest whose presence merely recapitulates themes better developed in earlier seasons. New characters are unnecessarily introduced and inconsequential subplots are given far more attention than necessary. And the inexplicable killing of perhaps the series' most beloved character is unforgivable, as is the puzzling final scene where the titular character escapes to become a lumberjack! It follows that the upcoming revival of the show is not only a relief to fans of *Dexter* but also necessary to cement the legacy of the show.
10. During his presidency, Trump generated more jobs, contributed to the growth of the economy, upheld rights guaranteed to citizens in the US Constitution, took measures to protect the country from unlawful intrusion, and always honestly spoke his mind. It follows that Trump was not such a bad president after all.
11. *Hamlet* is the name of a play written by William Shakespeare. It tells the story of a prince, Hamlet, who returns to Denmark to attend the funeral of his father and discovers that his uncle has married his mother and ascended the throne. As a result, he suspects foul play. Other works of literature adopted plot points from *Hamlet*, such as Hawthorne's *The Scarlet Letter* and Faulkner's *As I Lay Dying*. Tropes in popular films and television shows—such as Disney's *The Lion King* and FX's *Sons of Anarchy*—also borrow heavily from *Hamlet*.
12. Aristotle and Plato agreed that knowledge is intrinsically good, that philosophy is necessary for happiness, that there are transcendent absolutes, that ethics and morality are primarily matters of character and virtue, and that everything fits into a framework of purposes. However, Aristotle disagreed with Plato's theory that learning is recollection, rejected Plato's theory of the forms, denied that happiness is only a matter of virtue, and preferred a different style of writing and teaching.

II. **Deduction versus Induction:** Determine whether each of the following arguments is deductive or inductive.

1. All mammals are warm-blooded. All tigers are mammals. Therefore, all tigers are warm-blooded.
2. Most people who like Stephen King's novels and the original 1990 mini-series *IT* liked the new 2017 adaptation of *IT*. Doug is a fan of Stephen King and of the original adaptation of *IT*. So, he will probably like the new adaptation of *IT*.
3. An eyewitness said that the man who murdered the librarian had on a black T-shirt. But Joe does not like the color black, so, probably, he did not kill the librarian.
4. If there were an all-powerful God, there would be no instances of horrendous evil in the world. But there are instances of horrendous evil in the world. Thus, there cannot be an all-powerful God.
5. None of the cats at this address are named Myron. The collar of the cat in front of us reads Myron. So, Myron must not live here.
6. Most of the people who like John Carpenter's *Halloween* do not like most of the sequels. James not only likes John Carpenter's *Halloween*, but he thinks that it is the greatest horror movie of all time. So, he probably does not like *Halloween II*.

7. Most students who study logic get higher scores on the GRE. Mike studies logic, so he will most likely have one of the higher GRE scores this year.
8. Buddha Tagatha, originally named Siddartha Gautama, founded what is now known as Buddhism after working with several Hindu masters. And his religion was predominately Hindu. Plus, Hinduism has been an official religion for over 3,500 years. So, Buddhism definitely came from Hinduism.
9. The last time the projector stopped working, it had a defective bulb. So it probably needs a new bulb now.
10. Thomas Hobbes, Niccolo Machiavelli, and Hsun-Tzu all shared very similar ideas about human nature and political rule. It must be that there are ideas that apply to more than one place at more than one time.
11. After you identified the *deductive arguments*, try to determine whether each argument is valid or invalid. If you think the argument is invalid, provide a counterexample. If you think an argument is valid, then determine whether it is sound.
12. After you identified the *inductive arguments*, indicate whether each argument is strong or weak. If your argument is strong, determine whether it is cogent.

III. **Providing Counterexamples:** Each of the following arguments is invalid. Provide a counterexample to each, making the premises true and the conclusion false.

1. All cats are mammals. All leopards are mammals. Therefore, all leopards are cats.
2. All zebras are donkeys. All zebras are goats. Therefore, all goats are donkeys.
3. No gremlins are Kanamits. No Martians are gremlins. Therefore, no Martians are Kanamits.
4. All vampires avoid sunlight. No vampires are zombies. Therefore, no zombies avoid sunlight.
5. No Zed are Freds. Some Neds are not Zeds. So, Some Neds are not Freds.
6. If Joe went to the party, he saw Sally. Joe saw Sally. It follows that Joe went to the party.
7. If Nicky has his van, then he picked up the wedding cake. But Nick did not have his van. Hence, he did not pick up the wedding cake.
8. If Buster is a cocker spaniel, then he is a mammal. If Buster is a dog, then he is a mammal. Therefore, if Buster is a cocker spaniel, then he is a dog.

IV **Argument Diagramming:** Build a diagram for each of the following arguments. (There may be more than one suitable diagram in some cases.)

1. If Ryan wants Marni to find him interesting then he should do the following: visit an art museum at least once a month, visit a science museum at least once per month, read at least one book each week, read at least two different newspapers each week, watch at least one educational program each week, learn how to understand others' points of view, and attempt challenging activities that force him to think.
2. I told Matt that absence makes the heart grow fonder, so, if he truly wants Maci to be excited to see him, he should leave her alone for a couple of weeks.
3. Mathematics reflects universal truths. Mathematics also contains knowledge superior to that of the bodily senses. Moreover, mathematics is a distinctively human activity that no other animals participate in. Finally, some of the finest geniuses in history, such as Pythagoras, Euclid, Plato, Descartes, Pascal, Newton, and Einstein were mathematicians. It follows that everyone should study mathematics.
4. Through the progressive and attentive study of nature over many centuries, scientists were able to construct the periodic table, which describes all the elements that make up the physical world. It

follows that all physical objects can be broken down into more basic parts, that humans are naturally inquisitive, and that nature has an order beyond physical appearances designed for discovery.

5. If you start smoking cigarettes, then you will become addicted to them. And if you become addicted to smoking, you will damage your lungs. Damage to your lungs will make you more vulnerable to diseases such as asthma and COPD. And these diseases will inevitably lead to your untimely death.
6. A recent television program argued that the controversial issue of climate change is really a hoax invented by politicians to control people. The documentary cites various testimonies of former senators who remained anonymous. So, not all educated people believe that climate change is a genuine cause for concern. And if so, then not all educated people are inspired by scientific inquiry and experimental evidence for their beliefs.
7. Death does not hurt the one who dies, because to be hurt, one must feel pain, and one must already be alive to feel pain. And no one should fear anything that can cause no pain. So, no one should fear death.
8. It is safer to be feared than it is to be loved. First, people are inherently selfish and hostile; hence, they are only motivated by the threat of punishment or some other form of coercion. In addition, paying people for their loyalty makes a leader look weak, thereby inviting the desire for greater payments in the future, and contempt from one's subordinates. So, loyalty bought with money means nothing. Lastly, human beings are too fickle for love to last long.
9. All human beings are basically selfish, as suggested by the behavior of young children and the actions people take when they do not know they are being watched. Moreover, the only time an individual is likely to help others is if doing so benefits him or her in some way. Hence, there must exist a social contract by which people agree not to harm each other, which implies that there must be an all-powerful ruler to enforce such a contract.
10. Human beings have an instinct for generosity. For example, if anyone sees a child drowning, he or she would attempt to save the child without hesitation. Moreover, if a person is left alone, that person would never seek to harm or steal from anyone. Thus, human beings are inherently good, which means that people become evil through social institutions alone.
11. The world is illusory. I know this because pleasure does not last and is insufficient for happiness, because wealth is only a means to some other end, and because even civic and political achievements are only temporary and insufficient for happiness. So, the meaning of life must lie in a deeper reality, beyond life itself.
12. The laws of logic prove that no one has free will. For instance, the law of excluded middle says that every proposition must be either true or false, and the law of contradiction says nothing can both be and not be. So, for anything I do tomorrow, to attempt to do otherwise would violate one or both laws. And since no one has any free will, no one can be held responsible for their actions.
13. Go back to section I and build diagrams for those passages that you identified as arguments.
14. Build diagrams for each argument in section II.

## V **Miscellaneous Problems for Reflection and Discussion**

1. Suppose that an argument has no indicator words. How would you be able to tell that such a passage constitutes an argument? What does that mean about the nature of arguments as opposed to nonarguments? Explain.
2. A common misconception about deduction is that it consists of reasoning from general principles to specific concrete instances or claims. Also, a common misconception of induction is that it consists of the opposite process, reasoning from specific, concrete instances or claims to more general principles. Both ideas are mistaken, however. Give an example of (a) deductive reasoning that moves from

specific instances to a general claim and (b) inductive reasoning that moves from a general claim to a specific claim.

3. Deductive arguments may be valid even if their premises and conclusion are false. What, then, is the connection between validity and *truth*? Explain.
4. Consider the following inductive argument. Then, develop at least three sentences that strengthen the argument and at least three that weaken the argument.
    - John Q. Smith was murdered in the library at 1:30 a.m. on Friday, October 13. The only other person who had access to the building on that date at that time is Fred Jones, the custodian. So, probably, Fred Jones murdered John Q. Smith.
5. Find a complex argument in a book, newspaper, journal, magazine, or some other medium and build a diagram for the argument.

# 6

# Logic (II)

## Deductive Reasoning

INTRODUCTION

### Preparing to Read Chapter 6

The present chapter and the three that follow are extensions of the previous chapter. The current chapter emphasizes forms of *deductive reasoning* and *formal fallacies*, while those that follow emphasize forms of *inductive reasoning* and *informal fallacies*. This chapter covers the following topics:

- Elementary **categorical logic**, also known as Aristotelian logic, makes reference to Aristotle's three acts of the mind, categorical propositions, the traditional and modern squares of opposition, types of categorical syllogisms, and ways to test syllogisms for validity.
- Elementary **truth-functional logic**, addressing different types of propositions, basic translations from English to symbolic logic, truth-functional operators and the basic truth-tables for each operator, valid forms of truth-functional arguments, and formal fallacies.

## AS YOU READ, LOOK FOR THE FOLLOWING CONCEPTS AND TERMS

- Categorical Logic
- The Three Acts of the Mind:
    - Understanding
    - Judging
    - Reasoning
- Categorical Propositions:
    - A Propositions (Universal Affirmative)
    - E Propositions (Universal Negative)
    - I Propositions (Singular Affirmative)
    - O Propositions (Singular Negative)
- Properties of Categorical Propositions:
    - Quantity, Quality, and Distribution

- The Traditional Square of Opposition:
  - Contraries
  - Subcontraries
  - Subalternation
  - Contradictories
- Existential Import
- The Modern Square of Opposition
- Categorical Syllogism
- Figure and Mood
- Conditionally Valid versus Unconditionally Valid Syllogisms
- Counterexample
- Truth-Functional Logic
- Simple Sentence (Atomic Sentence)
- Compound Sentence (Molecular Sentence)
- Truth-Functional Connectives:
  - Negation
  - Conjunction
  - Disjunction
  - Conditional
  - Biconditional
- Truth-Table
- Valid Argument Forms:
  - Modus Ponens
  - Modus Tollens
  - Hypothetical Syllogism (Chain Argument)
  - Disjunctive Syllogisms
  - Dilemmas:
    - Simple Constructive
    - Complex Constructive
    - Simple Destructive
    - Complex Destructive
- Invalid Argument Forms:
  - Affirming the Consequent
  - Denying the Antecedent
  - Invalid Forms of Hypothetical Syllogism
  - Invalid Forms of Disjunctive Syllogism
  - Invalid Dilemmas

**KEEP THE FOLLOWING QUESTIONS IN MIND AS YOU READ**

- Why should I understand different forms of deductive reasoning?
- How can I apply the principles and rules of deductive reasoning to my everyday life and experiences?
- What are the shortcomings/limits of deductive reasoning?

# (I) Categorical Logic

This section focuses on the following topics of categorical logic:

- Aristotle's conception of the three acts of the mind.
- Categorical propositions and the relations between them.
- Categorical syllogisms and methods for assessing their validity.
- The traditional square of opposition and the relations it represents.

It is appropriate to begin with Aristotle since he is credited with establishing logic as a science, and he focused on categorical logic.

## (A) Aristotle: Three Acts of the Mind

If logic can be "invented," then, in effect, there could be no true logic, as logic would be whatever anyone wanted it to be. The word "logic" derives from the Greek term *logos*, which literally translates into "reason." Conventionally, logic refers to the science of reason and the rules that govern the mind and rules imply normative conditions of universality and objectivity. Hence, it would be improper to credit Aristotle with *inventing* logic, but he most certainly deserves credit for discovering the rules of logic and codifying logic as a science. Aristotle explicitly outlined the principles of logic in six books that collectively came to be called the *Organon* and governed the science of logic for nearly 2,000 years.

Since logic is a distinctively human endeavor, the science of logic constitutes a fundamental aspect of understanding human nature, in addition to understanding reality, truth, and knowledge. Succinctly, logic may be defined as the science of thinking. More specifically, Aristotle claimed that logic seeks three things: *clarity*, *truth*, and *proof*. Each item sought by logic corresponds to a fundamental act of the mind, each of which constitutes a way of thinking:

1) **Understanding:** Conceiving or understanding a concept that is neither true nor false (i.e., "human," "mortal," "mammal," etc.).
2) **Judgment:** Predicating one concept of another in a declarative sentence (i.e., "All humans are mortal," "All humans are mammals," etc.).
3) **Reasoning:** Drawing inferences from one proposition to another (i.e., from premises to conclusions), giving reasons for one's beliefs.

*Understanding* may also be called *simple apprehension*. This act of the mind involves grasping a single object of thought. Animals seem to be incapable of this act or at the very least are incapable of expressing understanding in words. Computers certainly seem to be incapable of understanding as well since they only perform operations based on what is programmed into them. Aristotle maintained that what is grasped or apprehended through the act of understanding is the *universal*. For instance, understanding the concept "human" means grasping or apprehending what all human beings have in common, thereby separating the essence of a thing from its object. In other words, understanding or conceiving of an object includes separating the *form* of the object from its *matter*. For Aristotle, understanding is made possible by distinctly human faculties, and the processes through which understanding occurs in addition to the concepts created by the mind establish that there is a *spiritual* component of humanity.

Next, *judging* is more complex than understanding since it involves more than one concept. The second act of the mind always involves the process of predicating one concept of another. For example, the statement "All dogs are mammals" involves the concepts "dog" and "mammal," through which dogs are affirmed as belonging to the class of mammals. Unlike concepts, judgments can be assessed as either true or false. Whereas understanding is concerned with separating essence or form from matter, judgment is concerned with *existence*, or whether declarative statements correspond to reality.

Finally, *reasoning* is the most complex process of the three since it involves multiple statements, multiple judgments. As judgment moves from one *concept* to another, reason moves from one *judgment* to another. Like concepts, reasoning cannot be true or false, but rather *valid* or *invalid* in deduction, or *strong* or *weak* in induction.

Each act of the mind corresponds to a different aim of logic. Understanding corresponds to *clarity*, as a concept must be clear if it is to be grasped properly. Judgments are concerned with the *truth* of declarative statements, whether one concept really can be predicated of another, and whether a specific concept corresponds to any concrete entity. Lastly, reason is concerned with arguments and the validity of inferences with *proof*. Moreover, each act of the mind also corresponds to an aspect of categorical logic. The three items of concern in categorical logic are the **term**, the **proposition**, and the **syllogism**.

- Understanding corresponds to the **terms**, each of which must be clear.
- Judgment corresponds to the **proposition**, which must be true.
- Reasoning corresponds to the **syllogism**, which must be valid.

The following sections emphasize first propositions and then syllogisms.

## (B) Categorical Propositions

A **categorical proposition** may be defined in the following way:

- A proposition that can be analyzed as being about classes, or *categories*, and as affirming or denying that one class, S, is included in some other class, P, in whole or in part.

There are four kinds of categorical propositions, traditionally abbreviated as A, E, I, and O:

- **A propositions** are *universal affirmative* and have the form, "All S are P" (i.e., "All dogs are mammals").
- **E propositions** are *universal negative* and have the form, "No S are P" (i.e., "No dogs are cats").
- **I propositions** are *particular affirmative* and have the form, "Some S are P" (i.e., "Some dogs are Labs").
- **O propositions** are *particular negative* and have the form, "Some S are not P" (i.e., "Some dogs are not Labs").

In categorical logic, the quantifier "some" just means "at least one." Hence, "Some S are P" just means that *at least one* S is P, whereas "Some S are not P" just means that *at least one* S is not P. The letters S and P, moreover, designate classes, categories, or groups of objects. For example, if the term S represents "Labs" and P represents "dogs," then the sentence "All S are P" would mean "All Labs are dogs." An additional subgroup of propositions are those that include specific, singular terms, for instance, proposition (a), "Josh Lott teaches philosophy," and proposition (b), "Josh Lott does not teach calculus." For the purposes of categorical logic, (a) may be translated as an I proposition and (b) may be translated as an O proposition.

Furthermore, categorical propositions have three properties: quantity, quality, and will distribute its terms in a specific way.

- The **quantity** of a proposition refers to whether it is *universal* or *particular.*
- The **quality** of a proposition refers to whether it is affirmative or negative.
- A term within a proposition is **distributed** if the proposition refers to *all of the members* under its class.

Distribution is most relevant to the current discussion of categorical logic and the validity of categorical syllogisms. *Universal affirmative propositions* (A) distribute only the subject term. For instance, the sentence "All dogs are mammals" refers to all dogs but not all mammals. *Universal negative propositions* (E) distribute both the subject and predicate terms. For example, the sentence "No dogs are cats" refers to all dogs and all cats. *Particular affirmative propositions* (I) distribute neither term. That is, the sentence, "Some dogs are Labs" refers only to individual dogs and Labs. Finally, *particular negative propositions* (O) distribute only the predicate term. For instance, the sentence "Some dogs are not Labs" excludes specific, particular dogs from the entire class of Labs. The following chart (Table 6.1) summarizes the properties of each type of proposition:

TABLE 6.1 Properties of Categorical Propositions

| Proposition | Quantity | Quality | Distribution |
|---|---|---|---|
| A | Universal | Affirmative | Subject term only |
| E | Universal | Negative | Both subject and predicate term |
| I | Particular | Affirmative | Neither term |
| O | Particular | Negative | Predicate term only |

Traditionally, Venn diagrams are used to diagram categorical propositions, in which circles represent each class designated by the terms. For example, the diagram of an A proposition, "All S are P," is the following:

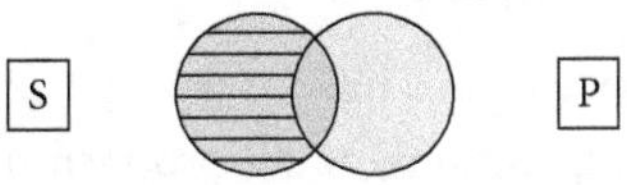


The lines in the left circle cross out any part of the class S that does not overlap with class P, while all that remains of S overlaps with P. For instance, in the sentence "All Labs are dogs," there are no Labs that are not dogs.

The diagram of E propositions, "No S are P," is the following:

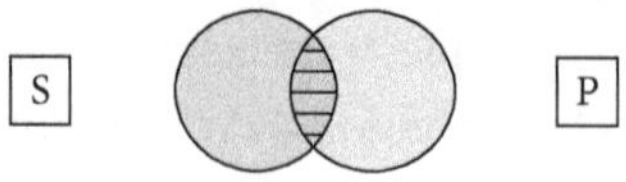


Here, the lines cross out any overlap between S and P, indicating that no members of class S belong to class P. For instance, the sentence "No dogs are cats" states that there is no overlap between the class of dogs and those of cats. No member of either belongs to the other.

The diagram for I propositions, "Some S are P," is the following:

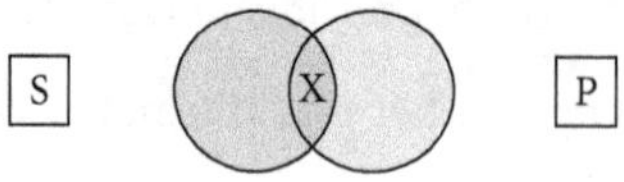


Here, "X" marks the overlap of some members of S with P. Since the sentence does not state that all S are P, no all of S can be crossed out. For example, the statement, "Some dogs are Labs" would have the diagram for I, since not all dogs are Labs and some would exist outside the overlap of the two classes.

Lastly, the diagram for O propositions, "Some S are not P," is the following:

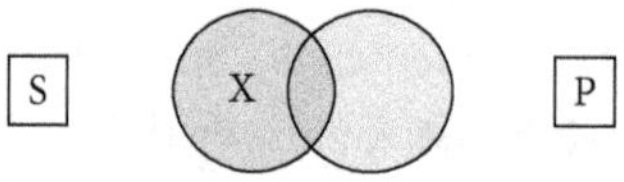


Here, "X" indicates those members of S that do not overlap with P. Since the sentence does not state that no S are P, the overlap between S and P cannot be crossed out, as all that can be inferred from the sentence is that there are members of S that are not P. For example, the sentence "Some dogs are not Labs" expresses that there are dogs that do not belong to the class of Labs, but it does not follow that there is no overlap whatsoever between dogs and Labs.

Traditionally, the following properties apply to the four categorical propositions:

- **Contradictories:** Two propositions are contradictories if they always have the *opposite truth-value*; whenever one is true, the other must be false, and vice versa. Traditionally, A and O propositions are contradictories, as are E and I propositions.
- **Contraries:** Two propositions are contraries if they *cannot both be true* but *can both be false*. Traditionally, A and E propositions are contraries.
- **Subcontraries:** Two propositions are subcontraries if they *cannot both be false* but *can both be true*. Traditionally, I and O propositions are subcontraries.
- **Subalternation:** Drawing an inference from a universal proposition to a particular proposition. Traditionally, A propositions subalternate to I propositions, and E propositions subalternate to O propositions.

Logicians used a square called the **traditional square of opposition** to represent these relationships:

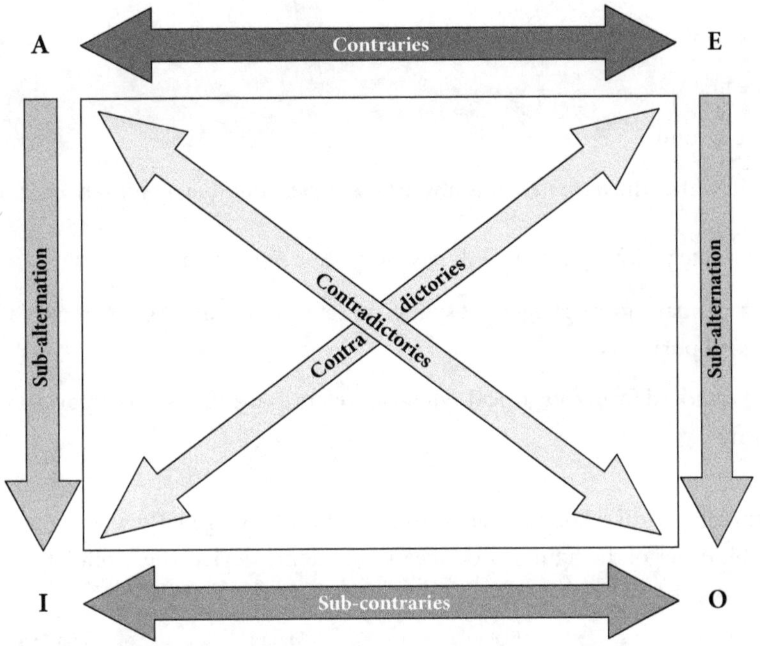


While much more can be said about categorical propositions, the discussion thus far adequately prepares the way for a discussion of categorical syllogisms.

## (C) Categorical Syllogisms

The term **syllogism** may be defined in the following way:

- An argument with only three propositions, two premises, and the conclusion.

A **categorical syllogism**, thus, is the following:

- A syllogism consisting entirely of categorical propositions.

Categorical syllogisms may be further analyzed into additional components. Every categorical syllogism has three terms—major, minor, and middle.

- The **major term** is the *predicate of the conclusion*; hence, it is designated by the letter P.
- The **minor term** is the *subject of the conclusion*; hence, it is designated by the letter S.
- The **middle term** appears in *both premises but not the conclusion* and is designated by the letter M.

Moreover, the term contained by each premise determines whether it is the *major* or *minor* premise.

- The **major premise** contains the major term.
- The **minor premise** contains the minor term.

Categorical syllogisms should be structured in **standard form**, which has the following order:

- Major premise first
- Minor premise second
- Conclusion—in which the *minor term* is always *the subject and the major term is always the predicate*

Every standard form categorical syllogism will have a specific *figure* and *mood.*

- The **figure** of a standard form categorical syllogism refers to the arrangement or placement of the terms in the argument's propositions.
- The **mood** of a standard form categorical syllogism refers to the kinds of categorical propositions contained by the syllogism.

Every standard form categorical syllogism will have one of the following *four figures*, summarized by the following diagram (notice that this order of the figures produces a mnemonic device, the "Split W"):

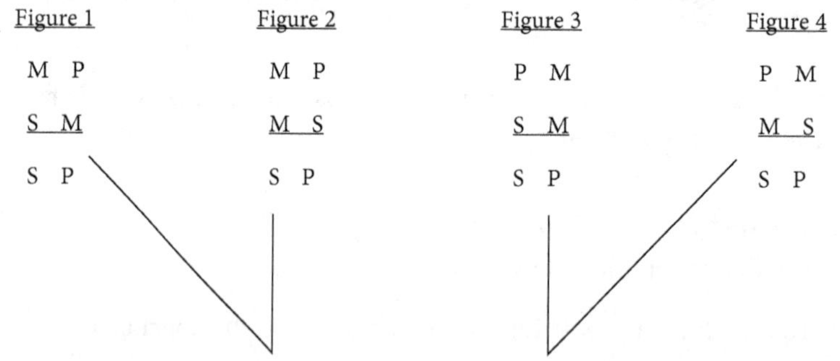


The mood of each categorical syllogism is determined by the types of propositions it contains and the order in which they appear. For example, consider categorical syllogism (1):

All M are P.

All S are M.

Therefore, all S are P.

This argument displays Figure 6.1 and has the mood AAA since it has three universal affirmative statements and may be abbreviated 1-AAA. Next, consider categorical syllogism (2):

No M are P.

Some M are S.

Therefore, some S are not P.

This argument displays Figure 6.2 and has the mood EIO, since it has a universal negative, particular affirmative, and particular negative proposition, in that order. It may be abbreviated 2-EIO. In addition, observe categorical syllogism (3):

All M are P.

Some M are S.

Therefore, some S are P.

This argument displays Figure 6.3 and has the mood AII. It may be abbreviated 3-AII. Finally, consider categorical syllogism (4):

All P are M.

No M are S.

Therefore, no S are P.

This argument displays Figure 6.4 and has the mood AEE. It may be abbreviated 4-AEE.

Each of the four figures will yield *unconditionally valid* categorical syllogisms only when combined with specific moods. Figures 6.1–6.3 may be combined with 4 moods each, while Figure 6.4 may be combined with 3 to produce a total of 15 unconditionally valid categorical syllogisms. The following chart summarizes the moods that may be combined with each figure to yield unconditionally valid categorical syllogisms (Table 6.2):

TABLE 6.2 The 15 Unconditionally Valid Standard Forms of Categorical Syllogisms

| FIGURE 6.1 | FIGURE 6.2 | FIGURE 6.3 | FIGURE 6.4 |
|---|---|---|---|
| M P<br>S M<br>∴ S P | P M<br>S M<br>∴ S P | M P<br>M S<br>∴ S P | P M<br>M S<br>∴ S P |
| **Valid Moods for Figure 6.1** | **Valid Moods for Figure 6.2** | **Valid Moods for Figure 6.3** | **Valid Moods for Figure 6.4** |
| AAA | EAE | IAI | AEE |
| EAE | AEE | AII | IAI |
| AII | EIO | OAO | EIO |
| EIO | AOO | EIO | |

With access to this table, one can determine whether a categorical syllogism is unconditionally valid by identifying its figure and mood. If it does not match one of these 15 forms, then it is not unconditionally valid.

Other forms of categorical syllogisms may also be valid, but only if specific conditions are met. Such syllogisms may be called *conditionally valid*. The following table designates the figure and moods of conditionally valid categorical syllogisms:

TABLE 6.3 Conditionally Valid Categorical Syllogisms

| Figure 6.1 | Figure 6.2 | Figure 6.3 | Figure 6.4 | Figure 6.5 |
|---|---|---|---|---|
| AAI<br>EAO | AEO<br>EAO | | AEO | S Exist |
| | | AAI<br>EAO | EAO | M Exist |
| | | | AAI | P Exist |

Understanding why these specific forms of syllogism require the conditions indicated demands a discussion of the difference between the traditional and modern squares of opposition and the meaning of categorical propositions under the modern interpretation, which will be discussed in Section II.

In addition to using the charts, there exist two other traditional methods of evaluating categorical syllogisms. First, one may check the argument to ensure that it follows the *six rules of categorical syllogisms.* If any of the rules are violated, then the argument is invalid. Second, one may represent the argument using a *Venn diagram.* If an argument's premises cannot be diagrammed properly, then the argument is invalid. Each of these methods will be briefly demonstrated.

First, the following list states the **six rules of categorical syllogisms** along with the associated fallacy that occurs if the corresponding rule is broken:

- **Rule (1):** The middle term must be distributed at least once.
  - Fallacy: Undistributed Middle
- **Rule (2):** If a term is distributed in the conclusion, then it must be distributed in the premises.
  - Fallacies: Illicit process of the major term, Illicit process of the minor term.
- **Rule (3):** Two negative premises are not allowed.
  - Fallacy: Exclusive Premises
- **Rule (4):** A negative premise requires a negative conclusion; a negative conclusion requires a negative premise.
  - Fallacy: Drawing an affirmative conclusion from a negative premise; drawing a negative conclusion from an affirmative premise.
- **Rule (5):** More than three terms are not allowed.
  - Fallacy: Four Terms
- **Rule (6):** If both premises are universal, the conclusion cannot be particular.
  - Fallacy: Existential Fallacy
  - **REMEMBER**, if only rule (6) is broken, the syllogism is *conditionally valid* from the Aristotelian standpoint if the term in question designates actually existing things.

As an example, consider categorical syllogism (5):

No mammals are lizards.

No turtles are mammals.

Therefore, no turtles are lizards.

Notice that this argument has two negative premises; hence, it violates rule (3). Categorical syllogism (6) provides a counterexample:

No cats are Labs.

No dogs are cats.

Therefore, no dogs are Labs.

Note that the premises of categorical syllogism (6) are true, while the conclusion is false, and (6) has the exact same form as (5), 1-EEE.

Categorical syllogism (7) provides an additional example:

All philosophers are wise.

All philosophers are courageous.

Therefore, all wise people are courageous.

This argument is also invalid, as it violates rule (2). The minor term "wise" is distributed in the conclusion but not in its premise (illicit process of the minor term, or "illicit minor" for short). Categorical syllogism (8) provides a counterexample:

All Labs are dogs.

All Labs are mammals.

Therefore, all mammals are dogs.

Note that categorical syllogism (8) has true premises and a false conclusion and is the exact same form as (7), 2-AAA.

Applying the **Venn diagram method** requires drawing a three-circle diagram that represents the argument in question. A Venn diagram for a categorical syllogism will have eight areas (although, technically, area eight constitutes everything outside the diagram) as shown next. Notice that each circle designates one of the three terms of the syllogism:

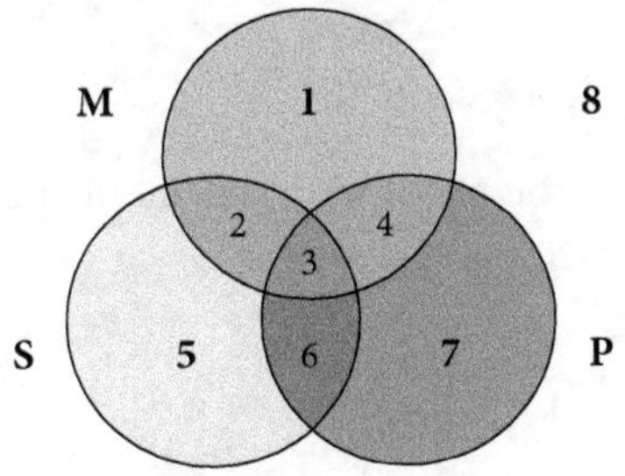


To use Venn diagrams to assess the validity of a categorical syllogism, follow these steps:

1. Only mark *premises*, focusing on their terms.
2. Always mark *universal statements* first.

3. Remember that particular statements assert that (a) at least one thing exists and (b) that thing is X.
4. When shading, the entire area in question must be shaded.
5. The area of an X, at first, occupies two areas. If one of those areas is shaded, the X should go in the non-shaded area.
6. Never place an X so that it hangs outside of a diagram.

Categorical syllogism (9) provides an example:

No weasels are courageous.

Some teachers are courageous.

Therefore, some teachers are not weasels.

The terms of syllogism (9) are *weasels*, the major term, P; *courageous*, the middle term, M; and *teachers*, the minor term, S. This argument can be diagrammed in the following way:

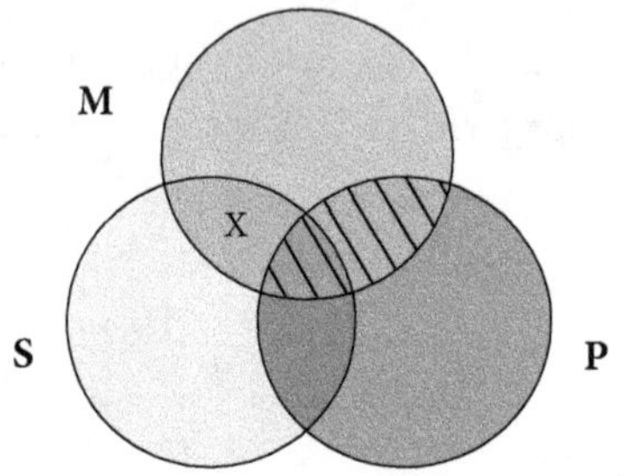


The entire overlap between P and M is crossed out (areas 3 and 4), representing the first premise. The “x” placed in area 2 represents the second premise. Since conclusions are not diagrammed, and there is an “x” within the S but outside the P, this diagram shows that categorical syllogism (9) is valid.

As a final example, consider categorical syllogism (10):

No leprechauns are tall.

Nothing tall spins gold.

Therefore, nothing that spins gold is a leprechaun.

This argument's terms are leprechauns, the major term, P; tall, the middle term, M; and spins gold, the minor term, S. It can be diagrammed in the following way:

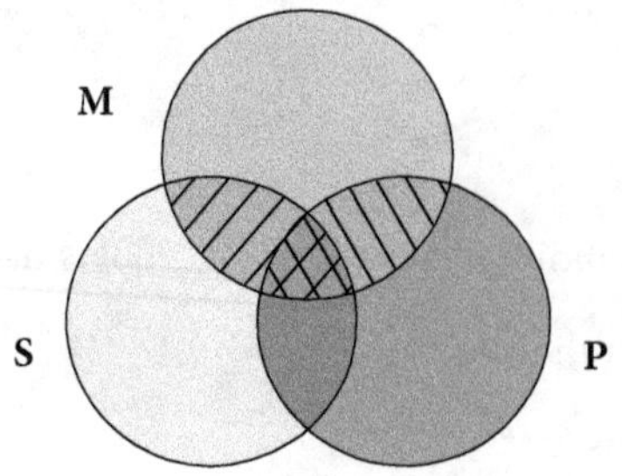

Propositions P and M overlap in areas 3 and 4, each of which are crossed out, representing premise 1. Propositions S and M overlap in areas 2 and 3, each of which are crossed out, representing premise 2. The conclusion states that nothing that spins gold is a leprechaun, translating into "No S are P." Hence, any overlap between S and P should be crossed out. But the two overlap in area 6, which is clear. Thus, the premises of syllogism 10 may be true while the conclusion is false. This diagram proves that the argument is invalid.

While the methods described allow for the assessment of any standard form categorical syllogism, not all arguments will be stated in standard form and not all arguments will contain only categorical propositions. Section II addresses modern truth-functional logic.

## (II) Truth-Functional Logic

Whereas the Aristotelian system of categorical logic dominated the Western world for over 2,000 years, truth-functional logic constitutes one of the primary systems favored by modern logicians. Truth-functional logic developed as the result of the work of several mathematicians, philosophers, and intellectuals, including Gottfried Wilhelm von Leibniz, George Boole, Gottlob Frege, Bertrand Russell, Alfred North Whitehead, Ludwig Wittgenstein, and Alfred J. Ayer. Truth-functional logic is comparable to computer programming and several forms of mathematics and is so named because through its principles, the truth-value of any sentence is dictated in a totally mechanical way, as a *function* of the *truth-values* of its components. In addition, truth-functional logic comprises part of modern symbolic logic, meaning that it allows for the representation of English sentences in terms of letters and various *operators*, also called *connectives*, that reveal the underlying logical form of sentences. This section emphasizes the following topics in truth-functional logic:

- The difference between simple and compound sentences
- The five basic truth-functional connectives
- Basic translations from English into symbolic form
- The most common valid truth-functional argument forms and formal fallacies
- The modern square of opposition, which details changes to the traditional square

### (A) Simple and Compound Sentences

A fundamental distinction in truth-functional logic is between two types of sentences: *simple* and *compound*.

- A **simple sentence** is a single independent, declarative, and affirmative statement. In truth-functional logic, such sentences may also be called **atomic sentences**.
- A **compound sentence** consists of multiple declarative sentences or independent clauses combined using one or more connectives or the negation of a simple sentence. In truth-functional logic, such sentences may also be called **molecular sentences**.

The sentences, "Josh teaches philosophy," "Sacred Heart University is located in Fairfield, Connecticut"; "A dog is a mammal"; and "Earth is a sphere" all are recognized as simple sentences in truth-functional logic. Moreover, modern logicians represent simple sentences using single letters from the English alphabet. The letters representing simple sentences are usually arbitrarily chosen, but the same letter should not be used twice when representing any compound sentence or argument. To illustrate, consider each of the following simple sentences:

1. Alex lives in Florida.
2. Maci earned an MA in criminal justice.
3. IAMX performed music for the show *How to Get Away with Murder.*
4. Smokey is a gray cat.
5. Lake Shirley has an irregular shape.

Sentence 1 may be represented by the letter "A." Sentence 2 may be represented by the letter "M." The letter "I" may be used for sentence 3. The letter "S" is the most obvious choice for 4. Finally, "L" seems the best choice for 5. Of course, different letters may be chosen for each sentence so long as no two sentences in this group have the same letter.

Simple sentences are always single, independent, and affirmative. Compound sentences, however, typically combine or negate simple sentences. Each of the following is an example of a compound or molecular sentence in truth-functional logic.

6. Sandy did not go to Las Vegas last weekend.
7. Becky and Trish went to the party.
8. Chris can either have an apple or an orange before going to bed.
9. If Judy goes swimming, then Megan will eat out tonight.
10. Pat can go to the Patriots game if and only if he finishes his homework by 5:00 p.m.

Each of these sentences can be reframed to expose their underlying logical form. Sentence 6 can be rephrased in the following way:

6. *It is not the case that Sandy went to Las Vegas last weekend.

   Sentence 6* more precisely reflects the *negation* of the following simple sentence:

   Sandy went to Las Vegas last weekend.

   Sentence 7 also can be analyzed into multiple components, the *conjunction* of the following simple sentences:

   Becky went to the party.

   Trish went to the party.

   Sentence 8 is a *disjunctive* statement composed of the following two simple sentences:

   Chris may have an apple before going to bed.

   Chris may have an orange before going to bed.

   Sentence 9, as one might recall from Chapter 5, is a *conditional statement* composed of the following two simple sentences:

Judy goes swimming (the antecedent).

Megan will eat out (the consequent).

Finally, sentence 10 is a *biconditional* statement whose simple components are the following:

Pat may go to the Patriots game.

Pat finishes his homework by 5:00 p.m.

Just as letters represent sentences, **truth-functional operators**, also called **connectives**, represent the logical form of compound sentences. Compound sentences, thus, are represented by a combination of letters, operators, and punctuation to eliminate ambiguity. There is an operator to represent each of the five types of sentences given in 6–10, and they are detailed in the next section.

## (B) Five Basic Truth-Functional Operators

Modern symbolic truth-functional logic consists of five basic truth-functional operators:

- The *tilde*, ~, representing **negation**, which may also be represented by the bent bar, ¬, or the straight bar, —.
- The *dot*, •, representing **conjunction**, which may also be represented by the ampersand, &, and the upside-down wedge, ^.
- The *wedge*, v, representing **disjunction.**
- The *horseshoe*, ⊃, representing **conditional statements**, also represented by the arrow, →.
- The *triple bar*, ≡, representing **biconditional statements**, also represented by the double arrow, ↔.

With these operators, the equipment necessary to translate English sentences into the symbolic language of truth-functional logic is available. Sentences 6–10 will be used as examples.

Sentence 6 can be translated by simply selecting a letter to represent sentence 11 and then placing a tilde in front of that letter. The letter "S" can represent sentence 11. Hence, the final translation would be truth-functional translation 1 (hereafter, TR1):

TR1: ~ S.

Notice that TR1 reflects the wording of sentence 6*, the negation of sentence 11.

Sentence 7 can be translated by first selecting a different letter to represent both 12 and 13. For 12, the letter "B" will suffice, while "T" seems the most suitable for sentence 13. Next, the conjunction between the two letters can be represented by placing the dot between them. Truth-functional translation 2 (TR2) represents sentence 7:

TR2: B • T.

In addition to the word "and," conjunctions may be indicated by the words "but," "also," "with," "in addition to," "in conjunction with," "combined with," or "along with."

As with the previous two examples, the translation for sentence 8 begins with selecting letters to represent its components, sentences 14 and 15. Sentence 14 may be represented with the letter "A," while "O" seems the most suitable for 15. Sentence 8 is disjunctive, so the wedge may be placed between its two components to represent this property. TR3 represents sentence 8: A v O. In addition to "either/or," the word "unless" usually designates the disjunctive relation as well. For instance, a sentence of the form "P unless Q" can be translated in the following way (TR4):

TR4: P v Q.

The terms of sentence 9 correspond to sentences 16 and 17. The letter "J" may represent sentence 16 while "M" is a suitable representation for 17. In conditional statements, the horseshoe typically comes between the antecedent and the consequent, representing the "if–then" relation. Truth-functional translation 5 (TR5) represents sentence 9:

TR5: J ⊃ M.

In addition to the terms "if …, then …," conditional statements may be designated by causal terms, such as "because," "since," "consequently," and "as a result of." For instance, the statement "P because Q," or "P as a result of Q," or "Q, consequently P," or "P since Q," may each be represented by the following:

TR6: Q ⊃ P.

Also, a statement of the form "P only if Q" designates a conditional as well. Recall from the previous chapter that in sentences like 9, the antecedent operates as a sufficient condition for the consequent. In the statement, "P only if Q," Q is a necessary condition for P and is best represented by the following:

TR7: P ⊃ Q.

Finally, biconditionals indicate both necessary and sufficient conditions, and that is the relation indicated by statement 10, whose components are sentences 18 and 19. Using the letter "G" for 18 and "F" for 19, the translation of 10 may be completed by placing the tribar between G and F, yielding the following:

TR8: G ≡ F.

More complex translations will require the use of additional punctuation to differentiate the sentences and components from each other, thereby eliminating ambiguity and exposing the primary operator within the sentence. Additional punctuation includes parentheses, ( ); brackets, [ ]; and braces, { }. As an example of a complex sentence, consider sentence 20:

20. If Toasty eats before Smokey, then Toasty will be satisfied and Smokey will go hunt for a mouse; however, both cats will be fed at 7:00 p.m.

To translate any sentence, no matter how complex, always begin by identifying the component sentences and designating a different letter to represent each. Sentence 20 has the following components:

- Toasty eats before smokey. (This statement may be represented by "T.")
- Toasty will be satisfied. (This statement may be represented by "S.")
- Smokey will go hunt for a mouse. (This statement may be represented by "H.")
- Both cats will be fed at 7:00 p.m. (This statement may be represented by "B.")

Now that we have the component sentences and letters, each letter may replace each statement in sentence 20. Consider 20*:

20. *If T, then S and H; however, B.

The most significant point in the sentence seems to be the break after H, the semicolon followed by "however," a word that functions as a *conjunctive adverb* in English. Hence, sentence 20 seems to be a rather long conjunction. Furthermore, there is a clear conditional statement in 20, given the "If T, then S and H." It seems that T is the antecedent of this conditional, while the consequent is a further conjunction between S and H. So, the final translation should reflect a conjunction between B and the conditional statement on its left. The dot will replace "however" and the word "and" between S and H. A horseshoe will be placed between T and its consequent, yielding a partial translation:

T ⊃ S • H • B.

Finally, punctuation must be introduced to eliminate ambiguity. To designate S and H as the consequent of T, parentheses may be placed around it. Then, lastly, to designate the dot between H and B as the main operator of the sentence, brackets may be placed around the conditional, "If T, then S and H." The result is the following translation:

TR9: [T ⊃ (S • H)] • B.

In addition to representing specific terms in the English language, each operator designates a logical relation between sentences that is true under specific conditions. In truth-functional logic, the truth-value of a sentence depends on the truth-values of its components and will reflect the truth-value of its main operator. Determining the truth-values for sentences in truth-functional logic requires a **truth-table.**

- A **truth-table** lists all the possible truth-values of the components of a sentence, which in turn dictate the truth-value of truth-functional operators. A truth-table may also be used for determining whether arguments are valid, whether sets are consistent, whether one statement implies another, and for investigating other truth-functional properties.

Every statement has two possible truth-values, True or False, represented by T or F. The formula for determining the number of rows in a truth-table is $2^n$, where *n* represents the number of component sentences and "2" the number of truth-values. For instance, building a truth-table for a sentence, argument, or set of sentences with two component sentences will require 4 rows ($2^2$). Building a truth-table for a sentence, argument, or set of sentences with three component sentences will require 8 rows ($2^3$). If a sentence has four components, its truth-table will require 16 rows ($2^4$), and so forth. Every truth-functional operator has a basic truth-table.

Beginning with the operator for negation, a negation represents the opposite of the sentence negated. Hence, a negation is true whenever its component sentence is false and false whenever it is true, as indicated in the following truth-table (Table 6.4), where "P" represents any simple sentence:

TABLE 6.4 Truth-Table for Negation

| P | ~ | P |
|---|---|---|
| T | F | T |
| F | T | F |

Conjunctions always state that all their components are true. Hence, a conjunction is true only when each of its components is true, and it is false otherwise. The following truth-table (Table 6.5) shows the conditions under which a conjunction is true, where P and Q represent any simple sentences:

TABLE 6.5 Truth-Table for Conjunction

| P | Q | P | • | Q |
|---|---|---|---|---|
| T | T | T | T | T |
| T | F | T | F | F |
| F | T | F | F | T |
| F | F | F | F | F |

Disjunctions, on the other hand, always assert that at least one of their component sentences is true. Hence, so long as at least one of the two components of a disjunction is true, the entire sentence is true, as the following truth-table (Table 6.6) indicates:

TABLE 6.6 Truth-Table for Disjunction

| P | Q | P | V | Q |
|---|---|---|---|---|
| T | T | T | T | T |
| T | F | T | T | F |
| F | T | F | T | T |
| F | F | F | F | F |

Notice that a disjunction is true even when both of its disjuncts are true since logicians typically assume the *inclusive or* when interpreting disjunctions. If a disjunction exhibits the *exclusive or*, then the sentence will only be true if one of the disjuncts is true while the other is false. It will be false otherwise.

Conditionals have the most controversial interpretation in modern logic. Conditional statements are understood to be false *only when the antecedent is true and the consequent false.* When both are true, obviously, the conditional is true. But when either both are false or the antecedent is false and the consequent true, the conditional is still understood to be true, as the following truth-table (Table 6.7) shows:

TABLE 6.7 Truth-Table for Conditional

| P | Q | P | ⊃ | Q |
|---|---|---|---|---|
| T | T | T | T | T |
| T | F | T | F | F |
| F | T | F | T | T |
| F | F | F | T | F |

Admittedly, this interpretation of conditionals is odd. For instance, if it is false that my uncle Don lives in Bridgeport, then the sentence, "If Don Lott lives in Trumbull, Connecticut, then chimpanzees are mammals" is true. Even more puzzling is that under the modern interpretation of conditionals, sentences such as, "If Don Lott lives in Trumbull, Connecticut, then there are green space aliens at the *Stop & Shop* on 100 Quality Street" are true!

Modern logicians seem inclined to err on the side of caution with conditionals. In part, their interpretation of conditionals reflects those assertions in ordinary language that state necessary truths. For instance, consider sentence 21:

21. If Buster is a dog, then he is a mammal.

Suppose that Buster is not a dog, but a cat. In that case, 21 would have a false antecedent but a true consequent. Nonetheless, 21 is still true. Moreover, imagine that Buster is a turtle, neither a dog nor a cat. Then, both components of 21 would be false. Despite the truth-value of its components, 21 remains a true conditional.

The final operator to consider is the biconditional, which serves as the symbol for logical equivalence. Thus, biconditionals are true in cases where its components have the same truth-value but are false otherwise. The truth-table for the biconditional is the following (Table 6.8):

TABLE 6.8 Truth-Table for Biconditional

| P | Q | P | ≡ | Q |
|---|---|---|---|---|
| T | T | T | T | T |
| T | F | T | F | F |
| F | T | F | F | T |
| F | F | F | T | F |

Notice that a biconditional is essentially the conjunction of two conditionals, asserting that each of its components implies or entails the other. That is, "P if and only if Q" really just means, "If P, then Q, and if Q, then P." In symbolic terms, P ≡ Q is logically equivalent to the following sentence: (P ⊃ Q) • (Q ⊃ P). The following truth-table (Table 6.9) demonstrates the equivalence:

TABLE 6.9 Using a Truth-Table to Demonstrate Logical Equivalence

| P | Q | P | ≡ | Q | (P | ⊃ | Q) | • | (Q | ⊃ | P) |
|---|---|---|---|---|---|---|---|---|---|---|---|
| T | T | T | T | T | T | T | T | T | T | T | T |
| T | F | T | F | F | T | F | F | F | F | T | T |
| F | T | F | F | T | F | T | T | F | T | F | F |
| F | F | F | T | F | F | T | T | T | F | T | F |

## (C) Existential Import and the Modern Square of Opposition

Modern logicians recognize a different square of opposition, given the insights of the mathematicians and logicians who developed truth-functional logic. Specifically, the **modern square of opposition** is connected with the conditions that dictate the truth-values of conditional statements and the concept of **existential import**, which may be defined in the following way:

- A proposition has **existential import** if it asserts the existence of some specified kinds of objects.

In traditional logic, universal sentences (A and E propositions) were understood to express existential import. However, under the modern interpretation—often called the Boolean interpretation after its founder, George Boole—universal propositions are interpreted in the following way:

- **A propositions**, statements of the form "All S are P" are understood to mean, "*For any object, x, if x is S, then x is P.*"
- **E propositions**, statements of the form "No S are P" are understood to mean, "*For any object, x, if x is S, then x is not P.*"

That is, universal propositions are interpreted as conditional statements. But remember that in modern symbolic logic, *conditional sentences are true whenever the antecedent is false*. Thus, if there are no objects under the class of S, then both A and E propositions may be true. Hence, they are no longer contraries. For instance, consider the proposition "All unicorns have wings." In modern logic, this sentence means, "For any object, x, if x is a unicorn, then x has wings." If there are no unicorns, then the component sentence "x is a unicorn" is always false and the statement "All unicorns have wings" is true. And the proposition "No unicorns have wings" is the modern equivalent of "For any object, x, if x is a unicorn, then x does not have wings" has the same antecedent. Thus, it, too, is true if there are no unicorns. This change undoes the relation at the top of the traditional square.

However, I and O propositions retain existential import in the modern interpretation:

- **I propositions**, statements of the form "Some S are P," in modern logic mean, "*There is at least one object, x, such that x is both S and P.*"
- **O propositions**, statements of the form, "Some S are not P," in modern logic mean, "*There is at least one object, x, such that x is S and x is not P.*"

But one cannot derive an I proposition from an A proposition or an O proposition from an E proposition without a statement explicitly affirming the existence of members under the class of the subject term. For instance, in modern logic, the proposition, "All frogs are amphibians" does not imply "Some frogs are amphibians." To yield the second sentence, one must add to the first, "Frogs exist," or, "There is at least one object, x, such that x is a frog." Hence, the inferences represented by the right and left sides of the traditional square of opposition are no longer valid in modern logic.

Finally, even though I and O propositions retain existential import in modern logic, they are no longer subcontraries since *they can both be false*. For instance, consider the sentence "Some unicorns fly." In modern logic, this sentence means, "There is at least one object, x, such that x is a unicorn and x flies." Since this statement is a conjunction, it is only true if both of its conjuncts are true. But if there are no unicorns, then the component sentence "x is a unicorn" is false, in which case, the I proposition is false. Moreover, the sentence, "Some unicorns do not fly," in modern logic, means, "There is at least one object, x, such that x is a unicorn and x does not fly." Once again, if there are no unicorns, the first part of the conjunction is false, in which case the entire sentence is false. Hence, in modern logic, the relation at the bottom of the square between I and O propositions is undone.

The only relations from the traditional square of opposition preserved in modern logic are those across the square. That is, A and O propositions are still contradictories, as are E and I propositions. Recall that two statements are contradictories if they always have the opposite truth-value. In other words, two statements are contradictories if one of the statements is the *negation* of the other. If one were to negate a statement of the form "All frogs are amphibians," it would, in modern logic, read in the following way: "It is not the case that for any object x, if x is a frog, then x is an amphibian." This sentence does not mean that no frogs are amphibians, as it only denies that all frogs are amphibians, which translates into the O proposition, "There is at least one object, x, such that x is a frog and x is not an amphibian." The same analysis applies to the relation between E and I propositions. For instance, the negation of the sentence "No dogs are reptiles" would read, "It is not the case that for any object, x, if x is a dog, then x is not a reptile." This sentence only implies that *not all dogs* are not reptiles, which translates into the I proposition asserting that *some* or *at least one* dog is a reptile.

The modern square of opposition is the following:

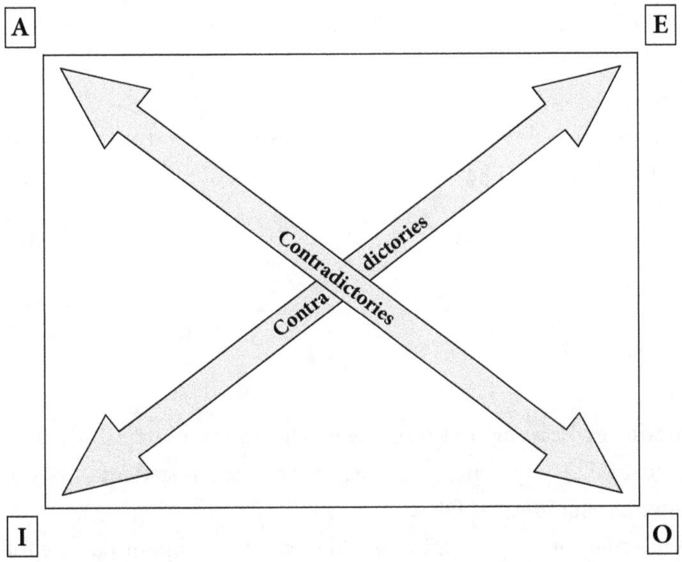


The question that remains is why all the fuss about existential import? Why cannot all statements simply assume existential import? For the following reasons:

- *First*, if all statements assume existential import, then there would be no meaningful way to formulate a proposition denying that a class has any members. That is, no one would ever be able to talk about imaginary objects that do not exist. Any single word that did not match up with a specific object would have no meaning. For instance, the author has used the word "unicorn" several times. Most people know what the term means even though no one ever discovered a real unicorn.
- *Second*, everyday ordinary language does not presuppose existential import. Novels, television shows, movies, theater plays, and various works of literature all construct imaginary worlds of events that did not in fact happen. But such works of imagination would not be possible to convey in language if every term had existential import.
- *Third*, science, philosophy, mathematics, and various other academic disciplines operate by constructing, testing, and evaluating theories. But theories do not always prove true. If every statement in language assumed existential import, hypotheses and theories that scientists debunked over history would be totally unintelligible. The same may be said about the thought experiments of philosophers and the imaginary numbers of mathematicians.

Perhaps the only benefit that would come from the assumption of existential import is that idols of the marketplace would be far less prevalent!

## (D) Common Valid Argument Forms and Formal Fallacies in Modern Logic

There is an *infinite* number of ways to combine statements to form different truth-functionally valid arguments in modern symbolic logic. However, there are several very common valid argument forms that everyone should know. They are the following:

- Conditional Syllogisms
- Disjunctive Syllogisms
- Dilemmas

The most common valid conditional syllogisms are **modus ponens, modus tollens**, and **hypothetical syllogism**. The term "modus ponens" translates from Latin into "the way of putting." It has the following form:

- Modus Ponens:

  If P, then Q.

  P

  Therefore, Q.

Given the nature of conditionals, if the first premise is true and the second is true (the antecedent of the first premise), the conclusion must follow. Remember that whenever the antecedent of a conditional is true, the consequent must be true or the whole statement is false.

The term "modus tollens" translates from Latin into "the way of taking." It has the following form:

- Modus Tollens:

  If P, then Q.

  Not Q.

  Therefore, not P.

Once again, considering the nature of conditionals establishes why this argument form is valid. If one assumes that both premises are true—meaning that both the conditional and the negation of its consequent are true—then the negation of the antecedent follows necessarily. Recall that a conditional is true when both the antecedent and the consequent are false.

The hypothetical syllogism consists entirely of conditional statements. It has the following form:

- Hypothetical Syllogism:

  If P, then Q.

  If Q, then R.

  Therefore, if P, then R.

This argument form is sometimes called the "chain argument," given that the consequent of the first conditional serves as the antecedent of the second conditional, in effect, chaining the antecedent of the first premise with the consequent of the second.

Each of these valid argument forms has an associated fallacy, an invalid counterpart. The first is **Affirming the Consequent**, which has the following form:

If P, then Q.

Q.

Therefore, P.

This argument form fails because the consequent of a conditional may be true while the antecedent is false, in which case the conditional statement would still be true. Since this argument form is invalid, a counterexample can be given with the same form. Suppose that "P" represents the sentence "Buster is a dog" and that "Q" represents "Buster is a mammal." These substitution instances yield the following:

If Buster is a dog, then he is a mammal.

Buster is a mammal.

Therefore, Buster is a dog.

The premises of this argument may be true while the conclusion is false since not all mammals are dogs. For instance, Buster could be a cat and still be a mammal.

The second kind of invalid conditional syllogism is **denying the antecedent**, which has the following form:

If P, then Q.

Not P.

Therefore, not Q.

This argument form fails, too, since the antecedent of a conditional statement may be false while the consequent is true. Using the same substitution terms as before yields the following counterexample:

If Buster is a dog, then he is a mammal.

Buster is not a dog.

Therefore, Buster is not a mammal.

Once again, the premises of this argument may be true while the conclusion is false, since Buster may be some animal other than a dog and still be a mammal.

In addition, there are invalid versions of hypothetical syllogism. First is the truth-functional version of the undistributed middle, which has the following form:

If P, then R.

If Q, then R.

Therefore, if P, then Q.

Suppose that "P" means "Buster is a dog," that "Q" means "Buster is a cat," and that "R" means "Buster is a mammal." These substitutions yield the following counterexample:

If Buster is a dog, then he is a mammal.

If Buster is a cat, then he is a mammal.

Therefore, if Buster is a dog, then he is a cat.

The premises of this argument are true, but the conclusion is clearly false.

A second invalid form of hypothetical syllogism has the following form:

If P, then Q.

If P, then R.

Therefore, if Q, then R.

Suppose that "P" means "Buster is a Lab," that "Q" means "Buster is a mammal," and that "R" means "Buster is a dog." These substitutions yield the following counterexample:

If Buster is a Lab, then he is a mammal.

If Buster is Lab, then he is a dog.

Therefore, if Buster is a mammal, then he is a dog.

The premises are true, but the conclusion is clearly false.

In addition to conditional syllogisms, there are also valid forms of **disjunctive syllogisms**. The most basic is the following:

Either P or Q.

Not Q.

Therefore, P.

Remember that a disjunction is true just in case at least one of the disjuncts is true. Hence, if the first premise of this syllogism is true but the second is also true, in which case Q is false, then P must be true. The following disjunctive syllogism is also valid:

Either P or Q.

Not P.

Therefore, Q.

Notice that the only difference between this syllogism and the previous example is that it negates disjunct P rather than Q.

A disjunctive syllogism is invalid if an unwarranted inference is made to a negative disjunct, such as in the following case:

Either P or Q.

P.

Therefore, not Q.

Remember that a disjunction may be true if both of its disjuncts are true on the assumption of the *inclusive or* unless there are instructions to do otherwise. Hence, both premises of this syllogism may be true while the conclusion is false.

Finally, there are several valid argument forms called dilemmas. Dilemmas may be simple or complex, constructive or destructive. Typically, dilemmas consist of a combination of conditional and disjunctive statements. There are four kinds:

- Simple Constructive Dilemma
- Simple Destructive Dilemma
- Complex Constructive Dilemma
- Complex Destructive Dilemma

The **simple constructive dilemma** has the following form:

If P, then R.

If Q, then R.

Either P or Q.

Therefore, R.

Next, the **simple destructive dilemma** has the following form:

If P, then Q.

If P, then R.

Either not Q or not R.

Therefore, not P.

Unlike the simple dilemmas, the complex will have four terms and will conclude with a disjunction. The **complex constructive dilemma** is the following:

If P, then R.

If Q, then S.

Either P or Q.

Therefore, either R or S.

Finally, the **complex destructive dilemma** has the following form:

If P, then R.

If Q, then S.

Either not R or not S.

Therefore, either not P, or not Q.

The most common of these four is the simple constructive dilemma, although typically anyone who constructs an argument in the form of a dilemma assumes a *false dichotomy*, an informal fallacy addressed in Chapter 9.

Even though the validity of the arguments presented here are common and well-known, their validity can be demonstrated using truth-tables. Remember that an argument is valid if and only if its premises jointly entail its conclusion. That is, whenever the premises of a valid argument are true, the conclusion is also true. There is no case in which the premises of a valid argument are true while its conclusion is false. Hence, if one translates the sentences of an argument into symbolic form and plots them on a truth-table, if there is no row on the table in which the premises are true and the conclusion false, then the argument is valid. For example, consider modus ponens. It has the following symbolic form:

$P \supset Q.$

$P.$

$\therefore Q.$

Since there are only two component sentences in this argument, its truth-table requires only four rows and looks like the following (Table 6.10):

TABLE 6.10 Truth-Table for Modus Ponens

| P | Q | P | ⊃ | Q | P | /∴ | Q |
|---|---|---|---|---|---|---|---|
| T | T | T | T | T | T | | T |
| T | F | T | F | F | T | | F |
| F | T | F | T | T | F | | T |
| F | F | T | T | F | F | | F |

Notice that in every row in which the premises are true, the conclusion is also true, demonstrating that the argument is valid.

Just as truth-tables can demonstrate validity, they can also demonstrate that an argument is invalid. To use a truth-table for this purpose, simply find a row in which all the argument's premises are true while its conclusion is false. For instance, consider denying the antecedent, whose symbolic form is the following:

$P \supset Q.$

$\sim P.$

$\therefore \sim Q.$

This argument's associated truth-table also will only require four rows, as Table 6.11 shows:

TABLE 6.11 Truth-Table for Denying the Antecedent

| P | Q | P | ⊃ | Q | ~ | P | /∴ | ~ | Q |
|---|---|---|---|---|---|---|---|---|---|
| T | T | T | T | T | F | T | | F | T |
| T | F | T | F | F | F | T | | T | F |
| F | T | F | T | T | T | F | | F | T |
| F | F | T | T | F | T | F | | T | F |

While it is not the purpose of this chapter to present a detailed introduction to symbolic logic, to construct and use a truth-table, follow each of these steps:

1. Identify the number of component sentences.
2. Determine the number of rows necessary using the formula 2n, where "2" represents the number of possible truth-values per component sentence letter, and "n" represents the number of component sentences.
3. On the left-hand side of the truth-table, assign truth-values to each component sentence. The top half of the rows for the first letter should be true and the bottom half false. The rest of the letters will alternate based on the number of rows. For instance, in a four-row table, the first letter will have two true on top and two false on the bottom while the second letter alternates one by one, true-false-true-false. In an eight-row table, the first letter will have four true on top and four false on the bottom, while the second letter alternates two by two all the way down, two true-two false-two true-two false, and the third letter alternates one by one all the way down. See Table 6.12 for an example of an eight-row truth-table.

TABLE 6.12 Example of an Eight-Row Truth-Table

| P | Q | R | |
|---|---|---|---|
| T | T | T | |
| T | T | F | |
| T | F | T | |
| T | F | F | |
| F | T | T | |
| F | T | F | |
| F | F | T | |
| F | F | F | |

4. If there are multiple sentences, devote a separate column for each sentence. If you are testing an argument, then the premises should come first, and the conclusion should be the last column.

5. Identify the main connective of your sentences, the operator with the broadest scope. With complex sentences, begin with the innermost connectives and work your way out. The truth-value of the sentence is determined by the truth-value of its main operator, which in turn is determined by its component sentences.

6. Some of the truth-functional relations truth-tables can reveal are the following:

   a. **Consistency:** If there is one row on a truth-table in which all the sentences in a set are true, then the sentences are consistent. They are inconsistent otherwise.
      - Retained from Aristotelian logic is the notion of *contraries*, statements that cannot both be true but can both be false.

   b. **Implication:** One sentence implies another if whenever the first sentence is true, the second is true. If there is no row on the truth-table where the first sentence is true while the second is false, then the first implies the second.

   c. **Equivalence:** Two sentences are logically equivalent if they always have the exact same truth-value. If two sentences are logically equivalent, they imply each other.
      - Retained from Aristotelian logic is the notion of a contradiction. Two sentences are *contradictory* if they always have *the opposite truth-value*, the opposite of equivalence.

   d. **Validity:** An argument is valid if its premises jointly imply its conclusion. Hence, if there is no row on the truth-table of an argument in which all its premises are true while its conclusion is false, then the argument is valid.

7. Truth-tables may also reveal whether an individual sentence is one of the following:

   a. **Contingent:** If there is at least one row on the truth-table in which a sentence is true and at least one in which it is false, then the sentence is contingent.

   b. **Tautologous:** If a statement is always true—that is, if every row of the truth-table for a sentence is true, then the sentence is a tautology.

   c. **Contradictory:** If a statement is always false—that is, if every row of the truth-table for a sentence is false, then the sentence is a contradiction.

## Chapter Summary and Key Points to Remember

This chapter provided a brief overview of two major systems of logic:

- Traditional, Aristotelian, **categorical logic**.
- Modern, symbolic, **truth-functional logic**.

I Categorical Logic

- Aristotle originally systematized categorical logic. He identified three acts of the mind:

1. **Understanding:** Conceiving of a concept
2. **Judging:** Predicating one concept of another
3. **Reasoning:** Inferring one proposition from another

- Each act of the mind corresponds to an aspect of categorical logic:
  - Understanding corresponds to **terms**, which must be formulated clearly
  - Judging corresponds to **propositions**, which are either true or false
  - Reasoning corresponds to the **syllogism**, which is valid or invalid
- There are four kinds of terms in categorical logic:
  - **A Propositions:** Universal affirmative, have the form "All S are P," and only S is distributed
  - **E Propositions:** Universal negative, have the form "No S are P," and both S and P are distributed
  - **I Propositions:** Particular affirmative, have the form "Some S are P," and neither S nor P are distributed
  - **O Propositions:** Particular negative, have the form "Some S are not P," and only P is distributed
- The **traditional square of opposition** designates relations between the four types of categorical propositions:
  - A and E are **contraries** in the traditional square; they cannot both be true but can both be false.
  - A and O are **contradictories** in the traditional square; they always have the opposite truth-value.
  - E and I are also **contradictories** in the traditional square.
  - I and O are **subcontraries** in the traditional square; they can both be true, but cannot both be false.
  - In the traditional square, A propositions imply I propositions, and E propositions imply O propositions. This relation is called **subalternation**.
- Every syllogism has three terms:
  - **Major Term:** The predicate of the conclusion (designated by "P")
  - **Minor Term:** The subject of the conclusion (designated by "S")
  - **Middle Term:** Appears in both premises but not the conclusion (designated by "M")
- Every syllogism has a standard form:
  - Every syllogism has a **major** and a **minor premise**.
    - The major premise has the major term.
    - The minor premise has the minor term.
  - In standard form, *the major premise* is first and *the minor premise is second.*
  - The conclusion of a categorical syllogism will always have the minor term as its subject and the major term as its predicate.
- Every syllogism has both a **figure** and a **mood.**
  - The *figure* of a syllogism is dictated by the way its terms are arranged.
  - The *mood* of a syllogism is dictated by the types of propositions it has in the order they are arranged.
  - There are four standard figures, and a limited number of moods are valid under each.

- There are three principal methods for evaluating the validity of categorical syllogisms.
    - One may simply match the figure and mood of the syllogism to the chart. If it does not match any of the valid forms, then the argument in question is invalid.
    - One may use a Venn diagram.
    - One may check to see if all six rules of categorical syllogisms are obeyed:
        1) The middle term must be distributed at least once.
        2) If a term is distributed in the conclusion, it must be distributed in the premises.
        3) Two negative premises are not allowed.
        4) A negative premise requires a negative conclusion, and a negative conclusion cannot be inferred from two positive premises.
        5) There can be no more than three terms.
        6) If both premises are universal, then the conclusion may not be particular, although such a syllogism may be conditionally valid if the terms of the premises denote objects that actually exist.

II Truth-Functional Logic

- Truth-functional logic is the basis for modern symbolic logic, which came to fruition in the late nineteenth and early twentieth centuries based on the work of the likes of George Boole, Gottlob Frege, Bertrand Russell, Alfred North Whitehead, Ludwig Wittgenstein, and A. J. Ayer, among others.
- Truth-functional logic is so named because based on its principles, the truth-value of a sentence depends entirely on the truth-value(s) of its components.
- Truth-functional logic allows for the translation of sentences from ordinary language into a symbolic form that reveals their underlying logical form, thus, constituting an artificial language.
- There are two kinds of sentences: **simple** and **compound**.
    - **Simple sentences** (sometimes called **atomic sentences**) are single, affirmative, declarative statements.
    - **Compound sentences** (sometimes called **molecular sentences**) are either negative or combine simple sentences.
- The symbolic language of truth-functional logic includes the following:
    - Single letters to represent simple sentences
    - Five truth-functional operators to represent compound sentences
    - Punctuation, such as parentheses, brackets, and braces, to eliminate ambiguity in statements
- The five truth-functional operators are the following:
    - The *tilde*, ~, representing **negation**, which may also be represented by the bent bar, ¬, or the straight bar, —
        - Negation represents the opposite of what a statement asserts; hence, it is true when a statement is false and false when a statement is true.
    - The *dot*, •, representing **conjunction**, which may also be represented by the ampersand, &, and the upside-down wedge, ^

        - Conjunctions affirm that two or more statements are true; hence, a conjunction is only true if all its components are true but false if any one of its components is false.

    - The *wedge*, v, representing **disjunction**

        - Disjunctions assert that either one or more statements are true; hence, a disjunction is true just in case at least one of its components is true but false only when all its components are false.

    - The *horseshoe*, ⊃, representing **conditional statements**, also represented by the arrow, →

        - Conditionals represent hypothetical, "If … then …" statements. They are false only when the antecedent is true and the consequent false but true in any other case.

    - The *triple bar*, ≡, representing **biconditional statements**, also represented by the double arrow, ↔

        - Biconditionals represent logical equivalence; hence, a biconditional is true when its components have the exact, same truth-value and are false otherwise.

    - The truth-value of a sentence is dictated by its **main operator,** which is the operator that has the broadest scope in a sentence.

- Truth-functional logic includes the use of **truth-tables** to assess the properties and relations of sentences and the validity of arguments.
- Based on the contributions of modern logicians, some changes were made to the traditional square of opposition, hence, the **modern square of opposition**.
    - In the modern square, universal propositions are translated as conditionals and, thus, lack **existential import**. As a result, they can both be true if the classes designated by their terms do not refer to objects that exist. Hence, A and E propositions are *not contraries* in the modern square.
    - In the modern square, particular propositions may not be inferred from universal propositions unless the universal proposition refers to objects that exist. Hence, the relations of subalternation are undone.
    - I and O propositions retain existential import but are interpreted as conjunctions. Hence, they may both be false if their terms do not designate existing objects.
    - The only relations that are retained in the modern square of opposition are that A and O propositions remain contradictories as do E and I propositions.

The following are the most common valid truth-functional argument forms:

- Modus Ponens:
  If P, then Q.
  <u>P.</u>
  Therefore, Q.
- Modus Tollens:
  If P, then Q
  <u>Not Q.</u>
  Therefore, not P.

- Hypothetical Syllogism:
  If P, then Q.
  If Q, then R.
  Therefore, if P, then R.
- Disjunctive Syllogism:
  Either P or Q
  Not Q*
  Therefore, P.
  *If the second premise were "Not P," then "Q" would follow.
- Simple Constructive Dilemma:
  Either P or Q.
  If P, then R.
  If Q, then R.
  Therefore, R.
- Simple Destructive Dilemma:
  If R, then P.
  If R, then Q.
  Either not P, or not Q.
  Therefore, not R.
- Complex Constructive Dilemma:
  If P, then R.
  If Q, then S.
  Either P, or Q.
  Therefore, either R or S.
- Complex Destructive Dilemma:
  If P, then R.
  If Q, then S.
  Either not R, or not S.
  Therefore, either not P or not Q.

The following argument forms are invalid:

- Affirming the Consequent:
  If P, then Q.
  Q.
  Therefore, P.
- Denying the Antecedent:
  If P, then Q.
  Not P.
  Therefore, not Q.

- Invalid Hypothetical Syllogisms:

  If P, then R.
  If Q, then R.
  Therefore, if P, then Q.

  If P, then Q.
  If P, then R.
  Therefore, if Q, then R.

- Invalid Disjunctive Syllogism:

  Either P or Q.
  P.*
  Therefore, not Q.

  *If the second premise were "Q," it would also be fallacious to infer "not P."

## Exercises for Practice and Application

**Instructions:** Use what you learned in Chapter 7 to solve each of the following problems.

I. Categorical Syllogisms: Using one of the methods described in the chapter, determine which of the following arguments are valid. If an argument is invalid, provide a counterexample showing that it is invalid.

1. No sailboats are bicycles. No sailboats can fly. Therefore, nothing that flies is a bicycle.
2. All employees who work in produce are associates of *Shop & Save*. All employees who work in produce work at a grocery store. Therefore, all associates of *Shop & Save* work at a grocery store.
3. Some philosophers are not soldiers. All philosophers are courageous. Therefore, some people who are not soldiers are courageous.
4. All athletes lift weights. All professional wrestlers lift weights. Therefore, all professional wrestlers are athletes.
5. No dogs are reptiles. All Labs are dogs. Therefore, no Labs are reptiles.
6. No eels are wolves. No eels are birds. Therefore, no birds are wolves.
7. No cowards are virtuous. Some scientists are virtuous. Thus, some scientists are not cowards.
8. No educated people are impatient. All teachers are educated. Therefore, no teachers are impatient.
9. Some physicists are theists. All physicists are naturalists. So, some naturalists are theists.
10. All philosophers have meaningful lives. Some physicians are philosophers. So, some physicians have meaningful lives.
11. No one loyal is a liar. Some politicians are liars. Therefore, no politicians are loyal.
12. All kings are noble. Some philosophers are not noble. Hence, some philosophers are not kings.

II. Truth-Functional Logic:

(A) Translations: Translate each of the following sentences into symbolic form.

1. Traci is a detective.
2. Eric is not a police officer.

3. Traci is a detective and Rob is a businessman.
4. Either Rob is a businessman or Steve is a salesman.
5. If Steve is a salesman then Tim is wealthy.
6. Tim is wealthy if and only if either Traci is a detective or Rob is a businessman.
7. If Tim is wealthy, then Rick is either his bodyguard or his associate, but Traci does not work for them.
8. If Traci and Jim are detectives, then Eric is not a criminal if and only if Rob and Tim are his business associates.
9. If Traci has dinner with Kevin then Eric and Tim will be jealous; however, Rob will be jealous if and only if he is not married.
10. Either Traci and Jim are detectives and Eric is a criminal, or if Tim and Rick are not criminals, then Rob is their associate if and only if he is a salesman.

(B) <u>Arguments:</u> Determine whether the following arguments are valid. If an argument is invalid, provide a counterexample showing that it is invalid.

1. If Buster is a Lab, then he is a mammal. If Buster is a dog, then he is a mammal. Therefore, if Buster is a Lab, then he is a dog.
2. If John sees Alice, then he went to the birthday party. If John went to the birthday party, then he met Maci. Thus, if John sees Alice, then he met Maci.
3. If Raphael is a turtle, then he is an amphibian. If Raphael is a turtle, then he is an animal. So, if Raphael is an amphibian, then he is an animal.
4. If season 6 will be the final season of *Lucifer*, then Netflix is ending a great series. Season 6 will be the final season of *Lucifer*. It follows that Netflix is ending a great series.
5. If the production schedule for *The Batman* is on track, then the movie will come out in 2022. But the movie will not come out in 2022. Hence, the production schedule for *The Batman* is not on track.
6. Either *Cobra Kai* will have at least two more seasons or the series will end too soon. However, the series will not end too soon. Consequently, *Cobra Kai* will have at least two more seasons.
7. If Shawn's review of the script is accurate, then *Halloween Kills* will be the best sequel to *Halloween!* But Shawn's review of the script is not accurate. So, *Halloween Kills* will certainly not be the best sequel to *Halloween*.
8. If Sheppy is a robot, then Sheppy is a machine. Sheppy is a machine. Therefore, Sheppy is a robot.
9. If I get a donut, then I will have an iced coffee tomorrow morning. If I get a bagel twist, then I will have an iced coffee tomorrow morning. I will either get a donut or a bagel twist. Thus, I will have an iced coffee tomorrow morning.
10. If I have salmon for dinner, then I will have a baked sweet potato on the side. If I have steak for dinner, then I will have tater tots on the side. I will either have salmon or steak for dinner. So, I will either have a baked sweet potato or tater tots on the side.

III. Categorical and Truth-Functional Concepts:

(A) Concepts in Categorical Logic:

1. Explain why the following two statements are *not contraries* in the modern square of opposition: (a) The hydra is a seven-headed monster. (b) The hydra is not a seven-headed monster.
2. Explain why the following two statements are *not subcontraries* in the modern square of opposition: (a) Some unicorns can fly. (b) Some unicorns cannot fly.

3. Give at least three examples of how you used words or terms in your everyday speech that *do not* have existential import.
4. Rewrite the following argument into a standard form categorical syllogism, reducing the number of terms to three. Then, determine if it is valid or invalid. If it is invalid, provide a counterexample.

Atheists do not favor the teaching of intelligent design. Nothing should be taught that undermines modern science. Whatever does not favor the teaching of intelligent design obstructs the learning of cosmology. Anything that enhances the understanding of modern science does not obstruct the learning of cosmology. Therefore, atheism should not be taught.

(B) Concepts in Truth-Functional Logic:

1. Use a truth-table to do each of the following:
   a. Find a sentence that is a *tautology*—that is, whose main operator is always true.
   b. Find a sentence that is a *contradiction*—that is, whose main operator is always false.
   c. Find a sentence that *implies* a second but is *not implied by* that second sentence. That is, whenever the first is true, the second is also true.
   d. Find two sentences that are *equivalent*—that is, whose main operators always have the exact same truth-values.
   e. Find any two sentences in truth-functional logic that are *contradictories* (that is, their main operators always have the *opposite truth-value*) but *do not* have the form P and ~ P.
   f. Find any two sentences in truth-functional logic that are *contraries* but *not contradictories*.
2. First, symbolize the following three sentences:
   a. If Alex loves Rob and Rob loves Blake, then Jack will be jealous.
   b. Either Alex does not love Rob or Rob does not love Blake, or Jack will be jealous.
   c. It is not the case that Alex loves Rob and Rob loves Blake and that Jack will not be jealous.

Then, build a truth-table and use it to answer each of the following questions:

   i. Are these sentences *consistent* with each other? That is, is there at least one row on the truth-table in which all three are true?
   ii. Do any of these sentences imply any others?
   iii. Are these sentences logically equivalent?
   iv. Are any of these sentences tautologies?
   v. Are any of these sentences contradictions?
   vi Are any two of these sentences contradictories?

3. The following argument makes several inferences. Use your knowledge of truth-functional logic to determine whether it is valid or invalid. If it is invalid, explain where the fallacy occurs and provide a counterexample. If it is valid, explain whether you believe the argument is sound.

If life is meaningless, then no one should be afraid to die. But either life is meaningless or everyone should be afraid to die. And if everyone should be afraid to die, then some things must have intrinsic value. But everything in life eventually perishes. And if everything in life eventually perishes, then nothing has intrinsic value. Therefore, no one should be afraid to die.

4. Use your knowledge of both categorical and truth-functional logic to determine whether the following complicated argument is valid. If it is invalid, provide a counterexample:

   All Sneeches are predatory if and only if all Martians are quaint. And if all Martians are quaint, then no Rhinos are treacherous. Either some Kanamits are treacherous or some Sneeches are not predatory. But all Sneeches are predatory. It follows necessarily that some Kanamits are not Rhinos.

5. Explain why any deductive argument whose premises are *inconsistent* is necessarily valid.
6. Given the interpretation of conditional statements in modern truth-functional logic, explain (a) why *any sentence implies a tautology* and (b) why a *contradiction implies any sentence.*
7. The **law of disjunctive addition** states that any true statement may be disjoined with another. That is, if S is true, then the statement "Either S or P" is true as well. Explain why this inference is valid.
8. Recall from Chapter 4 the three laws of thought: (a) the **law of noncontradiction**, which states that it is impossible for something both to be and not be at the same time and in the same respect; (b) the **law of the excluded middle**, which states that between being and nonbeing there is no middle ground; and (c) the **law of identity**, which states that each thing is what it is and no other thing. These principles are necessarily true. That is, they cannot be false. Use this information to answer the following questions:

   a. How can one thing become another without violating any of these laws?
   b. Reality seems to be made up of opposing forces. Explain why such phenomena do not violate any of these laws.
   c. The law of excluded middle implies that every statement must be either true or false. But what about statements whose truth-values are unclear? Are they simultaneously true and false? Explain.

# 7

# Logic (III)

## Forms of Induction—Analogies and Causes

INTRODUCTION

## Preparing to Read Chapter 7

### RATIONALE AND PURPOSE FOR CHAPTER 7

The previous two chapters emphasized different forms of deductive reasoning and deductive arguments. Recall that inductive reasoning is *probabilistic*, meaning that inductive arguments and inferences establish claims that are probably or likely to be true. The current chapter emphasizes two of the most common forms of *inductive* reasoning:

- **Analogical Reasoning:** A form of inductive reasoning that draws inferences based on *analogies*, similarities between two or more objects or ideas. This form of reasoning frequently occurs in legal settings, politics, science, literature, philosophy, history, and ordinary everyday conversations.
- **Causal Reasoning:** A form of inductive reasoning that attempts to establish causal connections between two or more objects, events, or phenomena. This form of reasoning is specifically crucial for developing and testing scientific hypotheses and theories; hence, it will be supplemented with a presentation of scientific reasoning and the criteria for scientific theories. Mill's methods will be presented and explained as techniques for identifying causal relationships.

A firm understanding of each basic form of reasoning lends itself as the basis for versatility, proficiency, and literacy in diverse fields.

### AS YOU READ, LOOK FOR THE FOLLOWING TERMS

- Analogy
- Analogical Argument
- Dis-analogy
- Counter-analogy

- Unintended Consequence
- Enumerative Induction
- Causal Chain
- Contributing Causes
- Causal Cycle
- Aristotle's Four Kinds of Cause
    - Material Cause
    - Efficient Cause
    - Formal Cause
    - Final Cause
- Hume's Criteria for Causation
    - Temporal Contiguity
    - Constant Conjunction
    - Necessary Connection
- The Law of Association
- Mill's Methods
    - Agreement
    - Difference
    - Joint Method of Agreement and Difference
    - Residues
    - Concomitant Variation
- Abductive Reasoning (Inference to the Best Explanation)
- The Scientific Method
- Criteria for a Scientific Theory
    - Empirical Adequacy
        - Verifiability
        - Falsifiability
    - Coherence
    - Fertility
    - Unification (Scope)

**KEEP THE FOLLOWING QUESTIONS IN MIND AS YOU READ**

- How can I distinguish deductive from inductive arguments in my everyday experiences?
- If inductive reasoning cannot produce claims that are certain and indubitable, then what good is it?
- How can I use inductive reasoning in my everyday life?
- How can I use analogical reasoning in my everyday life?
- How can I develop strong analogical arguments?

- How can I critique analogical arguments that seem dubious?
- How can I effectively employ Mill's methods?
- If scientific reasoning is inductive, then what does that mean about the laws and knowledge yielded by science?
- How can I distinguish scientific from nonscientific theories?

## Analogical Reasoning

Analogical reasoning, succinctly stated, consists of drawing inferences based on **analogies**:

- An **analogy** is a comparison between two or more items; a list of ways that two or more items are similar.

Since items usually are not totally identical, analogical reasoning is inductive, the inferences drawn from it are merely probabilistic. The following scenario presents an example of an analogical argument:

Alex and Bill both watch horror movies. They both enjoy *Halloween, Friday the 13th, A Nightmare on Elm Street, The Texas Chainsaw Massacre,* and *The Exorcist*. Alex also likes *Child's Play*. Since Alex and Bill have so many preferences in common, Bill probably likes *Child's Play* too.

All analogical arguments will share the form of the Alex and Bill scenario, despite how complicated they can become. Structurally, analogical arguments resemble inductive syllogisms in which the first premise lists the similarities between the items being compared while the second premise attributes an additional property to one of the items that the other(s) may or may not possess. Finally, the conclusion infers that the other item(s) probably has the additional property. The following represents the form of an analogical argument:

(P1) X and Y have *a, b, c* … in common.

(P2) X also has *n.*____________________

Therefore, probably, Y has *n*, too.

Formally structuring the Alex/Bill argument, one can designate "A" for Alex and "B" for Bill, as well as *h* for *Halloween*, *f* for *Friday the 13th*, *n* for *A Nightmare on Elm Street*, *t* for *The Texas Chainsaw Massacre*, *e* for *The Exorcist*, and *c* for *Child's Play*. The argument would have the following structure:

(P1) A and B have *h, f, n, t*, and *e* in common.

(P2) A also has *c.*____________________

Therefore, probably, B has *c* too.

While one can arbitrarily choose the letters to represent the terms and items, one should avoid using the same letter for different objects.

Recall that inductive arguments are neither valid nor invalid, neither sound nor unsound. Rather they are *strong* or *weak*, *cogent* or *uncogent*. The strength of an analogical argument depends on the following factors of analysis:

- **The *number* of items being compared.** Generally, the greater the number of objects compared in an analogical argument, the stronger the argument.

- **The number of *similarities* between the items.** The more that any objects have in common, the stronger the argument will be.
- **The *variety* between the items being compared.** The concept of variety in analogical reasoning is difficult both to grasp and convey, but basically, it refers to the ways in which the objects being compared are *different*. That is, analogical arguments attempt to infer a conclusion based on a specific set of similar properties. If the objects of comparison differ in many ways beyond those properties, then it strengthens the argument, increasing the probability that the *very properties in question* sufficiently justify the conclusion. An example will be given later in the chapter.
- **The *relevance* of the similarities to the argument's conclusion.** As one might expect, the more relevant the similarities between the objects to the argument's conclusion, the stronger the argument will be.
- ***Dis-analogies* between the items.** Dis-analogies are the opposite of analogies, the ways in which the objects of comparison are dissimilar. The more dis-analogies between objects, the weaker an analogical argument, while fewer dis-analogies equal a stronger argument. However, dis-analogies should not be confused with variety between the objects of comparison. Typically, the *variety* between objects in an analogical argument consists of differences that should not be relevant to the argument's conclusion. *Dis-analogies* between the objects of comparison usually consist of differences within the scope of properties that are relevant to the argument's conclusion, too many of which could weaken the argument substantially. Again, an example will be given later in the chapter.
- **The availability of *counter-analogies*.** A counter-analogy is a comparison between one of the objects in an analogical argument to an external object, not part of the original comparison, that weakens the argument in question. That is, one of the objects in an analogical argument is stated to have *more in common with the external object,* which *lacks the crucial property* in the argument's conclusion. See the example in the chapter.
- ***Unintended consequences* of the initial comparison and its implications.** Often, comparisons between objects will yield undesirable or disadvantageous consequences or implications, those that the author of the argument would not want to accept. Such consequences may demand that an author reject the analogy on which his or her argument is based.

These points of analysis may now be applied to the Alex/Bill scenario.

First, two items are compared in the argument, two people, Alex and Bill. Since there are not many items being compared, the argument is weaker than it could be with more objects. The argument states that they have five traits in common, essentially that they both enjoy the same list of horror movies. There is a saying that everyone should value *quality* over *quantity*, but it is generally advisable to list at least three points of comparison in an analogical argument. For current purposes, five is a decent number.

This argument does not indicate much about Alex and Bill personally but suppose that Alex and Bill are both single, 21-year-old Caucasian American college students from middle-upper class families. In this case, there is not much variety between the items being compared. However, suppose that Alex is a single, 21-year-old Caucasian American college student from a middle-upper class family while Bill is a married 35-year-old African American insurance salesman with two children. The second characterization has much more variety and, thus, an analogical argument comparing the second Alex and Bill would be stronger based on the listed points of comparison. It would make the argument even stronger to compare several other people with equal levels of variety *but who shared* Alex and Bill's taste in horror movies. Such an argument would imply that such differences are not relevant to the conclusion, but the points of comparison between the objects being compared are and, thus, support the conclusion.

Speaking of relevance, since the conclusion of the argument simply states that Bill probably likes a horror movie that Alex also likes, and since the points of comparison listed in the argument's first premise simply name horror movies mutually enjoyed by both subjects, the points of comparison are indubitably relevant to the argument's conclusion. However, if the argument's first premise stated that Alex and Bill both drive Honda Civics, eat lunch at Subway, go on vacation at Disneyworld, shop at Old Navy, and attend Brown University, then the traits that the subjects have in common would seem totally irrelevant to the argument's conclusion and would not be sufficient to justify it.

To take stock so far, the Alex/Bill argument compares two subjects, asserts that they have five traits in common (sharing a mutual enjoyment of five specific horror movies), has very little variety, if any, and states points of comparison between the subjects that are relevant to its conclusion. The next step is to search for *dis-analogies* between Alex and Bill. In this case, dis-analogies would consist of additional horror movies that one of the two subjects enjoys but that the other does not. Suppose that Alex also enjoys *The Conjuring, Insidious, The Ring, The Grudge, Annabelle, Dead Silence, Resident Evil, Underworld,* and *28 Days Later* but that Bill hates each of those movies. Such a disparity would weaken the argument.

Like dis-analogies, *counter-analogies* emphasize differences between the subjects or objects compared in analogical *arguments.* But rather than only listing relevant differences between the items listed, counter-analogies create an entirely new analogy that yields the opposite conclusion of the original argument, undermining it entirely. For example, suppose that Bill and Charles each enjoy following horror movies: *Red Dragon, Seven, Saw, Scream, The Hills Have Eyes, Jaws, House of 1,000 Corpses, The House by the Cemetery,* and *Creepshow.* However, Charles does not like *Child's Play.* One can argue that Bill has more in common with Charles than he does with Alex, but Charles *does not* have the property attributed to Bill. Hence, probably, Bill does not like *Child's Play* either.

The final step in the analysis of analogical arguments consists of the search for *unintended consequences* of the initial comparison. Suppose one argued that based on the comparison between Alex and Bill and the conclusion inferred from it, one too hastily assumes that individuals who have similar tastes for specific movies share preferences for all movies. After all, taste is a subjective property and varies with little predictability. Suppose, also, on that basis, one suggests that we might as well infer that based on their shared preferences in horror movies Alex and Bill enjoy the same kinds of food, prefer the same kinds of cars, wear the same kinds of clothes, and date similar kinds of women. If the author of the argument wishes not to accept these possibilities, he or she might consider amending the original argument. The main problem with such a criticism, however, is that the alleged unintended consequences are not as relevant to the conclusion as the points of comparison between Alex and Bill.

In short, even the Alex/Bill argument constitutes only one example of analogical reasoning, all analogical arguments will generally have the same structure and can be analyzed using the criteria put forth here. Often, analogical reason coincides with causal and scientific reasoning, each of which is addressed next.

## Causal Reasoning

Aristotle is one of the first philosophers to think and write extensively about the nature of causation. He distinguished four kinds of causes:

- **Material Cause:** The *matter* or *physical substance* of which an object is constituted.
- **Efficient Cause:** The *agent* or *force* that brought an object into existence.
- **Formal Cause:** The *essence* of an object, what an object *is.*
- **Final Cause:** The *end* or *purpose* of an object, *that for the sake of which* it exists.

For example, consider a golden statue of Abraham Lincoln. The material cause of the statue is the gold itself. The efficient cause is the artist, the sculptor who created the statue. The formal cause of the statue is the image of Abraham Lincoln. Lastly, the final cause of the statue is to remind people of Abraham Lincoln, paying homage to his legacy as the 16th president of the United States. Aristotle's four kinds of causes may also be deemed a fourfold analysis of objects.

Modern scientists emphasize *efficient cause* and *natural forces.* Efficient causes in modern science may be understood in at least three ways:

- **Causal Chains:** A casual sequence in which an initial event leads to a second, which in turn leads to a third, which in turn leads to a fourth, and so on; causal chains are comparable to a "domino effect" or a "chain reaction."
- **Causal Collaboration:** A scenario in which multiple events or phenomena combine, contributing in varying degrees to produce a result; causal collaboration may also be called the phenomenon of *contributing causes.*
- **Causal Cycles:** A sequence in which an initial event or phenomenon leads to a second, which in turn produces a third, which in turn produces a fourth, which, finally, circles back to reinforce and perpetuate the initial event; causal cycles differ from causal chains in that cycles are circular and self-perpetuating.

Given the complexity of causal relationships, the remainder of this section will emphasize simple causal chains and the process of inductive reasoning that detects them. First, Hume's analysis and critique of causality and induction will be presented to establish criteria for a causal connection. Then, Mill's methods and scientific reasoning will be briefly presented and explained.

## Hume's Analysis of Causality and Induction

Typically, the idea of a causal relationship develops through the process of **inductive enumeration**, illustrated by the following process:

- <u>Instance (1):</u> B follows A.
- <u>Instance (2):</u> B follows A.
- <u>Instance (3):</u> B follows A.
- <u>Conclusion:</u> Therefore, A is probably the cause of B.

Despite this basic model, causal reasoning typically follows such a pattern. Essentially, if one event or phenomenon always seems to follow some other event or phenomenon, then the first event is likely the cause of the second. Such reasoning is inductive because there may be elements in apparent causal chains that cannot be readily observed. For instance, there may be a third factor causing both A and B, such as when the drop in atmospheric pressure causes a barometer to fall before a storm happens. Certainly, the barometer does not cause the *storm.* Moreover, there may indeed exist a causal connection between A and B, but A may not *directly* cause B, such as in the following instance:

- $A \rightarrow {}_{E1} \rightarrow {}_{E2} \rightarrow {}_{E3} \rightarrow B$

In this scenario, event A sets off a chain of several other unobservable events that culminate with B. Furthermore, even if one can uncover the chain of events beneath A and B, this extended sequence merely reduces the question of causality to a different level. The modified sequence may reveal how A causes B, but it does not show how E1 causes E2, or how E2 causes E3, or how E3 inevitably leads to B. Merely exposing a causal chain may only lead to an infinite regress of explanations.

Since causal relations are so elusive, many thinkers attempted to develop a list of criteria for causal relationships. One of the most famous analyses of causality derives from the thought and writings of the eighteenth-century Scottish philosopher David Hume, arguably the greatest mind ever produced by the United Kingdom. Historians traditionally characterize Hume as a *radical* empiricist, which, for current purposes, is acceptable. In the century prior to Hume's, Newton discovered the law of gravity and formulated his famous three laws of motion, essentially inventing mechanics and explaining how the universe works. Hume took as his goal discovering the laws by which the human mind work, seeking to become the "Newton of the mind." Ironically, he nearly undermined Newton's achievements! Given Hume's radical presuppositions, he carried the implications of empiricism further than Newton.

With respect to causality, two principal questions concerned Hume. First, what constitutes a causal relationship? Second, why do people necessarily believe in causal relationships? To answer the first question, Hume indicates that a causal connection between two events, A and B, consists of the following:

- **Temporal Contiguity:** A and B must be close together in time; when event A occurs, B must follow shortly thereafter.
- **Constant Conjunction:** B always follows A.
- **Necessary Connection:** B *must follow* from A; there *cannot* be an instance of A without B.

The main problem of inferring causal relationships is the third criterion, *necessary connection*, a problem that relates to Hume's answer to the second question.

As an empiricist, Hume maintained that all ideas derive from experience. Everything in the mind Hume labeled a *perception.* Hume subdivided perceptions into *ideas* and *impressions.* Impressions consist mostly of basic sensations. Hume insists that they are the more lively and powerful of our perceptions. Ideas are *copies* of impressions. According to Hume, there are no ideas that do not inevitably trace back to a single impression. With respect to causality, individual events, such as A and B, can be observed. We can have impressions of them. Hence, we can always infer when two events are temporally contiguous and constantly conjoined. However, what cannot be observed is the elusive *necessary connection.* All observations are part of a *contingent* experience. The observations conveyed through sense-impressions may always be incomplete or erroneous and, thus, no necessary connection may be inferred from them. Ultimately, no one can truly have any idea of a necessary connection. And since the idea of a causal connection hinges on the idea of a necessary connection, it seems to follow that *no one can have any idea of a causal relationship.* So, not only can one not observe directly what occurs between A and B, but even if one could make such observations, one's impressions of the events would not be sufficient to yield an idea of a necessary causal connection.

According to Hume, the reason that people believe in causal relationships is mostly due to the psychological *law of association.* If two events occur together enough times, eventually one develops the expectation of seeing one follow from the other. The problem, however, with Hume's analysis is that it seems to render the laws discovered by modern scientists, including Newton's, as mere psychological propensities that reflect more the order of the mind than that of the external world. Hume produced a similar critique of general induction, indicating that predictions about the future based on the past not only can never be certain but rest on an application of a law whose justification rests on circularity (see Chapter 4 for a more complete explanation of the law of induction).

Two caveats should be held with Hume's critique of causality. First, he did not believe that he disproved causality, nor did he intend to do so. He simply believed that he showed causal relations cannot be derived from sense-impressions. At best, the laws of causality that serve as the foundation of natural science are regularities that are subject to change. Second, as such regularities are subject to change, we should always be on the lookout for evidence that may require the modification of our conception of causal regularities. Ultimately, thus, Hume did not undermine natural science but established a justification for the modern scientific method.

Another empiricist who wrote extensively about causality also provided a foundation for scientific investigation: John Stuart Mill. Mill's methods for detecting causal relationships are explored in the next section.

## Mill's Methods

In addition to being a famous social and moral philosopher, John Stuart Mill developed five inductive methods for detecting causal relationships between empirical phenomena. They are the following:

- **The Method of Agreement**
- **The Method of Difference**
- **The Joint Method of Agreement and Difference**
- **The Method of Residues**
- **The Method of Concomitant Variation**

Each method will be more thoroughly explained with concrete examples of their application. Keep in mind that understanding the meanings of the terms describing each method is the clue to understanding the method itself.

### The Method of Agreement

This method may be defined as follows:

- When all occurrences of a phenomenon have only one common factor, then that common factor is probably the cause, effect, or at least part of the explanation of the phenomenon in question.

To simplify this method, consider the following scenario:

- Instance (1): *A B C* and *D* occur with *w x y* and *z*.
- Instance (2): *A E F* and *G* occur with *w t u* and *v*.
- Instance (3): *A H I* and *J* occur with *w q r* and *s*.
- Conclusion: Probably, A is the cause, effect, or part of the explanation of w.

Notice that this method alone does not license the conclusion that A is the definitive and complete cause or explanation of w, and vice versa. Consider the following scenario as a concrete application of Mill's method of agreement:

Adam, Brian, Dave, and John all eat dinner at Joe's Diner. Adam had a cheeseburger with fries; Brian had a T-bone steak with mashed potatoes; Dave had a fried chicken sandwich; John had meatloaf with mashed potatoes. All four individuals contracted food poisoning. They all had different entrées, but they all had the same appetizer—cheese fries. When they give their doctor this information, thus, he concludes that the consumption of the cheese fries accounts for their illness.

While the doctor's conclusion in this scenario is reasonable, there still is no conclusive proof that the cheese fries caused the food poisoning. Rather, there is only a potential variable to investigate. Typically, causal fallacies can occur if one misapplies any of Mill's methods, including the method of agreement. For example, suppose a young woman has the following beverages during the week and becomes intoxicated each night:

- Monday – Vodka and Soda
- Tuesday – Bourbon and Soda
- Wednesday – Gin and Tonic with Soda
- Thursday – Jack Daniels and Soda
- Friday – Wild Turkey and Soda
- Conclusion: By Mill's method, the soda causes the woman to become intoxicated.

Nonetheless, one can enhance one's search for causes by using a different method in different situations.

## The Method of Difference

This method may be defined as follows:

- When all occurrences of a phenomenon differ in only one way from those instances in which it does not occur, then the missing variable is either the cause, effect, or at least part of the explanation of the phenomenon in question.

To simplify this method, consider the following scenario:

- Instance (1): *A B C D* and *E* occur with *w v x y* and *z*.
- Instance (2): *B C D* and *E* occur with *v x y* and *z*.
- Conclusion: Probably, *A* is the cause, effect, or at least part of the explanation of *w*.

Note that once again, the application of this method does not warrant the conclusion that A is in fact the total and complete cause or explanation of w, and vice versa. Consider the following scenario as a concrete application of Mill's method of difference:

> Adam, Brian, Dave, John, and Kelly all eat dinner at Joe's Diner. While everyone had a different entrée, the men all ate the cheese fries as an appetizer, but Kelly did not. Each of the men contracted food poisoning, but Kelly did not. When they visited the doctor, thus, he concluded that the cheese fries are the source of the food poisoning.

While once again the doctor draws a very reasonable conclusion, one still cannot know with absolute certainty why the cheese fries caused the men to become sick. Perhaps each of the four men has a rare form of lactose intolerance, in which case the cheese fries are not alone the cause of the food poisoning. So, like the method of agreement, the method of difference by itself cannot isolate a critical factor involved in a causal relationship. However, these two methods combined can be very powerful.

## The Joint Method of Agreement and Difference

Succinctly, this method consists in the simultaneous application of the methods of agreement and difference, through which an investigator examines both instances in which a phenomenon occurs and compares them to those in which it does not occur. The following scenario illustrates the joint method of agreement and difference:

- Instance (1): *A B C D* and *E* occur with *w v x y* and *z*.
- Instance (2): *B C D* and *E* occur with *v x y* and *z*.
- Instance (3): *A F G H* and *I* occur with *w q r s* and *t*.
- Instance (4): *F G H* and *I* occur with *q r s* and *t*.
- Instance (5): *A J K L* and *M* occur with *w u n o* and *p*.
- Instance (6): *J K L* and *M* occur with *u n o* and *p*.
- Conclusion: Probably, A is the cause, effect, or at least part of the explanation of w.

Returning to the food poisoning scenario, suppose that someone from the Board of Health chose to investigate Joe's Diner based on the experiences of Adam, Brian, Dave, John, and Kelly. Suppose that they discover that every time a person ate cheese fries in the last month, they became sick, while no one who did not eat the cheese fries became sick after eating at Joe's Diner. Such an instance constitutes the joint application of agreement and difference. While one certainly can conclude that the cheese fries make Joe's patrons ill, however, this joint method still does not reveal why they do so. Further investigation into the matter would be necessary. Perhaps the method of preparing the fries contributes to the string of illnesses. Perhaps the cheese used has expired. The point is that Mill's methods, alone, cannot reveal everything relevant to an investigation of causes. Overconfidence in one's conclusion may stunt any investigation, since if one does not expect additional factors to play a role in causal relationships then one will not search for them.

## The Method of Residues

The term "residue" refers to some item or phenomenon that is left over from a previous event. For example, if a teacher writes with a red marker on a whiteboard and then erases the board, the faint red markings left over constitute residue, or a residual effect, the same sort of effect left over were one to spill coffee on one's clothes. Hence, Mill's method of residues may be defined as follows:

- One searches for all possible causes of a given phenomenon and applies a process of elimination until narrowing the search to the most viable explanation.

Typically, when applying the method of residues, the possible causes ruled out will be known to cause other given phenomena. Whichever possible cause remains will most likely explain the item in question. Consider the following scenario as a model for the method of residues:

- *A B C* and *D* occur with *w x y* and *z*.
- *B* is known to cause *x*.
- *C* is known to cause *y*.
- *D* is known to cause *z*.

Conclusion: Probably, A is the cause, effect, or part of the explanation of w.

Consider the following situation in which one applies Mill's method of residues:

> Roger develops a stinging pain in his back after his routine at the gym one day. He thinks that deadlifting caused the pain, so he ceases the exercise, but the pain persists. He then theorizes that heavy bench presses caused the pain. But when he stops bench pressing, the pain remains. Roger then stops doing shoulder presses, yet he still feels pain. The pain persists after Roger stops doing squats as well. However, Roger stops running uphill with a weighted vest. Shortly thereafter, the pain diminishes and ultimately vanishes. Roger concludes that his extreme cardio somehow led to nerve damage in his back.

As with the previous methods, even if Roger's conclusion is correct, his use of the method of residues does not in itself reveal the reason why running on the treadmill caused nerve damage, but it reveals the phenomena to investigate. The final method to be considered is Mill's method of concomitant variation.

## The Method of Concomitant Variation

Two items are said to be *concomitant* if they come together as a package of sorts. That is, one could not have the first item without the second. The term "variation" basically means change. Thus, the term "concomitant variation" refers to items or phenomena that vary together. Hence, the method of concomitant variation is the following:

- If a change in the occurrence of a given phenomenon always accompanies a proportional change in the occurrence of another phenomenon, then the two phenomena in question are causally connected.

Consider the following scenario as a model for the method of concomitant variation:

- <u>Instance (1):</u> *A B C* and *D* occur with *w x y* and *z*.
- <u>Instance (2):</u> $A^1$ *B C* and *D* occur with $w^1$ *x y* and *z*.
- <u>Instance (3):</u> $A^2$ *B C* and *D* occur with $w^2$ *x y* and *z*.
- <u>Instance (4):</u> $A^3$ *B C* and *D* occur with $w^3$ *x y* and *z*.
- <u>Conclusion:</u> Probably, A is the cause, effect, or at least part of the explanation of w.

Consider the following scenario that applies the method of concomitant variation:

> Two months after moving into his new apartment, Sam's new dwelling became a total mess. Not wanting to live in squalor, he decided to abide by a routine in which he would clean the apartment on a regular basis. The first cleaning took him approximately three hours, and his apartment looked as clean as the day he first moved. Sam's next cleaning took place one month later. This time, however, the cleaning only took approximately 90 minutes. Sam cleaned the apartment again two weeks later. This time, he finished in 45 minutes. Sam concluded that the less time he waits between cleanings, the shorter and easier will be the cleaning process.

Sam's conclusion is probably correct, as the amount of time between cleanings seems to vary concomitantly with the amount of time spent cleaning.

Not all instances of concomitant variation, however, will clearly indicate a causal connection between the phenomena directly observed. Psychologists often warn their students not to infer *causation* from *correlation*. For example, past statistical studies revealed strong positive correlations between the sale of ice cream and homicide rates. That is, as ice cream rates increase, homicide rates seem to increase. The two phenomena vary concomitantly and, thus,

Mill's method of concomitant variation may compel the statistician to conclude that ice cream consumption somehow causes people to become homicidal! But consider other variables, including the time during which the most ice cream is sold and the homicide rate rises—*summer*! Perhaps this third variable constitutes a common cause that explains both phenomena. Just as more people eat ice cream during the summer, rising temperatures likely drive people to be more aggressive as well. Like all of Mill's methods, the method of concomitant variation has limits.

### Taking Stock of Mill's Methods

Mill's methods are incredibly helpful to those working in all branches of natural science, aiding in the construction of hypotheses, experiments, and the detection of causal connections. They also apply to many common, everyday problems and are sufficiently flexible and accessible to be applied by laypersons and intellectuals alike. However, the following caveats must be kept in mind if Mill's methods are to be applied correctly:

- Any two objects will have many circumstances or variables in common and will usually differ in more than only one way, in which case Mill's methods may only help to narrow the search for causes.
- If Mill's methods are applied too liberally, they may lead to false cause fallacies and faulty induction, such as the confusion of correlation with causation, the post hoc fallacy, and hasty generalizations (each of which is addressed in Chapter 9).
- Even when observations are made correctly and Mill's methods are applied conservatively, there may still exist relevant critical factors that cannot be observed or detected by Mill's methods alone.

Mill's methods resemble the scientific method and in some ways are extensions of it. Hence, it is appropriate to address scientific reasoning before closing the current chapter.

## Scientific Reasoning and Scientific Theories

Since scientific reasoning typically is employed to detect causal relationships between various phenomena, scientists make frequent use of Mill's methods. However, more generally, scientific reasoning may be called **abductive reasoning,** which may be defined in the following way:

- Step 1: A surprising fact, event, or phenomenon, S, is observed.
- Step 2: It is inferred that if hypothesis, H, were true, S would not be surprising but would naturally follow as a matter of course.
- Conclusion: Therefore, probably, H is true.

Many famous and influential scientific theories developed through this very inferential process. Two of note are the Copernican heliocentric model of the solar system and Darwin's theory of evolution by way of natural selection.

Astronomers for centuries embraced the Ptolemaic model of the solar system, which is *geocentric*. That is, they mutually agreed that Earth is the center of the solar system, that the sun and the other planets revolve around it. The astronomer, Nicolaus Copernicus was not the first to suggest a heliocentric model of the solar system (that honor goes to Aristarchus of ancient Greece, refuted by Aristotle unfortunately!) but his challenge to the dominant paradigm of his day is the most famous. The modern heliocentric model of the solar system, thus, is often called the "Copernican model," and Copernicus's challenge, the "Copernican revolution."

Essentially, on the geocentric model of the solar system, many observable anomalies arise. For instance, Mars, which allegedly orbits Earth along with the sun and the other planets, often seems to stop and move backward. To explain such an anomaly, proponents of the geocentric model suggested that planets such as Mars move in *epicycles*, smaller revolutions within a longer more gradual revolution around its central planet. Such a modification, however, resulted in far too many complications with the geocentric model. Eventually, astronomers defending the geocentric model added as many as 40 epicycles to the motions of some of the planets. When a theory becomes too complicated, it is usually a sign that the theory is erroneous. Nicolaus Copernicus proposed a different model: *perhaps the planets, including Earth, orbit the sun*. This model is much simpler and more efficient. The Copernican hypothesis did not gain much support during Copernicus's lifetime, but his followers, Kepler, Brahe, and, ultimately, Galileo, proved his theory using more precise and refined observations and technology.

Like Copernicus, Darwin's voyage on the HMS Beagle afforded him the opportunity to observe many anomalies with both intelligent design and the accepted biological taxonomy of his day. Traditionally, theologians argued that God created Earth, the universe, and all its creatures with a plan in mind. During the eighteenth and early nineteenth centuries, a popular analogy for intelligent design was Paley's "Watch" analogy, comparing God to an omnipotent watchmaker. This idea coincided with both a literal reading of the Book of Genesis and the idea of the *fixity of species* perpetuated by the likes of Carl von Linne, the idea that species are fixed and eternal and, hence, do not change. On his famous voyage, however, Darwin made several observations that conflict with both ideas. For instance, Darwin noticed a completely uneven geographic distribution of life across the planet, in which some species seemed either to transform in significant ways or die out altogether. The fossilized remains of animals that no longer existed testified to such an anomaly. Moreover, many animals have rudimentary organs that no longer serve any specific purpose, such as wings on birds that do not fly, such as dodos and penguins. Darwin made his most crucial observations on the Galapagos Islands, in which he noted that several animals of the same species had characteristics that varied widely. Animals, he observed developed traits uniquely adapted to their needs and surroundings. For example, the finches on one of the islands had very long, thin beaks that enabled them to retrieve food at the bottom of shells. Finches on a different island, however, had short, thick beaks that allowed them to break hard shells. Ultimately, he proposed the idea of natural selection, the idea that species evolve via a chance process of adaptation to their surroundings. Those members of a species that have the traits necessary for survival live and pass on their traits to their offspring, whereas those that lack the traits go extinct. Hence, evolution occurs by the mechanism of survival of the fittest. Aware of the implications of his theory, Darwin waited nearly 20 years to publish his discoveries, until shortly after his friend and colleague, Alfred Russell Wallace, discovered virtually the same theory.

Each of these monumental discoveries occurred via the process of abductive reasoning, the foundation of the modern scientific method, which may be more precisely outlined in the following way:

- **Step 1:** A surprising phenomenon or observation occurs, which raises questions.
- **Step 2:** A hypothesis, or educated guess, is proposed to explain the phenomenon in question.
- **Step 3:** An experiment is established to test the proposed hypothesis.
- **Step 4:** Data is collected during the process of the experiment.
- **Step 5:** The experimental data is interpreted; it either supports or conflicts with the hypothesis.
- **Step 6:** If the data supports the hypothesis, further experiments are conducted. If the hypothesis continues to gather support, eventually it becomes known as a *theory*.
- **Step 7:** If the data does not support the hypothesis, the hypothesis is revised and new experiments are conducted to test the new hypothesis.

Typically, scientific experiments resemble one or more of Mill's methods. Often, empirical studies that test the effectiveness of new medications will resemble Mill's joint method of agreement and difference. For instance, suppose a pharmaceutical company wishes to test a new drug that reverses male pattern baldness. Typically, those conducting the experiment will gather two groups of participants:

- Those in the **control group** receive a *placebo*, a fake medicine.
- Those in the **experimental group** receive the medication whose effectiveness is being tested.

If those in the experimental group experience hair regrowth while those in the control group do not, then the experiment would provide evidence that the new medication is effective.

Not all scientific endeavors are experimental. Some are *theoretical*, designed to construct and enhance theories that explain natural phenomena. Not all theories, however, are purely scientific. For the scientific community to accept a theory as scientific, it must adhere to the following criteria:

- The theory must be **empirically adequate**, which means that the theory is stated in a way that is both **verifiable** through sense-experience and **falsifiable,** meaning that it is possible to conduct experiments that can possibly find evidence against the theory.
- The theory must be both **internally consistent**, formulated in a way that is both logically coherent and intelligible, and **externally consistent**, consistent with other known and accepted scientific theories.
- The theory must have a **broad scope**, such that it unifies phenomena previously believed to be unrelated (for example, Descartes's invention of analytical geometry, which unified algebra and geometry by plotting equations on graphs; Newton's discovery of gravity explained not only the motion of objects on Earth but also the motions of the other planets in the solar system; Maxwell's discovery that electricity can generate magnetic fields gave rise to the field of electromagnetism; Darwin's theory of evolution lacked a viable account of trait transmission, but his insights were eventually combined with the genetic theory of Mendel; Einstein's theory of special relativity required a reinterpretation of gravity, hence his general theory of relativity and the field of quantum mechanics).
- Finally, the theory must **generate research**. In other words, it must propose new insights that intrigue scientists enough to test them. It must not merely state trivial information.

Ultimately, despite the numerous triumphs of science in recent centuries, remember Einstein's famous quote, "Imagination is more important than knowledge." Experiments can reveal connections and may provide support for theories, but without the human element of curiosity and the drive for inquiry, there can be no progress, scientific or otherwise.

## Chapter Summary and Key Points to Remember

This chapter focused on two forms of inductive reasoning:

- **Analogical Reasoning**, in which one draws inferences based on a comparison between two similar objects
- **Causal Reasoning**, in which one infers that a causal relationship exists between two or more objects or events

**Analogical Arguments** consist of the following structure:

(P1) X and Y have *a, b, c*......in common.
<u>(P2) X also has *n*.</u>
Therefore, probably, Y has *n*, too.

- The *strength* of an analogical argument depends on the following factors:
  - The *number of items* being compared
  - *The number of similarities* between the objects
  - *Variety* among the objects
  - The *relevance* of the common properties to the argument's conclusion
  - The availability of **dis-analogies**, differences between the objects being compared
  - The availability of **counter-analogies**, in which one of the two objects is said to have more in common with an object that undermines the argument's conclusion
  - **Unintended consequences** of the comparison
- Aristotle distinguished between **four kinds of causes**:
  - **Material cause**, the physical substance or matter of an object
  - **Efficient cause**, the force or agent that produced an object
  - **Formal cause**, the essence of an object, what it is
  - **Final cause**, the end or purpose of an object
- Even though Aristotle privileged natural teleology, modern scientists emphasize material and efficient causes, best signified by a chain of events, or a "causal chain."
- David Hume suggested that a causal relationship must fit three criteria:
  - **Temporal contiguity**, the events must be close together in time
  - **Constant conjunction**, whenever one event occurs the second occurs
  - **Necessary connection**, if the first event happens, the second *must* happen
- Hume's critique of causality suggests that causal laws are largely produced by associations in the mind, implying that scientific laws reflect human psychology more than they do the physical world. Nonetheless, the attribution of causal laws to physical phenomena is crucial for the progress of science and, thus, must be pursued although one must always be open to change one's concept of a causal connection if relevant evidence presents itself.
- **Mill's Methods:** Named after their founder, John Stuart Mill, may be used to narrow the search for causes, although they are not infallible.
  - **Method of Agreement:** When all occurrences of a phenomenon have only one common factor, then that common factor is probably the cause, effect, or at least part of the explanation of the phenomenon in question.
  - **Method of Difference:** When all occurrences of a phenomenon differ in only one way from those instances in which it does not occur, then the missing variable is either the cause, effect, or at least part of the explanation of the phenomenon in question.
  - **Joint Method of Agreement and Difference:** The use of both agreement and difference simultaneously.

  - **Method of Residues:** One searches for all possible causes of a given phenomenon and applies a process of elimination until narrowing the search to the most viable explanation.
  - **Method of Concomitant Variation:** If a change in the occurrence of a given phenomenon always accompanies a proportional change in the occurrence of another phenomenon, then the two phenomena in question are causally connected.

- Mill's methods have limitations since any two objects or events will have multiple common factors, and false cause fallacies may occur if they are not applied conservatively.
- **Scientific reasoning** is basically a form of **abductive reasoning**, or **inference to the best explanation**, which consists of the following steps:
  - A surprising fact, A, is observed.
  - It is proposed that if hypothesis H were true, then A would not be surprising, but true as a matter of course.
  - Therefore, H is probably true.
- Many monumental scientific theories were discovered using this process, such as the Copernican model of the solar system and Darwin's theory of evolution.
- More specifically, scientific reasoning occurs when one takes the following steps:
  - An unexplained phenomenon occurs
  - A hypothesis is formulated as a possible explanation
  - An experiment is designed to test the hypothesis
  - If the experiment supports the hypothesis, then further experiments are done. If the hypothesis continues to acquire support, it becomes a theory
  - If the experiment shows the hypothesis to be erroneous, then the hypothesis is revised, and a new experiment is conducted to test the new hypothesis
- For a theory to be considered scientific it must have the following properties:
  - **Empirical Adequacy:** It must be both
    - **verifiable** by experience and
    - **falsifiable** in that it is possible to find evidence against it.
  - **Coherence:** It must be logically consistent and consistent with other accepted theories.
  - **Scope:** It must unify phenomena previously thought to be unrelated.
  - **Fertility:** It must be significant enough to generate research.

## Exercises for Application and Reflection

**Instructions:** Use what you learned in this chapter to complete the following exercises.

<u>Set I Analogical Reasoning:</u> For each of the following arguments, first give the *structure* of the argument and then *analyze* the argument by establishing the number of items being compared, number of similarities between the items, variety among the items, relevance of the similarities to the argument's conclusion, and availability of dis-analogies, counter-analogies, and potential unintended consequences.

1) Martin and Clifford both enjoy pancakes, waffles, French toast, and muffins. Martin also enjoys donuts. So, Clifford probably enjoys donuts too.
2) Jesse and David both took Professor Hay's literature course and received final grades of A. Each student also took Professor Bauer's philosophy course and received final grades of A. They also both took Professor Kapitan's course on cultural linguistics and received final grades of A. Furthermore, each student took Professor Robertson's course on art history, and once again, both received A's. Last semester, however, Jesse took a course on calculus for natural science and received an A. So, if David takes the course on calculus for natural science, he will probably receive an A too.
3) Gorillas and humans have much in common. They are similar in body size, have similar-sized brains, share 98 percent of their genetics, can recognize themselves in mirrors, and in some cases can even use sign language to communicate. Humans, moreover, are self-aware. Gorillas, therefore, probably are self-aware too.
4) Josh read three novels by Tom Savage—*Valentine*, *Precipice*, and *Scavenger*. Each novel constituted a realistic thriller that largely ignored supernatural elements, had a serial killer who operates on specific holidays, characters who used aliases based on anagrams, and a very surprising twist. Josh is now reading a novel titled *Inheritance*, also written by Tom Savage. Hence, it probably will have all the features of Savage's other novels.
5) Annie's dog, Buster, and Marcie's dog, Julie, are crosses between the breeds of dachshund and Chihuahua, enjoy Busy Bones®, eat Alpo®, play with the same chew toys, and graduated from the same dog school. Buster, moreover, has never bitten anyone. So, Julie probably will never bite anyone either.
6) Owning a gun and driving a vehicle are privileges society affords its citizens. Both require the development of specific skills and obedience to specific rules, and both can be dangerous to oneself and others if they are practiced irresponsibly. Before owning and driving a car, however, people must take both a written and practical exam to earn a license. So, people should have to take both a written and practical exam to earn a license before possessing and firing a gun.
7) Lifeboats have limited space and carrying capacities and finite resources, which should be given to their current members first and foremost. In these ways, lifeboats compare to most nations that also have limited space and finite resources. However, if a lifeboat takes on more people than it can carry, it will sink. Thus, if a nation tries to help more impoverished countries than it can help, it will probably "sink" as well.
8) If a woman's life is threatened and the only way to survive that threat is by killing her assailant, then she ought to have the right to kill her assailant without penalty. By comparison, there are cases in which a pregnant woman will die if she gives birth. In those cases, a woman ought to be allowed to terminate her "assailant."
9) In Golding's *Lord of the Flies*, when a group of children, aged 6–12, are stranded on an island without adult supervision, their attempt to establish a civil community descends into a "might makes right" driven chaos, given the scarcity of resources and the lack of any authority to distribute them properly. If our central government were to collapse, there would be a lack of central leadership to distribute resources, which would become increasingly scarce. It's very likely that such circumstances would also descend into a "might makes right" driven chaos.
10) Special Challenge—The Design Argument: Our cosmos and human artifacts are alike in many ways. Human artifacts, such as intricate machines and works of art, are far too complicated to have happened by a random chance process. The *Mona Lisa*, for instance, certainly could not have been created by a child randomly splashing paint on a canvas. Moreover, there is no known law or force of nature that could create such things, nor is it in their nature to exist necessarily. That is, clocks don't grow like trees,

nor do computers develop in the same way that tornadoes or hurricanes do. It certainly is the case that clocks and works of art are contingent, meaning that they could have been different and, thus, are not necessary. Furthermore, they conform to specified, recognizable, independently given patterns. A general mountain valley, for instance, is far different from the instantly recognizable faces carved into Mt. Rushmore. Anything that has these qualities was created by an intelligent being. And under close examination, we realize that our cosmos has these features. The mathematical laws and universal constants governing our cosmos are far too precisely and intricately calibrated with each other to have happened by chance. In fact, by chance alone, it would have taken an exponentially longer time for the conditions of our universe to emerge. In addition, we have not yet discovered any mechanism, or physical law, that would produce a universe. And since our universe could have been different than it is, it does not exist necessarily. Lastly, there are specified, independently given, recognizable patterns in our universe, such as the fact that its laws can be described mathematically, and the fact that irreducibly complex structures exist even at the microscopic level, such as bacterial flagella. Since items with these features have been designed by an intelligent agent, it follows that our cosmos, too, has been designed by an intelligent agent. The most simple, elegant, and rational explanation is that God is this intelligent agent.

<u>Set II—Mill's Methods:</u> For each of the following scenarios, state which of Mill's methods the investigator applies and then state the conclusion of the inquiry.

1) For two months, Simon set the thermostat in his house at 68 degrees. For each of those months, he slept comfortably, but the electric bill was nearly $300, a lot for a small house. For another two months, Simon set the thermostat at 74 degrees and found that for those two months, he slept just as comfortably, but the electric bill was under $200. Wanting to save money, Simon decided to set the thermostat no higher than 74 degrees.
2) John and Dan wanted to find an effective exercise routine for losing weight. For two weeks, John lifted weights, ran on the treadmill, performed bodyweight cardio, and ate a low-fat, low-calorie diet. Dan did the same, except he also began taking martial arts lessons. After two weeks, John lost 15 pounds, but Dan lost 25 pounds.
3) Jill noticed a rash forming on her foot. She stopped wearing nylons, but the rash persisted. She then began using a different skin lotion, and yet the rash remained. She switched body washes and still saw no results. She even changed her diet, but the rash did not budge. Finally, she switched to a new laundry detergent, and the rash gradually disappeared.
4) Maci's dogs, Jolie and Dre, became sick. They both ate different food, ate different dog treats, had baths at different times, used different shampoos, and were walked at different times of the day. However, Maci noted that the day they became sick, they both fought with a raccoon that invaded the backyard.
5) Tired of constantly waking up in the middle of the night, Ryan decided to eat his dinner earlier in the evening and go to bed earlier. On Sunday night, he ate dinner at 9:00 p.m. and went to bed at 11:00 p.m. He slept for three solid hours and woke up twice after that before getting up at 6:00 a.m. On Monday night, he ate dinner at 8:00 p.m. and went to bed at 10:00 p.m. He slept for five solid hours and woke up only once after that before getting up at 6:00 a.m. the next day. On Tuesday night, he ate dinner at 7:00 p.m. and went to bed at 9:00 p.m. He slept for seven hours and did not wake up at all in the night.

Set III—Reflecting on Causes

1) Use Aristotle's distinction between the four kinds of causes to explain at least three different items.
2) Explain how each of Bacon's idols of the mind can present obstacles to causal reasoning and the search for causal laws.
3) In the late fifteenth century, intellectuals and scientists stopped emphasizing final causes and placed greater emphasis on efficient and agent causes. Provide at least one defense of this shift and then explain at least one reason why the search for final causes should guide scientific inquiry.
4) If Hume's analysis of causality is correct, then what does that imply about science and the physical world? How are the efforts of scientists legitimate if Hume is right?
5) Besides Hume's critique of causality, explain at least one additional problem with the search for efficient causes in nature.
6) The doctrine of causal determinism suggests that since nature is subject to causal laws, no natural object is "free" to do otherwise, including people and nonhuman animals. Explain why if everyone were completely and fully determined, then scientific inquiry would be impossible and no one ever would have proposed causal determinism.
7) Explain how Mill's methods take Hume's critique of causality into account.
8) Explain whether you believe that Mill's methods address each of Bacon's idols of the mind.
9) Since abductive reasoning can be used in other contexts besides scientific inquiry, what distinguishes a scientific application of abduction from any ordinary abductive inference?
10) Find a scientific experiment and identify the experiment's hypothesis, prediction, conclusion, and whether the experiment contributes to contemporary scientific knowledge.

# 8

# Logic (IV)

## Informal Fallacies

INTRODUCTION

### Preparing to Read Chapter 8

Previous chapters highlighted many **fallacies:**

- In general, a **fallacy** constitutes an error in either deductive or inductive reasoning.
- There are two very broad types of fallacies, **formal** and **informal**:
    - A **formal fallacy** is an error in the form or structure of a deductive argument.
    - An **informal fallacy** is an error in reasoning that typically occurs in ordinary, everyday language.

An example of a formal fallacy is an argument form such as undistributed middle, affirming the consequent, or denying the antecedent, as addressed in previous chapters. An argument may be structurally correct but still commit an informal fallacy. For instance, consider the following argument:

If John is obese then he is wrong that President Biden should be removed from office.
John is obese.
Therefore, John is wrong that President Biden should be removed from office.

Notice that this argument has the form *modus ponens*; hence, it is valid. However, the issue of John's obesity does not at all seem relevant to Biden's presidency. This argument, thus, seems to commit a fallacy of relevance commonly called *abusive ad hominem*.

Previous chapters addressed *formal fallacies*. The present chapter aims to highlight and explain the most common *informal fallacies*, specifically each of the following:

- Appeals to factors irrelevant to an argument's conclusion (**fallacies of relevance**). Such fallacies include,
    - Personal Attacks
    - Emotional Appeals
    - Diversionary Tactics

- Faulty generalizations and faulty causal reasoning (**fallacies of weak induction**)
- Making assumptions that need proof (**fallacies of presumption**)
- The use of vague or misleading language (**fallacies of ambiguity**)

Some informal fallacies can be spotted more easily than others but knowing and understanding such fallacies will make them easier to recognize and avoid.[1]

## AS YOU READ, LOOK FOR THE FOLLOWING TERMS

- Personal Attacks
    - Ad Hominem, Abusive
    - Ad Hominem, Circumstantial
    - Poisoning the Well
    - Tu quoque
- Emotional Appeals
    - Appeal to the People
        - Group Solidarity
        - Bandwagon
        - Elite Person
        - Appeal to Tradition
    - Appeal to Pity
    - Appeal to Fear or Force
    - Appeal to Flattery
    - Special Pleading
- Diversion
    - Red Herring
    - Straw Man
    - Misleading Precision
    - Missing the Point
- Weak Induction
    - Fallacy of Accident (Sweeping Generalization)
    - Hasty Generalization
    - Fallacy of Composition
    - Fallacy of Division
    - Biased Sample

1 I compiled my list of fallacies from multiple sources, including Baronett's *Logic,* (New York: Oxford University Press, 2019), Patrick Hurley's *A Concise Introduction to Logic,* (Belmont, CA: Wadsworth-Cengage, 2008), Irving Copi, Carl Cohen, and Kenneth McMahon's *Introduction to Logic,* (New York: Routledge-T&F Group, 2010), John Chaffee's *Thinking Critically*, (Belmont, CA: Cengage, 2019), and Julian Baggini's *The Philosopher's Toolkit,* (Malden, MA: Blackwell, 2003). While my classification of the fallacies may differ slightly from these authors, my explanation of the individual fallacies mostly aligns with the general consensus of others in the field.

- False Cause Fallacies
  - Post Hoc Fallacy
    - Coincidence
    - Common Cause
  - Slippery Slope
- Fallacies of Presumption
  - Begging the Question
  - False Dichotomy
  - Appeal to Ignorance
  - Complex Question
  - Appeal to Unqualified Authority
- Fallacies of Ambiguity
  - Equivocation
  - Amphiboly
  - The "Masked Man" Fallacy

**KEEP THE FOLLOWING QUESTIONS IN MIND AS YOU READ**

- Why should I learn the most common informal fallacies?
- Do I ever commit any of the informal fallacies I learned in this chapter?
- How often do I encounter the informal fallacies I learned in this chapter?
- Are there cases in which the appeals made by any informal fallacies are relevant or important?
- Are there any famous disputes that could have been resolved more easily if people could more easily avoid and recognize informal fallacies?

## Fallacies of Relevance

In general, a fallacy of *relevance* occurs when the author of an argument appeals to reasons that either do not at all pertain to or directly support its conclusion. Hence, it is also appropriate to label the tactics addressed in this section fallacies of *irrelevance*. This section focuses on three types of fallacies of relevance:

- **Personal attacks,** which occur when an individual's characteristics or life circumstances are invoked as reasons for rejecting that individual's position or argument, even though the position or argument is not properly engaged
- **Emotional appeals,** which occur when one uses psychological tactics to elicit an emotional response, and based on that emotional response, one is expected to accept or reject an argument or position
- **Fallacies of diversion,** which occur when one distracts an audience from the primary focus of an argument, focusing instead on a side issue and then using that side issue as a basis for rejecting the original argument

## Personal Attacks

The general pattern of a personal attack is the following:

- **Step 1:** Person A presents an argument.
- **Step 2:** Person B refers either to undesirable character traits or controversial life circumstances of Person A.
- **Step 3:** Person B rejects Person A's argument based on the personal attack.

There are four major personal attacks:

- **Abusive Ad Hominem**
- **Circumstantial Ad Hominem**
- **Poisoning the Well**
- **Tu quoque**

The term "ad hominem" is Latin for "against the person." Ad hominem attacks, thus constitute the most basic forms of personal attack. Each can be defined as follows:

- The **abusive ad hominem** occurs when an argument or claim is rejected based on some purported character flaw or undesirable attribute of the person who made the claim or argument.
- The **circumstantial ad hominem** occurs when an argument claim is rejected based on controversial life circumstances surrounding the person who made the claim or argument.

It can be difficult to distinguish these two fallacies, but the following illustrations are helpful in doing so. Suppose Alex claims Rob is a poorly dressed degenerate and, thus, concludes that his argument in favor of ethical vegetarianism should be rejected. This example constitutes an *abusive* ad hominem. However, if Alex claimed that police recently arrested Rob for leading a protest outside a factory farm and, thus, his argument for ethical vegetarianism should be rejected, Alex invokes a *circumstantial* ad hominem.

**Poisoning the well** differs from both abusive and circumstantial ad hominem attacks in one important respect:

- **Poisoning the well** occurs when either a person's character or life circumstances are attacked *before* the person has a chance to present their claim or argument.

Consider each of the following examples.

- **PW1:** Before you read his new nonfiction book, you should know that I once met Shawn Davis and he totally snubbed me.
- **PW2:** Before you read his new nonfiction book, you should know that police once arrested Shawn Davis for assault.

Notice that the word "before" appears in each example and nothing specifically is mentioned about the Shawn Davis nonfiction book to which each passage refers. Hence, the "well" is poisoned, as the content of his new nonfiction book is dismissed before it is known by the person to whom each appeal is made.

Finally, the term "tu quoque" is Latin for "you also." The fallacy of **tu quoque**, thus, could also be deemed the "two wrongs do not make a right" fallacy. It can be defined as follows:

- **Tu quoque** occurs when a person attempts to avoid accepting a claim, appeal, or argument by claiming that the person making the claim, appeal, or argument is a hypocrite.

Typically, adolescents make such appeals when protesting the boundaries set by their parents, such as when a father catches his son smoking an illicit recreational drug such as marijuana. When the parent begins to lecture, the teenager will likely exclaim, "But I learned it from you, Dad!" Any appeal of this form constitutes a tu quoque, although, like many informal fallacies, they can occur in more subtle ways and may be disguised in longer more complicated passages.

Often, personal attacks may inspire additional personal attacks from the opposing side of a debate or discussion, as personal attacks give rise to emotions. Emotional appeals, however, constitute an independent class of fallacies of relevance that are addressed next.

## Emotional Appeals

The following constitutes the general pattern of emotional appeals:

- **Step 1:** Person A employs psychological tactics known to give rise to powerful emotions.
- **Step 2:** Person B is supposed to accept Person A's claim or argument based on those emotions.

There are five major emotional appeals:

- **Appeals to the people**, of which there are four subtypes:
  - **Group Solidarity Appeal**
  - **Bandwagon Appeal**
  - **Elite Person Appeal**
  - **Appeal to Tradition**
- **Appeals to Pity**
- **Appeals to Fear or Force**
- **Appeals to Flattery**
- **Special Pleading**

To begin with **appeals to the people**, since there are several variations of this appeal, it is useful to present a general definition. While each of the fallacies in this section appeal to a specific emotion, appeals to the people emphasize the universal human desire to *belong*. The humanistic psychologist Abraham Maslow famously outlined a hierarchy of needs, of which *belongingness* came third, after basic physiological needs (food, water, sleep, shelter, sex) and safety needs (protection from harm, a steady source of income to meet one's physiological needs, etc.). Belongingness basically consists of the desire for friendship, love, and being desired by others. Such a need also leads to the desire to be part of a community or a cause. Hence, the following general definition of appeals to the people can be provided:

- An **appeal to the people** occurs whenever an argument hinges on arousing in others the strong desire to belong or be part of a community or cause.

The clearest example of an appeal to the people is the **group solidarity** appeal, which may be defined as follows:

- **Group solidarity** consists in the attempt to justify a claim or a course of action because doing so serves the greater good for one's group.

Hitler famously used the group solidarity appeal. Germany shouldered most of the blame for instigating World War I, after which Hitler rose to prominence. Many of his appeals cultivated and emphasized the perception of victimhood held by Germans, epitomized by the idea that their country became a target as the rest of the world bullied them. Hitler attempted to unify the Germans by compelling them to revolt against their oppressors. More recently, in US history, Donald Trump's campaign "Make America Great Again!" also constitutes an appeal to solidarity, an attempt to unify a group against all potential threats.

The **bandwagon** appeal is a common tactic in advertising, just as the expression "jumping on the bandwagon" is commonly used. This appeal consists of the following:

- The **bandwagon appeal** consists in the attempt to justify a claim or a course of action because it is popular or because "everyone else believes it" or "everyone else is doing it."

The bandwagon appeal perpetuates that which is popular and the universal human desire to belong, to be wanted and desired by others. The appeal to "jump on the bandwagon" is so effective because embracing that which everyone else loves serves as the path of least resistance to belonging and being loved.

The **elite person appeal** emphasizes not merely the universal human desire to belong but the desire of many people to be or feel *special*. It can be defined in the following way:

- The **elite person appeal** consists in the attempt to justify a claim or a course of action by suggesting that only special or unique people hold such a claim or act in such a way.

Often, cults and various fringe groups will recruit members by using such an appeal and typically the targets for recruitment are loners, people with few friends, if any. For instance, suppose that the leader of the hypothetical cult "Transcend" considers Sam for recruitment and he dispatches one of his emissaries to make the following appeal:

> Sam, the reason you have no friends is that you are *special*. You are not only different, but you are *better* than everyone else. You were born to serve a higher purpose, like us. You should join us and we'll be a *true family*.

Elite person appeals can also mirror bandwagon appeals, attempting to make some product or behavior popular by linking it with an elite person, such as if a celebrity wears a specific brand of clothing or drinks a specific nutrition beverage. The difference between the bandwagon appeal and elite person appeal is that the former appeals to the popularity of an item, whereas the latter appeals to its alleged unique attributes that make the user special in some way.

Finally, the **appeal to tradition** may also be deemed the appeal to historical customs and practices. It may be defined in the following way:

- The **appeal to tradition** consists in the attempt to justify a claim or a course of action because it has been held or done for a long time.

For example, if a group of people indulged in cannibalism merely because the custom dated back several centuries, such a justification would constitute an appeal to tradition, hardly a reason for consuming members of one's own species!

The meaning of the remaining emotional appeals can be understood simply by understanding the terms that describe them. For example, the **appeal to pity** can be defined as follows:

- An **appeal to pity** consists of an emotional plea that relies entirely on arousing a sense of pity, sympathy, guilt, or sorrow.

In essence, appeals to pity "pull on the heartstrings" of individuals. Many classic appeals to pity occur in legal disputes, such as when an individual is on trial for murder. Suppose that a defense attorney makes the following appeal:

> Ladies and gentlemen of the jury, I know that my client allegedly carried out a shooting spree and murdered 27 people, but his stepfather severely emotionally abused him as a child. Moreover, his classmates relentlessly bullied him his entirely life. Even worse, he has no friends and has never even had girlfriend! You simply cannot find him guilty!

Other appeals to pity seek to elicit charity donations or some form of special treatment from others. Often, ads from the ASPCA feature pictures of neglected animals gazing longingly into the camera. And many students attempt to elicit feelings of pity from their teachers to raise their grades or be granted extensions on late assignments.

The **appeal to fear or force** in Latin is known as *ad baculum*, "appeal to the stick." Behavioral psychologists distinguish between both *positive reinforcement* and *punishment*. Positive reinforcement attempts to produce a specific behavior by reward. Punishment attempts either to eliminate or produce specific behaviors by using an aversive stimulus of some kind. The two are sometimes distinguished as "carrot" (positive reinforcement) and "stick" (punishment). In other words, the rabbit *chases the carrot* but *avoids the stick*. Appeals to fear or force typically attempt to provoke a specific response by making a threat. Specifically, such an appeal may be defined as follows:

- An **appeal to fear or force** consists of threatening some form of harm—usually either physical, emotional, psychological, or economic—to instigate a course of action that may or may not be acceptable.

Whereas appeals to fear or force elicit negative feelings in people, **appeals to flattery** are more positive and consist of the following:

- **Appeals to flattery** appeal to a person's vanity to entice them to act a specific way or embrace a specific claim.

In other words, an appeal to flattery "butters a person up." Appeals to flattery can be very effective because people universally want to feel good about themselves. For example, if I were to approach my department supervisor and say, "Dr. Kelly, you look great in that new suit! You have great taste in clothes! Oh, and by the way, you should consider giving me a raise!" Granted, my appeal was not very smooth, but it effectively demonstrates how an appeal to flattery works. Typically, such an appeal works best on those who already have a strong sense of vanity.

The final emotional appeal, **special pleadings**, like appeals to pity, may elicit feelings of guilt or sorrow, but tend to be more general and can be defined as follows:

- A **special pleading** occurs whenever an individual tries to make him or herself an exception to the rules for arbitrary reasons.

For example, if Simon says, "I refuse to wash my dishes tonight because I had a difficult exam," Simon's appeal would be a *special pleading*, but it overlaps with an appeal to pity. However, if Simon were to say, "I refuse to wash my dishes tonight because I'm taller than anyone in the house," Simon specifically commits the fallacy of special pleading.

Emotional appeals are effective and even more powerful than logic and reason, so powerful in fact that the Scottish philosopher David Hume famously remarked, "Reason is and ought to be the slave of the passions." Nonetheless, because emotional appeals often are not relevant to a position, debate, or discussion, Hume's claim most certainly seems at least partially incorrect. Reason sometimes is the slave of the passions, but said passions and emotions should not be the universal standard for the assessment of arguments. However, what makes emotional appeals so effective is that they disrupt one's ability to focus and, thus, create a *diversion.* Other fallacies of diversion are addressed in the next section.

## Fallacies of Diversion

This subsection addresses the following fallacies of diversion:

- **Red Herring**
- **Straw Man**
- **Misleading Precision**
- **Missing the Point**

The most common and basic of these fallacies is the **red herring,** which can be defined as follows:

- The **red herring** occurs when someone ignores an argument entirely and instead changes the subject, deflecting attention to a side issue.

The term "red herring" derives its name from a fish that is normally a silvery hue but turns a reddish-brown when it is smoked. It is believed that prisoners used such fish to cover their tracks, as the scent would throw off the dogs. Red herrings are common in literature, specifically in crime and mystery novels. Typically, a "red herring" is a false suspect introduced to distract the audience from the true culprit. Unfortunately, red herrings are also common devices used in constructing and responding to arguments. Consider the following retentionist argument (in favor) for the death penalty:

> When a person is convicted of a capital offense, such as first-degree murder, and is sentenced to life imprisonment, it places an enormous burden on the taxpayers. It costs hundreds of thousands of dollars—in some cases, millions—to pay for room and board, food, utilities, and health care for one person, let alone for thousands of inmates. It would greatly reduce the financial burden on law-abiding, taxpaying citizens if those convicted of capital offenses were executed rather than given life sentences. Hence, the death penalty should be a mandatory sentence for anyone convicted of a capital offense.

This passage deflects attention from the main issue, which should be the morality of the *death penalty.* If the death penalty is immoral, then it should be avoided *regardless* of the cost, just as no parent should murder their children because doing so would make the lives of the parents less expensive! Similar arguments are often made by abolitionists (against the death penalty). The following example focuses on race:

Statistical studies of the death penalty reveal two things:

1) The death penalty is always more likely to be imposed when the offender is non-Caucasian, such as black, Asian, or Hispanic.

2) The death penalty is always more likely to be imposed when the victim is Caucasian rather than black, Asian, or Hispanic.

Hence, the death penalty is imposed with racial bias and, therefore, should be abolished.

Like the previous example, this argument deflects attention from the morality of the death penalty to a side issue: *the way it is imposed*. If a convicted offender truly deserves the death penalty, if the death penalty truly is necessary to balance the scales of justice, then the practice itself should not be abolished. *How the practice is imposed* is a related but different matter.

Another common fallacy of diversion is the **straw man**. Just as it is very easy to defeat an inanimate scarecrow in a physical fight, it is equally easy to defeat an argument specifically constructed in its weakest possible form. This fallacy may be defined as follows:

- The **straw man** fallacy occurs when one's argument, claim, or position is purposefully distorted or incorrectly interpreted to create a weaker argument easier to attack and reject.

Usually, a straw man will consist of an extreme interpretation of an argument or position. Typically, the more extreme a position is, the less plausible it is. Consider the following example:

Senator Johnson recently argued that intelligent design should not be taught in classrooms alongside evolutionary biology, as he feels that the religious implications of the former could dissolve the separation between church and state. Obviously, Johnson wants us to live in a godless, secular world with no foundation for our values!

This passage blatantly portrays a straw man against the hypothetical Senator Johnson. There is an important difference between maintaining a separation between church and state and banning religion from a country altogether. The more extreme claim, though, is much easier to attack and reject. Notice that the more extreme claim that Johnson wishes to ban religion also will elicit strong emotional reactions from most people since most people hold *some* religious beliefs.

Just as extreme positions easily grab the attention of an audience, numbers and empirical data can be very persuasive. Tangible evidence equals results! However, if it is not clear what the data in question means, then such data functions only as a distraction. The most common diversionary tactic relies on the use of quantitative and statistical data, **misleading precision**:

- **Misleading precision** occurs when an argument invokes numbers or quantitative data to make an argument seem statistically significant when it is not entirely clear what the data in question means.

For example, suppose that an advertisement for a new beverage claims that the product has 50 percent less sugar than the leading brand. If the amount of sugar in the leading brand is not known, then the advertisement is misleading.

The final fallacy of diversion addressed here is **missing the point**. This fallacy has the Latin alias, "non sequitur," meaning, "It does not follow." **Missing the point** may be defined in the following way:

- **Missing the point** occurs when an argument's premises seem naturally to imply an obvious conclusion, but instead either the opposite or a totally unrelated conclusion is drawn.

For example, consider the following argument:

My students in PHI 100-01, Intro to Philosophy, did excellent work for the spring 2021 semester. They all attended every class, completed all the assignments on time, scored highly on all the exams, wrote excellent, scholarly essays, and participated in every discussion. Thus, I failed every student in my section.

This argument's conclusion literally follows from nothing stated prior, as though the author draws it out of thin air. The diversion in arguments that "miss the point" consists of the premises that obscure the author's true intentions.

While the discussion of the most common fallacies of diversion and general relevance is now complete, there are several other types of fallacies of which one must be aware and avoid. The following subsections address those most prominent and common.

## Fallacies of Weak Induction

Recall that an inductive argument is strong when its premises make its conclusion likely to be true and weak when its premises do not make its conclusion likely to be true. As the title of this category of fallacies suggests, the fallacies in this section consist of forms of inductive reasoning that fail to establish a high probability for the truth of their conclusions. There are two main types of inductive fallacies:

- **Generalization fallacies**, which occur when one makes an error either by inferring a general principle from too few specific observations to support it (a "bottom-up" inference) or by applying a general principle to cases that are an exception to the rule (a "top-down" inference)
- **False cause fallacies**, which occur when one mistakenly infers that a causal relationship exists where there is no such relationship

### Generalization Fallacies

This subsection will address the following generalization fallacies:

- **The Fallacy of Accident**
- **Hasty Generalization**
- **The Fallacy of Composition**
- **The Fallacy of Division**
- **Biased Sample**

Beginning with a "top-down" fallacy, the **fallacy of accident** has several other labels, including the "sweeping generalization" and the "rigid application of a generalization." This fallacy is "top-down" because it moves from a general principle or rule to a concrete, individual situation or set of circumstances. In other words, it moves from the *general to the specific*. It may be defined in the following way:

- The **fallacy of accident** occurs when a general principle or rule is applied to instances that should be exceptions to that principle or rule.

For example, if a police car, an ambulance, or a fire truck speed through a red light, they are probably responding to an emergency. It would be totally inappropriate to suggest that either vehicle deserves a speeding ticket. Generally, it is illegal to use a sharp instrument to cut people, but a surgeon certainly should not be charged with a crime for using surgical tools to perform a procedure necessary to save a life.

A famous case of the fallacy of accident occurs in the field of moral philosophy, specifically with the moral theory of Immanuel Kant. Kant insisted that all people have a perfect duty to be honest and never to lie under any circumstances. However, if there is a murderer at one's door asking for the whereabouts of one's friend, it seems that the situation constitutes an exception to the rule.

While the fallacy of accident moves from the general to the specific, other fallacies of weak induction move in the opposite direction, from the *specific to the general,* such as the **hasty generalization:**

- The **hasty generalization** occurs when an argument attempts to create a general principle or rule from too small a sample.

Like other informal fallacies, the meaning of "hasty generalization" can be inferred from the meanings of its terms. The word "hasty" refers to an action that is done too quickly or impulsively, and a "generalization" is an inference developed from a set of individual concrete observations. Hence, a "hasty generalization" consists of formulating a general principle or rule too quickly.

The fallacies of **composition** and **division** parallel those of hasty generalization and accident. The first, *composition,* like hasty generalization, moves from specific to general, while the second, *Division,* like the fallacy of accident, moves from general to specific. The **fallacy of composition** can be defined in the following way:

- The **fallacy of composition** occurs when either (a) the properties of the *parts* of an object are attributed to the *whole* object or (b) the properties of the *individual members* of a class are attributed to the *entire class.*

In other words, composition can occur as a "part-to-whole" or as a "member-to-class" inferential process. For instance, suppose that someone builds a sandcastle and then claims, "Each grain of sand in the sandcastle is very small. Hence, the entire sandcastle itself is very small." This fallacy is an example of composition type (a). However, if an individual suggests that a garbage truck uses more gasoline than a car and, thus, that the entire class of garbage trucks consumes more gasoline than cars, one commits composition fallacy type (b) since there are more cars than garbage trucks. The *class of cars,* thus, consumes more gasoline overall.

The **fallacy of division** is essentially the inverse of the fallacy of composition. It may be defined as follows:

- The **fallacy of division** occurs when either (a) the properties of the whole object are attributed to its parts or (b) the properties of an entire class of objects are attributed to its individual members.

Hence, division may occur as a "whole-to-part" or as a "class-to-member" inferential process. For example, if someone were to say, "My apartment building is made of bricks, and thus, the building itself is as small as a brick," they commit the division fallacy type (a). For an example of type (b), suppose that someone inverts the garbage truck example, reasoning instead in the following way: "Since the class of cars consumes more gasoline than the class of garbage trucks, an individual car uses more gasoline than a garbage truck." Clearly, this conclusion is erroneous.

The final generalization fallacy occurs in statistics, **biased sample**. Statistical studies usually consist of a *sample* of individuals selected from a *population*. A population is simply any group of objects. For instance, imagine a box of cookies. All the cookies in the box represent a population. If someone were to reach in and withdraw ten cookies, those ten cookies are a sample. The size of a population can vary, as can the size of samples. However, the data collected in a statistical study must come from a *representative sample*, or it cannot adequately support an argument.

- A **representative sample** is a sample that accurately reflects the population such that all members of the population had an equal chance of being selected.

For example, suppose that a student at Farmington University wishes to conduct a study by surveying the student body about their religious affiliations. If the student advertises the study in a wide variety of locations on campus, collects data from students majoring in many different subjects in addition to members of various clubs and the athletic team, and the number of students surveyed is high and proportional to the population, then the sample is representative. However, if the student only collects data from students in the drama club and surveys no one else, then the sample is *biased*. The fallacy of **biased sample**, thus, may be defined as follows:

- A **biased sample** consists of a sample that does not accurately reflect the population from which its members are selected.

Another common example of the fallacy of biased sample may occur in politics, for instance, if a poll only collects information from Democrats but does not include Republicans.

## False Cause Fallacies

This subsection emphasizes the following false cause fallacies:

- **The "post hoc" gallacy**, of which there are two versions:
    - **Coincidental Post Hoc**
    - **Common Cause Post Hoc**
- **The Slippery Slope Fallacy**

The "post hoc" fallacy is an abbreviation for the Latin phrase, "Post hoc, ergo propter hoc," which means, "After this, therefore because of this." Hence, the **post hoc** fallacy generally occurs whenever one event, x, occurs before some second event, y, and since y happened after x, an observer assumes that the first event caused the second. On this basis, each type of post hoc fallacy may be defined as follows:

- The **coincidental post hoc** fallacy occurs whenever some prior event is said to cause a later event when in fact there is no causal connection.

For example, suppose that one of your professors scratches his head during class, and approximately five seconds later, an earthquake destroys a small Mexican village. There probably is no causal connection between the actions of your professor and the earthquake. Similar instances of this fallacy occur when one believes that one's dreams or one's horoscope reading may predict the future simply because they happen to come true once. Typically, the person ignores the thousands of other times that their dreams or horoscopes did not accurately predict the future.

The second type of post hoc fallacy usually occurs when one does not consider the possibility of an additional *common* factor that may account for an apparent causal connection:

- The **common cause post hoc fallacy** occurs when one attributes a causal connection to two or more events when there is an additional unseen common factor that accounts for all the events in question.

For example, suppose that the oil light in your car flashes on precisely two minutes before your car's engine seizes. The oil light did not cause the engine to seize, but a lack of oil would cause both events. A similar process applies to the falling of a barometer before a storm occurs. The falling barometer does not cause the storm, rather both may be attributed to the fall in atmospheric pressure. Recall from Chapter 8 that *correlation* must not be confused with *causation*, as can happen with Mill's methods and with scientific inquiry.

The final inductive fallacy treated in this subsection is the **slippery slope fallacy**, the most common form of which assumes a false causal connection. It can be defined as follows:

- The **slippery slope fallacy** occurs when a person assumes that an initial event sets off a chain reaction sequence leading to an inevitable but implausible outcome.

Given its nature, this fallacy may also be called the "chain reaction" fallacy. For example, suppose one of my students indicates that he or she wishes to change majors, from the natural sciences to a liberal arts field, and I make the following appeal:

> You should not change your major to a liberal arts field. If you do so, all your classes will be in fields that have no practical value. If none of your courses have practical value, then when you graduate from college, you will not be able to procure a job that pays a substantial salary. And if you cannot earn a substantial salary each year, you will not be able to live in a nice neighborhood. You will never have your own home, and you will not be able to pay for a vehicle or groceries. If you cannot afford to pay for a home, a vehicle, and groceries, then eventually you will be homeless.

Clearly, this argument jumps to many conclusions whose connections with the initial event are not obvious, especially since many thriving businesses demand employees with a broad education and problem-solving skills. In essence, any sort of appeal that resembles this example commits a slippery slope fallacy.

Other versions of the slippery slope fallacy occur because of the mistaken transference of *potentiality* to *actuality*. For example, an acorn is a potential tree. However, if one has an acorn in one's pocket, one certainly should not claim to have a tree in one's pocket. Some professors refer to the slippery slope fallacy as the "bald man" fallacy. That is, many individuals are potentially bald, specifically males with a family history of hair loss. But merely having the potential to be bald certainly does not make an individual bald.

Many of the informal fallacies presented in this chapter overlap with each other. Fallacies of weak induction, for instance, may overlap with fallacies of relevance since the evidence for an inductive inference may not be relevant to a conclusion. Or one might make assumptions that stand in need of further proof, fallacies of presumption. Fallacies of presumption tie into many other fallacies and are closely examined in the following section.

## Fallacies of Presumption

Fallacies of presumption occur when an argument assumes premises that demand proof or additional support, premises without which the conclusion may not be inferred. This section addresses the following fallacies of presumption:

- **Begging the Question**
- **False Dichotomy**
- **Appeal to Ignorance**
- **Complex Question**
- **Appeal to an Unqualified Authority**

The most common fallacy of presumption is **begging the question**, also known by its Latin alias "petitio principii," which means, "assume at the beginning." There are three variations of **begging the question**:

- The first and most basic form of begging the question occurs when an argument merely **assumes a conclusion** without proof.
- The second form of begging the question occurs when **an argument's conclusion merely restates one of its premises**, typically by using different words that have the same meaning.
- The third form of begging the question occurs when an argument employs **circular reasoning**.

An example of the first form of begging the question is the following argument:

<u>Josh Lott was born in Leominster, Massachusetts.</u>

Therefore, he robbed the federal armored car!

Notice the similarity between this form of question-begging and fallacies of relevance, such as the diversionary fallacy, missing the point. This tactic occurs more commonly than one might assume. Even those well-versed in philosophy sometimes commit this fallacy. For instance, consider the common argument against abortion:

A fetus is a person.

<u>All persons have a right to life.</u>

Therefore, a fetus has a right to life.

What is in question here is the first premise, whether a fetus truly is a *person* or merely a biological human organism that lacks the rights of full-fledged persons. Many ethicists maintain that simply to assume so begs the question.

The following exchange constitutes an example of the *second* form of begging the question:

Person A: Simon is honest.

Person B: Why?

Person A: Because Simon never lies.

In this exchange, verifiable evidence of Simon's honesty must be marshaled. Simply to state the definition of honesty using different terms merely assumes what one attempts to prove.

Finally, *circularity* is quite common as well. Typically, circularity occurs whenever at least one premise in an argument depends on the truth of the conclusion it purports to establish, and vice versa. For example, consider the following sentences:

(A) God exists because the Bible says so.

(B) You can believe the Bible because God wrote it.

To accept sentence (A) is to assume that the Bible is true. On the other hand, to accept sentence (B) is to assume God exists as the author of the book. There are many examples of this form of question-begging in the history of philosophy. A famous alleged example occurs in Descartes's *Meditations on First Philosophy.* In developing his central argument, Descartes seems to assent to the following two claims:

(M1): God exists because I have a clear and distinct idea of Him.

(M2): I can trust my clear and distinct ideas because they come from God and He would not deceive me.

Whether Descartes truly employed circular reasoning is the subject of much scholarly debate, but on the surface, it certainly seems that these two statements reflect a vicious circle.

In addition to various forms of begging the question, **false dichotomies** also reflect fallacies of presumption:

- A **false dichotomy** occurs whenever a person presents two alternatives as though they are (a) exhaustive and (b) mutually exclusive when other options are available.

Two options are exhaustive if they represent all possible choices. Moreover, two options are mutually exclusive when if one is true, the other must be false. Such conditions would obtain in a *true dichotomy,* such as the law of excluded middle. However, usually, any issue or problem will have more than only two alternative solutions. Consider the following example:

Either humans evolved from apes over the course of millions of years, or they were created by God on the sixth day of creation, as indicated by the Bible.

This sentence clearly overlooks many alternatives. For instance, perhaps the teachings of a different religion, such as Hinduism, are true. Or, perhaps evolution and Christianity are compatible, as several philosophers such as Teilhard de Chardin and Richard Swinburne argued. There is also the position of teleological panpsychism developed by Tom Nagel. Moreover, those who favor a secular explanation for the appearance of design may find multiverse theory promising. The point is that there are options besides only these alternatives.

Another fallacy of presumption is the **appeal to ignorance**, also known as "ignoratio elenchi" in Latin. An **appeal to ignorance** may take one of two forms:

1) A person assumes that some claim is true because there is no proof against it.

2) A person assumes that some claim is false because there is no proof for it.

Such appeals are common in debates about religion and the existence of aliens. For instance, a theist might argue that God must exist since no one can disprove His existence, whereas an atheist might invert such an argument, asserting that God must not exist since no one can prove His existence. Substituting the word "aliens" or "UFOs" for "God" in each of these arguments would produce additional examples. In other contexts, such as court cases, a prosecutor might claim that since there are no other possible suspects, the defendant in his case must be guilty of the crime of which he is accused. On the other hand, a defense attorney might profess the innocence of his client on the grounds that the defendant has no discernible motive for the crime of which he is accused.

The next fallacy of presumption usually occurs in the form of a question, a **complex question**:

- A **complex question** occurs when an individual asks a question that has multiple questions built into it such that no matter how a respondent answers, he or she is forced to make an undesirable or embarrassing admission.

Complex questions are sometimes also called "loaded questions," not because they are difficult to answer, but because they have multiple questions built into them, questions that reflect unwarranted assumptions. For example, imagine that I ask one of my students the following question: "Do you still plagiarize your research papers?" This question really asks two separate questions:

1) Did you ever plagiarize your research papers?

2) Do you still plagiarize your research papers?

If the student replies, "Yes," obviously, he or she admits to an offense that at most universities and colleges is grounds for expulsion. But even if the student replies in the negative, he or she still admits to cheating in the past! The unwarranted assumption built into this question is that the student cheated at some point in his or her academic career.

This fallacy can also occur in much more subtle ways and is a tactic commonly used by law enforcement agents. For instance, suppose a homicide detective suspects a specific person of murder but has no concrete evidence and, thus, no grounds for a search warrant. Typically, detectives will invite the suspect on a "fishing trip." That is, the lead detective will call or approach the suspect and politely ask them to come to the station to "ask a few questions" and state that the interview will not take long. During the interrogation, the officers usually lull the suspect into a false sense of security and try to finagle the suspect into slipping up, attempting to catch him or her in a lie. Consider the following hypothetical exchange:

**Detective:** You have a great body! You run at Willow Creek Park often, right?

**Suspect:** Yes, I do.

**Detective:** So, you could have been present at that park on the seventh, between the hours of 8 and 10 a.m.?

**Suspect:** Yes, it's possible.

**Detective:** And it's possible that you saw the woman in this photograph, as she runs at that park often. (The detective shows the suspect the photograph.)

**Suspect:** Yes, she looks familiar.

**Detective:** She disappeared on the seventh, and her body was found on the ninth in the woods. Do you know anything about that? (The detective then shows the suspect a photograph of the woman's dead body, trying to elicit an emotional response.)

These elements of a hypothetical exchange are sufficient. Notice that the detective began by appealing to the suspect's vanity (appeal to flattery) and got the suspect to make many seemingly innocuous admissions that draw him into more damning admissions later in the conversation. While the detective does not ask any one question, the questions he asks have multiple parts (i.e., "Is it possible you were at the park?" combined with "Were you at the park?" and "Is it possible you saw this woman?" combined with "Did you see this woman?"), and they lead the suspect to answers that he already believes are true. Moreover, while the suspect's answers are vague in some respects (he refers to the "possibility" that he ran at the park that morning and says that the victim "looks familiar"), that will not stop the police from using his answers against him (i.e., since he can be placed at the crime scene, he had opportunity; since he knew the victim, he possibly had a motive, etc.) Tactics such as those employed in this scenario are the reason why lawyers recommend that suspects never voluntarily talk to the police!

The final fallacy of unwarranted assumption to be addressed here is the **appeal to an unqualified authority,** whose process is essentially conveyed by the terms of its label:

- An **appeal to an unqualified authority** occurs when an authority figure endorses a claim, position, or product that pertains to an area in which the authority figure lacks significant expertise.

For example, if one asked Mike Tyson about how to pursue a career in professional boxing, or if one approached Connor McGregor for his advice about pursuing a career as a professional Mixed Martial Arts fighter, one would probably receive valuable advice. However, were one to ask either of these gentlemen to endorse a medication that prevents heart failure in those with cardiac problems, such endorsements would likely carry little merit. In such cases, those in charge of marketing a product hope merely to associate the face of a celebrity with their product, thereby eliciting a positive emotional response. The *assumption* built into such appeals is twofold. On the one hand, the individuals marketing the product or making the claim in question provide no legitimate evidence for the effectiveness of their product or the truth of their claim. On the other hand, those who accept the endorsement assume that a product is worth buying or that a claim is true merely because a celebrity says so! Thus, such appeals "beg the question" on both sides.

Often, fallacies can be avoided simply by clarifying one's claims and terms, especially if one wishes to avoid the fallacies of ambiguity addressed in the final section of this chapter.

## Fallacies of Ambiguity

The term "ambiguous" literally refers to a term or word that can have multiple meanings, in which case the term's or word's meaning must be precisely clarified. For example, the word "bark" can refer to at least three different items: the hard substance that covers a tree, the sound made by a dog, or shouting at someone (in which case the term applies metaphorically). If one were to say, "Ted is barking at me again," one might mean that they have a dog named Ted who is barking or that one has a human associate named Ted who is shouting at them. The meaning of the sentence, thus, is not entirely clear given the ambiguity of the word "barking." Fallacies of ambiguity, hence, occur when an argument's terms lack clarity, leading to faulty inferences. This section addresses the following fallacies of ambiguity:

- **Equivocation**
- **Amphiboly**
- **The "Masked Man" Fallacy**

**Equivocation** is the most common fallacy of ambiguity. Analyzing the word itself into its component parts, "equi" and "vocal," elucidates its meaning:

- **Equivocation** occurs when a person uses a word with multiple meanings in two different senses in the same argument, resulting in a faulty inference.

Thus, "equivocation" literally means treating the meanings of a word as if they are *equal*. For example, suppose someone were to say, "Kelly is hot! Therefore, her body temperature must be well over 100 degrees Fahrenheit!" The inference made by this person uses the term "hot" in two different senses: first in a metaphorical sense indicating that someone is physically attractive and then in a literal sense referring to physical temperature. Any time an inference reflects an error of this type, the person who made the inference is guilty of equivocation.

The fallacy of **amphiboly** also consists of a faulty inference resulting from a lack of clarity but not merely because of the ambiguity of individual words. Amphiboly involves misplaced modifiers and sentence structures that obscure the meanings of terms as well:

- **Amphiboly** occurs when an inference is drawn erroneously from an ambiguous sentence.

For example, consider the following sentence: "Standing on the luxury yacht traveling through the Mississippi River, the Sears Tower can be seen. So, the yacht must have been the size of an entire city block to hold the Sears Tower!" Given the structure of this sentence, one can easily misinterpret what the word "standing" refers to, the Sears Tower or the person describing the tour. Both equivocation and amphiboly can occur in very subtle ways. One can more easily avoid each by understanding the different meanings of words and structuring sentences to clearly reflect the meaning one intends to convey.

The final fallacy of ambiguity and, in fact, the final fallacy addressed in this chapter is typically called the **masked man fallacy.** While stating a concise definition of this fallacy is extremely difficult, understanding **Leibniz's law** can expedite one's understanding of it. **Leibniz's law** is the following:

- If two objects, X and Y, are identical, they have all their properties in common.

Leibniz's law is also known as the **indiscernibility of identicals**. To explain the fallacy in question, imagine that Dave and Dan are best friends. One night, while Dave is walking to his car after buying groceries, a masked assailant holds him up at gunpoint demanding his wallet, keeping his voice low but intense and sinister. Dave quickly hands over the wallet and the masked man disappears into the night. Quite shaken by the event, Dave cannot sleep that night. He lies awake wondering about the identity of his victimizer. But Dave knows one thing with absolute certainty: the culprit could not possibly be his best friend, Dan, since Dave *knows* who Dan is and does not know the identity of the masked man. In other words, Dave believes that Dan has a property that the masked man lacks, the property of *being known* by Dave. Hence, by Leibniz's law, Dan is not the masked man. But it is still entirely possible that Dan is still the masked man, as the perpetrator concealed both his face and voice so that he *would not be identified even by those who know him*. On this basis, the "masked man" fallacy can be succinctly defined as follows:

- The **masked man fallacy** occurs when one misapplies Leibniz's law, resulting in a faulty inference.

Descartes's *Meditations* may be revisited here for an example of another famous case of an informal fallacy (logical target practice!). In the second *Meditation*, Descartes put forth his initial argument for substance dualism:

1) It is possible to doubt the existence of one's body.
2) One cannot enter into the process of doubt without a mind, and hence, it is impossible to doubt the existence of one's mind.

Therefore, the mind and the body are not identical.

If one understands Leibniz's law, one should be able to spot the flaw in this argument. Just like Dave, Descartes misapplies the law (long before Leibniz discovered it!), suggesting that the ability to doubt the existence of some object confers a property on that object. A common counterexample to Descartes's argument concerns a famous comic book superhero, Super Man! Suppose Super Man saves Lois Lane, who then draws the following inference: since I am certain that Super Man saved me, and I doubt that Clark Kent saved me, Superman is not Clark Kent. But of course, Super Man moonlights as Clark Kent by day!

While the version of Descartes's argument presented here certainly seems flawed, he presents a stronger argument at the end of his classic work, one that integrates other aspects of his argument, which should be assessed by reading the *Meditations* as a whole. Nevertheless, most philosophical works have multiple interpretations, all of which have their strengths and weaknesses. By becoming aware of common formal and informal fallacies, students are better equipped to form their own interpretations of literature and reality in addition to impartially evaluating information and arguments.

## Chapter Summary and Key Points to Remember

This chapter presented and explained several **informal fallacies,** which contrast with **formal fallacies**.

- A **formal fallacy** occurs when an argument is structurally incorrect and is, thus, invalid.
- An **informal fallacy** occurs when an argument may be structurally correct but commits an error in ordinary language by either appealing to irrelevant factors, making a weak inductive inference, making assumptions that require proof, or using ambiguous language.

The most common informal fallacies are the following:

- **Fallacies of relevance** occur when an argument appeals to factors that are not relevant or significant to the argument's conclusion. There are three general types:
    - **Personal attacks,** the general pattern of which is the following: Person A presents an argument; Person B attacks either the character or life circumstances of Person A; Person A's argument is rejected based on Person B's attack. The most common personal attacks are the following:
        - **Ad hominem, abusive**, in which one attacks the character of the person making an argument
        - **Ad hominem, circumstantial**, in which one attacks the controversial life circumstances of the person making an argument
        - **Poisoning the well**, in which one attacks either the character or life circumstances of an individual *before* that person has a chance to state their position
        - **Tu quoque**, Latin for "You, too!" A fallacy in which one's argument is rejected on the grounds that he or she is a hypocrite
    - **Emotional appeals**, the general pattern of which is the following: Person A uses psychological tactics to arouse strong emotions in Person B; Person B accepts Person A's claims based on those emotions. The most common emotional appeals are the following:
        - **Appeals to the people**, in which one attempts to stimulate in others the desire for belongingness; usually, this fallacy occurs in one of three ways:
            - **Group solidarity**, in which one argues that some course of action or claim is necessary to maintain the integrity of a group
            - **Bandwagon**, in which one argues that some course of action or claim should be accepted because it is popular
            - **Elite person**, in which one argues that some course of action or claim should be accepted because exceptional people do so, and by engaging in the activity, one can be special too
            - **Appeal to tradition**, in which one argues that some course of action or claim should be accepted because it has been embraced for a very long time

        - **Appeals to pity**, in which one attempts to justify some claim or course of action by eliciting sympathy from an audience
        - **Appeals to force**, in which one makes threats to justify some claim or course of action
        - **Appeals to flattery,** in which one attempts to justify some claim or course of action by appealing to an audience's vanity, "buttering them up"
        - **Special pleading**, in which one makes oneself an exception to the rules for arbitrary reasons
    - **Fallacies of diversion,** which distract attention from the issue at hand to a less relevant or totally unrelated issue. The most common are the following:
        - **Red herring**, in which one diverts attention from the focus of an argument to a side issue
        - **Straw man**, in which one reconstructs an opponent's argument in the weakest way possible so that it is easy to attack and refute
        - **Misleading precision**, in which one uses numbers and statistical data that seem significant but are unclear
        - **Missing the point**, in which one's premises lead to a seemingly obvious conclusion but instead the exact opposite conclusion or a totally unrelated conclusion is drawn
- **Fallacies of weak induction** occur when an argument makes a weak inductive inference, of which there are two very general types:
    - **Fallacies of generalization**, which may occur in the formulation of a general principle (from specific to general, bottom-up) or by misapplying a general principle (from general to specific, top-down). They include the following:
        - **Fallacy of accident (aka sweeping generalization)**, in which a general principle is applied to a case that should be an exception to the rule
        - **Hasty generalization**, in which one infers a general principle without an adequate sample or without sufficient evidence to justify it
        - **Fallacy of composition**, which may occur in two ways:
            - **Part to whole**, in which one infers that the properties of an object's parts are true of the whole object
            - **Member to class**, in which one infers that the properties of the individual members of a class are true of the entire class
        - **Fallacy of division**, which may occur in two ways:
            - **Whole to part**, in which one infers that the properties of an object are true of the object's parts
            - **Class to member**, in which one infers that the properties of an entire class of objects are true of its individual members
        - **Biased sample**, in which one makes an inference based on statistical data collected from a *non-representative sample* of participants—that is, from a sample that does not accurately reflect the population to which the inference applies
    - **False cause fallacies**, which occur when one infers the existence of a causal relationship where there is no such relationship. The most common are the following:

- **Post hoc fallacy**, abbreviation for the Latin, "Post hoc, ergo propter hoc," meaning, "After this, therefore because of this." Generally, it is the inference that because one event, B, happened after a prior event, A, the first event caused the second. It has two versions:
    - **Post hoc – coincidence**, in which one event happens after another but the two are totally unrelated.
    - **Post hoc – common cause**, in which one event happens after another, but some third event caused both.
- **Slippery slope (aka, the "chain reaction" fallacy)**, which occurs when one infers that some initial event sets off a sequence of events that leads to an allegedly inevitable but unlikely outcome

- **Fallacies of presumption** occur when an argument makes assumptions that require proof or further explanation. The most common are the following:
    - **Begging the question**, which generally occurs when an argument assumes its conclusion without proof. There are three forms of question-begging:
        - **Simple assumption of a conclusion**, in which a conclusion is put forth either without evidence or without relevant evidence
        - **The conclusion merely restates a premise using different words**
        - **Circularity**, in which an argument's conclusion seems necessary to justify one or more of its premises
    - **False dichotomy**, which assumes that there are only two mutually exclusive options when in fact there are additional alternatives
    - **Appeal to ignorance**, which has two forms:
        - The argument that some belief or claim must be true because it cannot be or has not been disproven.
        - The argument that some belief or claim must be false because it cannot be or has not been proven.
    - **Complex question**, in which one asks a single question that has multiple questions built into it. Usually, no matter how the interlocutor answers, he is forced to admit to an assumption made by his interrogator
    - **Appeal to an unqualified authority**, in which one uses an authority figure to justify a claim on a topic outside that figure's area of expertise
- **Fallacies of ambiguity** occur when an argument's terms or premises are unclear, and this lack of clarity results in a faulty inference. The most common are the following:
    - **Equivocation**, in which an argument uses one term or word in at least two different senses
    - **Amphiboly**, in which the structure of one or more of an argument's premises obscures their meaning
    - **The "masked man fallacy,"** a fallacy of attribution in which one misapplies **Leibniz's law**, the **indiscernibility of identicals**, which states that any two objects that are identical have all their properties in common

## Exercises for Application and Reflection

**Instructions:** Use what you learned in this chapter to answer the following questions and solve the following problems.

**Set I:** Identify the informal fallacy committed in each of the following arguments. Be as *specific* as possible!

1. Because Sandy does not watch Fox News and is not a registered voter, we should ignore anything she says about social and legal policies.
2. My uncle, Ernie, was a chain-smoker who went through three or four packs of cigarettes a day. He is, thus, nothing but a hypocrite for lecturing me about the dangers of smoking, and I should ignore him!
3. Even though Leonard spent his wife's paycheck on lottery and scratch tickets, he should not be blamed. After all, compulsive gambling is a sickness. He needs our sympathy and support!
4. St. Bernard's football team beat us by a landslide last year, 48–0! They humiliated us in our own stadium! This season it's our turn! We can't just beat them! We must humiliate them and make them suffer, too!
5. Louis, I have many longtime friends and colleagues at Johns Hopkins Medical School. If you do not break off your engagement with my daughter, I could simply make a couple of phone calls to have your admission revoked.
6. Professor Capuletti insisted that the so-called evidence for intelligent design may be explained by purely mechanical laws governing universal constants without appealing to God. But he is an arrogant, self-important miscreant. I don't care what he says!
7. Before you read John Douglas's book, *Mindhunter*, you should know that he and his friends took a joy ride in a stolen car during their college years.
8. The Good Samaritan who performed CPR on that fallen young woman cracked her sternum in the process! That's assault! He should be arrested and prosecuted to the full extent of the law!
9. A fortune cookie from last week read that I would soon meet a person with whom I would have a significant, close relationship. And then today, I met someone at Starbucks, and we seem to have a lot in common! The fortune cookie came true!
10. Every Lego® in Anthony's set is very small. Therefore, whatever he is building will also be very small.
11. Brock Lesnar is enormous! Thus, he must have an enormous spleen!
12. On eight separate days, a rabbit scurried past me just before a thunderstorm. A rabbit just hopped past me. So, I should probably cancel my afternoon walk. I don't want to be drenched!
13. Andy, you did not replace my tools properly. If you don't return items to their proper place, you will not be able to organize your house or your personal property. And if you are not organized, then you will not be able to manage your money. Moreover, if you cannot manage your money, then you will eventually end up destitute and homeless!
14. Everyone in my art club says that it is OK to throw rocks at birds. Hence, everyone else must think that such behavior is acceptable too!
15. I learned that Hyundai Sonatas consume more gasoline each year than 18-wheel semitrailer trucks. Hence, my mom's new Sonata must use more gasoline than that big rig truck Joe drives!
16. Joe's engine light flashed right before his car stalled. Those darn lights should be taken out of vehicles since they cause them to stall all the time!

17. The highest homicide rates coincide with the highest ice cream sales each year. It must be all that sugar in the ice cream that causes people to commit murder!
18. Either you accept every passage in the Bible literally or you are not a good Christian. You did not follow the instructions in Deuteronomy that said you should stone your child to death if he or she disobeys you! Therefore, you are not a good Christian.
19. My uncle Don is the coolest guy I know. He must spend a lot of time in the refrigerator!
20. Since no one ever disproved the Hindu doctrine of reincarnation, it is a fact that everyone will be reborn after death.
21. Since Judo, Brazilian Jiu-Jitsu, and Catch Wrestling were all very easy for you, and you won many competitions in all three, I think that you should give them up and become a ballet dancer instead!
22. Do you still con people into giving you money so that you may buy illegal drugs?
23. The label on that bag of potato chips says that they have 40 percent less fat per serving than the leading brand! So, if I eat the new potato chips I won't gain any weight!
24. Senator Richardson never tells the truth because he fabricates stories that no one in their right mind would believe!
25. John, you have been a reliable and flexible employee for the last four years. You are a very passionate teacher and always receive the most positive evaluations from students. Your courses always have good enrollment, and recently you accumulated some impressive publications. You are just what our department needs. But there are hundreds of thousands of people in this country who are unemployed and would not only be happy to have your job but would do it for less money. Hence, we cannot justify giving you a raise.
26. Because Warwick is a master chess player, you should take him seriously when he says that the United States should implement the same social and legal policies as Singapore.
27. On the sidewalk, Joe could easily see the White House. The sidewalk must have been huge, though, if the White House can fit on it!
28. My psychology professor recently conducted an experiment designed to increase our knowledge about romantic relationships. Obviously, he wants to find ways to control the wills and emotions of other people. So, we should all be very careful of him.
29. Last night, Greg was assaulted and robbed by an assailant in a ski mask. Because he didn't see the perpetrator's face, Greg could not identify him. However, he knows the identity of his best friend, Rupert. So, obviously, Rupert cannot be the one who accosted Greg!
30. The government's spending of our income tax money on public education without our permission is wrong; therefore, the government's actions are a violation of our human rights. Furthermore, since the government's actions are a violation of our human rights, it follows that the government's spending of our income tax money on public education without our permission is wrong.

**Set II:** Answer each of the following questions as completely as possible.

1. Choose one of the fallacious arguments from section I and reconstruct it into an argument that commits no fallacy.
2. Do the following:
    a. Choose one informal fallacy and explain how it commits all four of Bacon's idols of the mind.
    b. For each of Bacon's idols of the mind, find a specific fallacy that best represents it (a different fallacy should represent each idol).

3. Do the following:
   a. Choose one informal fallacy and explain how it commits at least four different cognitive biases.
   b. Choose four different cognitive biases and match each one to a different informal fallacy, explaining how the fallacy perfectly represents its associated bias.
4. Explain how informal fallacies may be committed in each of the following fields and suggest how to avoid such occurrences: philosophy, religious studies, literature, history, art, music, theater, biology, chemistry, physics, psychology, sociology, anthropology, political science, mathematics, economics, and business management and administration.
5. Choose one of your favorite books, stories, movies, celebrities, or activities, and then use three different informal fallacies to convince your professor that he or she should like them.
6. Watch the American crime show *The People vs. O.J. Simpson* and explain how at least one informal fallacy from each category is committed.
7. Find an example of an argument in a recent newspaper or magazine article, speech, movie, or television show (other than *The People vs. O.J. Simpson*!) that commits an informal fallacy. Then, try to reconstruct the argument so that it commits no fallacy.
8. Write a dialogue between two people on any topic of your choice. Have one character appeal to at least one informal fallacy from each category to defend their position and then have the second character refute the arguments by showing them to be fallacious.

# 9

# Morality and Moral Reasoning

INTRODUCTION

## Preparing to Read Chapter 9

Recall that a fundamental principle of Socrates is that justice is good for the human soul, while injustice is bad for the human soul. In other words, living a righteous and just life is always in a person's best interest, while living in a corrupt and malicious way is always harmful to a person despite the perceived instrumental value achieved by harming others. Thus, living a moral life should be a top priority for everyone and a goal toward which one's critical thinking skills should be directed. This chapter attempts to improve students' understanding of the very deep and complex question, "How should I live?" Specifically, the following questions will be addressed:

1) How can I determine the difference between right and wrong?
2) How should I act in any given situation?

A plethora of answers have been proposed to answer the first question. Moreover, it further complicates matters that however one answers the first question influences how one answers the second. Several answers to the first question will be addressed, including each of the following:

- Whatever I think is right is right for me.
- Whatever my social group says is right is right for me.
- Whatever my religion says is right is right for me.
- Whatever is in my own best interest is right for me.
- Whatever produces the best overall results for everyone is right.
- The rules of the social contract reveal right and wrong.
- Only those actions that prevent the collapse of civilization into a state of nature are right.
- Only those actions that can be chosen from behind a veil of ignorance are right.

- Only those actions that everyone can do universally are right.
- Instead of figuring out the difference between right and wrong, I will just focus on becoming a good person by developing virtues of character.

As is the case in most areas of philosophy, the problem with the study of morality is not that there are too few answers but that there are too many! Even this list of answers to the central question of morality is not exhaustive. Nonetheless, each of these answers has strengths and weaknesses. Each theory will be concisely explained and assessed.[1]

## AS YOU READ, LOOK FOR THE FOLLOWING TERMS

- Moral Nihilism
- Moral Skepticism
- Moral Dogmatism
- Moral Objectivism
- Moral Relativism
    - Individual Relativism
    - Ethical Relativism
    - Cultural Relativism
- Emotivism
- Divine Command Theory
- Infallible Guide Theory
- Natural Law Theory
    - Teleology
- Consequentialism
    - Ethical Egoism
    - Psychological Egoism
    - Utilitarianism
        - Act-Utilitarianism
        - Rule-Utilitarianism
- Social Contract Theory
    - Hobbesian Contract Theory
    - The Original Position
    - The Veil of Ignorance
    - Rawlsian Ideal Contract Theory

1 For more detailed examinations of these theories, see James Rachels, *Elements of Moral Philosophy*, 9th ed. (New York: McGraw-Hill, 2019). An additional useful text is Jonathan Wolff, *An Introduction to Moral Philosophy* (New York: Norton & Norton, 2020). Moreover, I am indebted to Professor Mylan Engel of Northern Illinois University for supplying many of the formal criteria of rightness in his course, "Contemporary Moral Issues," specifically for relativistic theories, divine command theory, infallible guide theory, act and rule-utilitarianism, and Rawlsian ideal contract theory.

- Kantian Ethics
  - Goodwill
  - The Categorical Imperative
  - The Universal Law Formula
  - The End-in-Itself Formula
  - Perfect versus Imperfect Duties
- Virtue Ethics
  - The Meaning of "Virtue"
  - The Four Cardinal Virtues
    - Justice
    - Courage
    - Moderation
    - Prudence (Wisdom)
  - The Problem of Incompleteness

**KEEP THE FOLLOWING QUESTIONS IN MIND AS YOU READ**

- Why should anyone be moral?
- Which moral theory do I think is best?
- How can I address the problems with my chosen theory?
- Can any of these moral theories be put together to form a new theory?
- How can I apply any of these theories to issues in my everyday life?

## Moral Relativism

**Moral relativism** generally may be defined in the following way:

- The idea that there are no *universal* moral absolutes.

This doctrine should be distinguished from each of the following positions:

- **Moral Nihilism:** The idea that there are *no* moral absolutes whatsoever.
- **Moral Skepticism:** The idea that there *may be* moral absolutes, but such principles *cannot be known to us.*
- **Moral Dogmatism:** The uncritical, unreflective acceptance of moral principles taught by the authorities of one's culture.
- **Emotivism:** The idea that moral principles are merely expressions of one's emotions, one's "feelings."

While each of these positions differs from moral relativism, each is usually embraced either based on a more general relativistic outlook or is marshaled as an unwarranted assumption to justify such an outlook. With respect to *moral nihilism*, proponents of this doctrine usually adopt it because there is no general agreement about right and wrong. The fact that people disagree about morality leads many to the conclusion that there are no moral standards. Even if people have different moral standards, there are still *individual* moral standards, just not *universal moral standards*.

As for *moral skepticism*, the lack of consensus about morality leads its proponents to the more plausible but still erroneous conclusion that there *may be moral standards* but they cannot be *known* to anyone. Once again though, even if moral standards differ from person to person, from social group to social group, or from culture to culture, one can know those standards simply by conversing with the individuals who hold them. Moreover, skepticism itself is a flawed view, as addressed in Chapter 4.

Turning to *moral dogmatism*, this doctrine essentially encourages people to accept blindly what they are taught by various authority figures without ever subjecting such teachings to question. Hence, moral dogmatism gives people permission not to exert the effort of thinking for themselves in trying to discern right from wrong. The social institutions and authorities of one's culture did all the work for them! This doctrine, thus, really is no different than the doctrine of ethical relativism to be defined shortly.

Lastly, *emotivism* suggests that moral principles are merely expressions of emotion. For instance, if an action elicits a positive emotion, such as pleasure, then that action is morally permissible, or morally right. If an action causes a negative emotion, such as pain, then that action is morally impermissible, or wrong. On another school of thought, moral assertions merely express one's feelings. For instance, suppose Andy has an extra $100, and he decides that the right thing to do is to give the money to charity. Proponents of emotivism would suggest that the statement "The right thing for Andy to do is to donate his money to charity" translates into "Donating the money to charity makes Andy happy." Regardless, what causes pleasure and other positive experiences vary from person to person, as do the causes of pain. Hence, by emotivism, the standards of right and wrong will vary from person to person. This doctrine is very similar to individual relativism, defined as follows:

In general, there are three forms of moral relativism:

- **Individual Relativism:** Act x is right for person S if and only if S believes that x is right.
- **Ethical Relativism:** Act x is right for person S if and only if the social group to which S belongs says that x is right.
- **Cultural Relativism:** Each culture has different moral standards. (Note the difference between *ethical* and *cultural* relativism. The former is a *normative, prescriptive* theory, indicating what people ought to do, whereas the latter is a *factual, descriptive* theory, reporting peoples' lives and behaviors.)

Each of these theories will be addressed in turn.

## Individual Relativism

Beginning with *individual relativism*, the first and most obvious problem with this theory is that *certain obviously wrong actions become right* if one embraces them. For instance, if Joe Smith simply believes that it is morally permissible to rape and torture people, then such actions are morally permissible for Joe Smith, even though the general consensus is that such acts are morally reprehensible. A second problem with individual relativism is that if everyone embraced it, no one could ever criticize anyone else's moral principles, even if two people hold completely contradictory beliefs. For example, if Alice Jones believes that it is not morally permissible to rape people, but Joe Smith assents to the opposite, then Alice cannot object to Joe's actions should he try to rape anyone, including herself. Nonetheless, most people intuitively recognize the principle that no one ought to harm anyone else. Hence, most people would likely object to being harmed or raped and, thus, would dismiss individual relativism if the theory allowed one to be harmed in any way. A third problem with individual relativism parallels that of alethic relativism: *if individual relativism is true, then no one can ever be wrong in one's moral judgments.* In other words, individual relativism implies that everyone is infallible. But as noted in the discussion of alethic relativism, no one is infallible. Everyone errs in judgment on occasion. Furthermore, if two people hold contradictory beliefs—i.e., "rape is morally permissible" versus "rape is not morally permissible"—they cannot *both* be true. The only coherent way to hold such incompatible principles would be to add a qualifier specifying the person who holds each belief—i.e., "rape is morally permissible for Joe Smith" versus "rape is not morally permissible for Alice Jones." Even such qualifications result in statements that are *logically* compatible, they assume a principle of comparative injustice that no one would or should want to embrace.

## Ethical and Cultural Relativism

Turning now to *ethical relativism*, similar problems abound. Although ethical relativism at least places the criteria for the permissibility of actions in the hands of a group rather than the whims of an individual, groups can still err in judgment. A group's decision may still yield actions that are obviously wrong. For instance, anti-Semitism in Nazi Germany and the fact that slavery was legal in America prior to the country's civil war are glaring examples of the leaders of nations making decisions that are morally reprehensible. Moreover, like with individual relativism, if all people embrace the precepts of their group and the doctrine of ethical relativism itself, then no members of a group can ever criticize the moral decisions of any other group. And once again, ethical relativism implies that every group is infallible, that no group can ever be wrong in their moral decisions.

An additional troubling implication of ethical relativism is that the group to which an individual belongs is never entirely clear. Every individual seems to belong to many different groups and organizations. Return to the hypothetical Joe Smith. Suppose that Joe Smith lives in the United States of America, specifically in Fairfield, Connecticut, has a family, belongs to a specific school, plays basketball, participates in student government, is a member of a specific church, and assists his neighborhood in their crime watch program. There are, thus, at least seven different groups to which Joe belongs and from whom his moral principles may derive. Which group is *the* basis for Joe's morals and values? Moreover, even if Joe can narrow down his specific group, how did that group decide which moral principles to accept and implement? They likely took a vote and the majority ruled, in which case the group simply adopted the opinions of the most individuals possible. But what if a group cannot form a consensus? What if a group cannot determine a single view with a simple vote? It seems that a coup, or a hostile takeover, would be necessary, in which case the dominant view of the group is determined via a "might makes right" mentality. But using physical force to develop institutional principles *undermines the very idea of moral progress.* People and the various institutions they serve want to improve upon the past. But if the best that can be done is to bully those physically weaker into accepting one's point of view, then the group that subscribes to such a mantra is no better than the barbarians and tyrants of eons past.

It seems that neither individual nor ethical relativism provides solid foundations for morality. But is ethical relativism not implied by *cultural relativism*? Have not anthropologists and sociologists observed that all cultures around the world significantly differ from each other in important ways? Specifically, do not all cultures have different customs and moral principles? Aboriginal people in Australia, for instance, kill their elders at the age of

60! Many other indigenous cultures force their children to partake in very painful and dangerous rites of passage into adulthood, such as surgeries without anesthesia. Moreover, many countries outside the United States, such as Canada, do not have the death penalty for capital crimes. In Sweden, physician-assisted suicides are legal. Does not the acceptance of such different practices imply a form of ethical relativism, that people should generally follow the dictates of their social group?

First, even if one accepts that cultural relativism implies a form of ethical relativism, such an inference does not resolve the problems facing ethical relativism itself. Second, and more importantly, recall that cultural relativism is a *descriptive* but not a *prescriptive* theory; it describes only *what* people do but not what they *should* do. Part of the description of a culture's behaviors and rites, however, is the worldview behind them. Imagine, for instance, a culture of people who eat the remains of their dead. While this practice seems at worst horrific and at best very strange to people in the industrialized West, suppose that the reason for this practice is that the members of this culture *do not want the remains of the dead to go to waste*. Thus, they feel that eating their remains is *necessary to respect human life*. Moreover, the Aborigines of Australia believe that in the afterlife, people will possess the same bodies they occupy in this lifetime. Thus, they determined that after 60 years, a person has lived in this lifetime long enough but is still in reasonably good shape for eternity. In both cases, *respect for human life* is a value that motivates the ritual, and generally, all cultures share such a value, even though they do not necessarily share the same overall worldview. Moreover, the rituals that allow adolescents of many cultures to pass into adulthood constitute tests of *courage* and *resilience*. It seems that all cultures value such virtues as courage and resilience. Hence, on close inspection, while the practices and worldviews of cultures may differ, *all cultures still have some values in common*, and if so, then not all morality is merely a matter of what individuals or any one specific group dictate.[2]

By finding what people have in common, perhaps some common ground for the basis of morality in addition to common moral principles can be ascertained. Most cultures have some form of religion. Perhaps religion can provide a basis for moral principles.

## Religious Moral Theories

As the title of this category of moral theories suggests, religious moral theories attempt to justify moral absolutes based on the teachings of a religious worldview. The English word "religion" derives from the Latin words "re" and "ligare." Together, these terms translate into "linking back" or "to link back." The etymology of "religion" implies that embracing and following the doctrines of a religion reconnects an individual with the primal source of their being, with the world and reality. If religion truly does link people to reality in rich ways, then it should make available moral absolutes. To paraphrase John Arthur,[3] people traditionally believe that religion is the basis of morality for three kinds of reasons:

1) **Psychological Reasons:** Religion is necessary to motivate people to live morally (i.e., the good are rewarded in heaven, and the wicked are punished in hell).
2) **Epistemological Reasons:** Religion is necessary so people will know the difference between right and wrong (i.e., the Bible, Koran, Upanishads, Dhammapada, Analects of Confucius, Tao Te Ching, etc., teach people how to live).

2 See the discussion of the relationship between cultural and ethical relativism in Rachels, *Elements*, 21–7.
3 See John Arthur, "Morality, Religion, and Conscience," in *Morality and Moral Controversies: Readings in Moral, Social, and Political Philosophy, eds.* John Arthur and Steven Scalet (New York: Routledge, 2016), 25–32.

3) **Metaphysical Reasons:** Religion is necessary for there to be moral absolutes (i.e., God somehow sets moral standards).

This section addresses three major religious moral theories:

- **Divine Command Theory**
- **Infallible Guide Theory**
- **Natural Law Theory**

Divine command and infallible guide theory will be addressed first.

## Divine Command Theory and Infallible Guide Theory

The distinction between *divine command* and *infallible guide theory* rests on an ambiguity in the following statement:

**$R_A$:** Everything God tells us to do is right.

This statement may be interpreted in two ways. It might mean the following:

**$R_1$:** Act x is right because God commands it.

Or, it could mean,

**$R_2$:** God commands act x because it is right.

The statement R1 represents **divine command theory** (hereafter, DCT) whereas R2 represents **infallible guide theory** (hereafter, IGT). This dilemma is sometimes called the "Euthyphro problem," as Plato's dialogue *Euthyphro* contains a similar presentation of the distinction. Each theory, however, faces serious obstacles.

Prima facie, DCT has problems like those of individual relativism, except that the individual in this case is the omnipotent, omniscient, and infallible God, the will to whom we mere mortals must bend. What if God, for instance, commanded a person to do something horrific, such as torture an innocent person? Just like individual relativism, DCT seems to make certain obviously wrong actions right. The obvious objection from proponents of DCT, however, is that "God would not command obviously wrong actions." But this objection implies that morality, right and wrong, what agents ought to do, *are not solely determined by God's will.* If actions are right *merely because* God commands them, then anything God commands is right solely in virtue of God's will. But if God would not command specific actions because they are wrong, then *there must be an independent moral standard apart from God's will.*

Proponents of IGT accept that there is an independent standard of morality apart from God's will. They maintain that God commands actions to people because those actions are right. In other words, God knows moral standards perfectly, and his infinite and perfect wisdom is necessary to impart morality to humans. However, the main obstacle for IGT, which also serves as a challenge to DCT, is that there are problems determining just *what* exactly God commands. Typically, proponents of any religious theory would suggest that its practitioners consult a religious text to determine the commands of God. The Jews have the Hebrew Bible (basically, the Old Testament known as the Tanakh), while Christians have the Judeo-Christian Bible. Muslims have the Koran. Hindus have the Upanishads. Buddhists have the teachings of the Buddha. Followers of Confucius have his Analects and what Confucius referred to as the "Decree of Heaven." However, simply listing these alternatives underscores the problem: Which should an agent choose? The Judeo-Christian Bible seems replete with contradictions, specifically between the Old and New Testaments. Many Islamic beliefs overlap with those of Judaism and Christianity but many differ as well. How does one decide between them? The teachings of Confucius differ starkly from those of the Buddha, whose teachings largely derive from Hinduism. It seems that the best the individual can do is choose the religion that he or she prefers, but to do so dangerously approximates individual relativism or perhaps ethical relativism, given that religions tend to amass very large, complicated social groups.

Moreover, which of these religions have the correct conception of God? And if one rejects religious texts because God somehow communicates with them directly, how can anyone verify that one really can communicate with God? How can we determine that the conduit between God and the rest of humanity is being truthful? What if the person "hearing God" is only hallucinating, in which case he or she is probably mentally ill?

Lastly, if there is an independent moral standard apart from God's will, why can people not access such a standard without God? How can anyone even have the idea of such a standard if one cannot determine the nature of God or how the process of communication with this being occurs? In addition, the idea that religion is necessary to motivate people to live just and righteous lives raises additional problems. People are motivated by many different internal and external factors, not solely by the desire to be rewarded or to avoid punishment in a possible afterlife. Even those who subscribe to such a notion often do not live as if it is in fact true. Moreover, obedience to a God merely because one wishes to avoid punishment seems to differ very little from living under the ministrations of a tyrant. Those in favor of a secular foundation for morality maintain that any such religious basis for morality undermines the possibility of moral integrity since it justifies morality through the concepts of reward and punishment. It seems that neither DCT nor IGT provides solid foundations for morality, but perhaps natural law theory can be of some usefulness.

## Natural Law Theory

**Natural law theory** has its roots in both the Christian philosophy of Thomas Aquinas and the virtue ethics of Aristotle (considered in more detail later in the chapter). It is difficult to do this theory justice with limited space, but despite its complexities, this natural law theory can be understood as affirming three concise theses[4]:

**NL1:** Everything in nature is designed to fulfill a specific purpose.

**NL2:** Nature sets normative and prescriptive standards.

**NL3:** The faculty of reason allows people to discern the normative standards of nature.

In essence, proponents of natural law theory (hereafter, NLT) maintain that morality comes from humans but only because God made humans. Morality, thus, is not merely arbitrary but built into human nature and the nature of the world. Furthermore, morality is not merely a matter of reward and punishment but part of a divine plan. For a creature to flourish, it must fulfill its natural purpose. What a thing is determines what it needs and its goal. A dog, for instance, cannot flourish if it is fed the diet of a rabbit or a beaver. The same is true for humans. Humans cannot be happy if they pursue only those items that would satisfy dogs, cats, chickens, squirrels, or any other nonhuman animal. Humans cannot hope to be happy if they stray from the dictates of nature. However, through the natural light of reason God gifted humanity, people can discern their natural purpose and how to achieve it. In other words, God gave humans the ability to figure out how to be truly and fully happy. We can discern that nature is the product

4 See Rachels, *Elements*, 56–9, for a similar explanation of natural law theory,.

of design with purpose and intent and, thus, that human beings have a purpose. For religious thinkers, such as St. Thomas Aquinas, ultimate happiness requires union with God and, thus, cannot be achieved in the present lifetime.

Proponents of NLT maintain that actions that contradict nature are immoral in some way. For instance, typically, religious proponents maintain that specific kinds of sexual persuasion and behaviors are "wrong" because they are unnatural, such as homosexuality and masturbation. But herein lies one of the major problems with NLT: *not all actions that are unnatural are immoral.* For instance, dancing is not a natural activity, but it is not immoral. Performing cartwheels, handstands, or gymnastics does not constitute natural human behavior but such things are not immoral. In addition, contemporary scientists generally reject the idea of *teleology*, the notion that everything exists to serve a purpose, that the world and universe at large are products of design. Instead, contemporary scientists favor a mechanical and evolutionary understanding of reality as having developed as the product of a series of glorious accidents in a causal chain that took several billion years without the guidance of an infinitely powerful being.

Before closing this discussion of religious moral theories, it is important to note that there remains a contingent of scientists and intellectuals who strongly favor the idea of intelligent design given the minuscule probability that a planet like Earth, a planet that can give rise to and sustain complex intelligent life, can emerge without some guiding intelligence. Moreover, most religions of the world, specifically, Christianity, maintain that humans are fallen creatures, imperfect. Hence, they are bound to engage in activities that run contrary to their nature. Finally, many intellectuals argue that even if morality cannot be grounded in religion, religious beliefs can enhance morality in many ways. Louis Pojman, for instance, argues that religious beliefs assure people that living a moral life is not in vain, that religion assures people that good will prevail over evil, and that cosmic justice reigns in the universe. Nonetheless, many popular moral theories are secular in nature and must be addressed.

## Consequentialism

In general, **consequentialism** may be defined in the following way:

- The idea that actions should be judged based on their *results*. An action is good if it has good results and bad if it has bad results.

Like NLT, consequentialism is rooted in *teleology*, though in a purely secular, quantitative, situation-relative sense. This section addresses two major versions of consequentialism:

- **Ethical Egoism**
- **Utilitarianism,** which may be broken down further into two sub-theories:
    - **Act-Utilitarianism**
    - **Rule-Utilitarianism**

### Ethical Egoism

As with previous moral theories, understanding the meaning of the terms that label each theory in addition to the general meaning of consequentialism can function as a helpful guide to learning and remembering the theories. For instance, **ethical egoism** may be defined in the following way:

- **Ethical egoists** maintain that act x is right for person S if and only if x produces the *best* results for S.

In other words, everyone ought to do whatever is best for herself or himself. This doctrine should not be confused with individual relativism, which holds that any individual may do whatever he or she *thinks* or *believes* to be right. One might think that an action is right, but that action may not be in one's best interest, such as an individual who believes that it is permissible to drive while intoxicated.

Typically, the ethical egoist will say, "I have a right to do what is best for me." In fact, many believe that such a doctrine is not only perfectly natural but entirely necessary. Moral philosophers generally agree with the principle "ought implies can." Suppose that a person, S, ought to do act x. In this case, S is responsible for doing x. S can be praised for doing x and blamed for not doing x. If so, then S must at least be *able* to do x. For instance, if a teenager works a summer job landscaping but the crew falls behind because of frequent and unpredictable inclement weather, it is absurd for the leader of the crew to blame his workers for the job not being finished on time, as no one can control the weather. However, many thinkers believe that no one can completely control their actions, that people instinctively do what is in their own self-interest and avoid anything that conflicts with self-interest. This doctrine is called **psychological egoism:**

- **Psychological egoism** is the doctrine that people are incapable of behaving in ways that conflict with their own self-interest.

If psychological egoism is true, then no one can be held responsible for an action if that action conflicts with their self-interest. Hence, the *only* moral theory that can accommodate the "ought implies can" principle is ethical egoism. Psychological egoism, thus, seems to justify ethical egoism.

Nonetheless, ethical egoism has several problems. First, like the relativistic theories, *it seems to permit obviously wrong actions*. For example, if John and Dave are competing for a promotion and a 20 percent increase in their salaries. It is in the best interest of both agents to eliminate the competition to achieve the promotion. John, however, is the more aggressive of the two. So, he decides to push Dave out of a very high window and make the event look like a suicide. John's actions, however, a clearly morally despicable. Doing what is best for oneself, thus, does not always equate to doing the right thing.

Second, *psychological egoism seems to be erroneous*. That is, people often seem quite capable of acting against their own self-interest. Heroic individuals often put their own well-being at risk to save the lives of others. Such actions include rushing into a burning building to save those inside, diving into a stream headed toward a waterfall to save a drowning child, or a soldier jumping on top of a grenade to save his platoon. Proponents of psychological egoism may respond that such actions, at bottom, truly extend from the motive of self-interest. For instance, no one would risk one's life if one did not desire the recognition, status, and respect of being a hero. Moreover, soldiers are trained and conditioned to sacrifice themselves for the good of the group. However, a soldier sacrificing his or her own life for the good of others still conflicts with one's *self-interest*. Furthermore, psychological egoism is allegedly a scientific theory. As such, it should be a *falsifiable* theory. But if its proponents construct the theory and the idea of human motivation such that no action conflicts with self-interest, then their theory seems to resist being stated in a falsifiable way. If that is the case, then it should either be rejected or at least evaluated with skepticism.

Finally, *many ethicists deny that ethical egoism is a true moral theory*. That is, a moral theory is supposed to address not only the well-being of oneself but of others as well. As such, it should address how one's actions affect others. But ethical egoists are concerned only with the well-being of the individual, hence why it permits obviously wrong actions in many cases. Ultimately, thus, ethical egoism does not seem to be a suitable moral theory.

# Utilitarianism

**Utilitarianism** constitutes a more popular and plausible consequential alternative among moral philosophers. Like ethical egoism, it has roots in naturalism and empiricism, ideas favored by Jeremy Bentham, a pioneer of the theory. Bentham lived in the mid-nineteenth century, a time during which intellectuals began to embrace evolutionary theories that placed human beings on a continuum with all other animals and the natural world. Humans were no longer understood as special, privileged creatures created in the image and likeness of divinity but merely apex predators atop the food chain. All animals universally seek pleasure and avoid pain, humans included. In the early twentieth century, the behavioral psychologist E. L. Thorndike coined the **law of effect**, which states that all living creatures will continue to act in ways that produce pleasure and avoid acting in ways that produce pain. Recognizing this principle in the previous century, Bentham used it as the foundation of his moral theory hoping to inspire social and legal reform. His version of utilitarianism may be called **hedonistic act-utilitarianism:**

- **Hedonistic act-utilitarianism** (HAU) is the idea that act x is right for person S if and only if, out of all options available to S, x maximizes pleasure and minimizes pain for all affected by x.

In other words, in any given situation, one should choose the action that produces the greatest amount of pleasure and minimum amount of pain. In essence, this theory seeks to make as many people happy as possible. Since situations will vary, the action that is consequentially the best will vary as well. A classic problem that applies to HAU is the "trolley problem." Suppose that there are two sets of divergent tracks and a trolley that cannot be stopped. On the first set of tracks stands one person while on the second stand five people. Imagine that you have the power to pull a lever to divert the trolley. Traditional HAU implies that you should divert the trolley to the first set of tracks, killing only one person but saving five, yielding a net gain of four.

Generally, utilitarians, including those of the HAU variety, insist that people rely on general rules of thumb and only make exceptions in extreme situations, such as the hypothetical one involving the trolley. HAU has many benefits since it is a flexible, quantifiable, and results-oriented theory. However, it has many problems as well. Traditionally, critics make the following criticisms of HAU:

- **HAU permits morally reprehensible actions.**
- **HAU is too narrow since pleasure and pain are not the only factors relevant to moral decisions.**
- **HAU is too demanding since it makes supererogatory actions obligatory.**
- **HAU forces agents to violate their special obligations to others.**

Each of these objections deserves to be further explained.[5]

## HAU Permits Certain Obviously Wrong Actions

Its critics assert that, in at least three ways, HAU permits morally reprehensible actions:

1) HAU cannot accommodate individual rights.
2) HAU cannot accommodate justice.
3) HAU cannot accommodate backward-looking reasons.

5 Rachels, *Elements*, 119–31. See also Wolff, *An Introduction*, 197–211 for his discussion of these and additional objections to utilitarianism.

With respect to the problem of individual rights, utilitarians typically deny that there are any natural rights, that talk about rights is merely fictitious, "idols of the market-place," perhaps. Suppose, however, that five young men brutally rape a young woman. Since there are five rapists and one victim, the pleasure experienced by the rapists most likely outweighs the pain and suffering experienced by the victim. According to HAU, it seems that the actions of the rapists are not merely permissible but *obligatory.* But their actions are not only clearly wrong but despicable!

Furthermore, objections to HAU based on justice usually invoke the "scapegoat" problem. Imagine that there is a serial killer at large in a small community. Because law enforcement agents failed to identify the assailant, vigilantes gather into groups and seek out the perpetrator independently. To stop the riots, the sheriff decides to frame an innocent person, a scapegoat, as more people are dying from the vigilantes than from the crimes of the unknown subject. The attempted damage control succeeds, at least temporarily, but the killer is still at large. And what would happen if anyone uncovered the conspiracy? Certainly, that would not maximize utility.

In addition, *backward-looking reasons* contrast with *forward-looking reasons.* Recall that HAU is a consequential theory, meaning that it determines the value of an action based on its results. Thus, when applying HAU to decide how to act, one must think about the *future* and act on reasons that are *forward-looking,* such as pulling the switch to kill one person on the tracks and allowing five to live. A *backward-looking* reason justifies an action by appealing to something in the past. For example, physicians take a Hippocratic oath before practicing medicine, by which they pledge to do no harm. However, if a physician were to use a drug to assist a terminally ill patient in committing suicide, then the physician violates his oath, even though the action ends the pain and suffering of the patient. In that case, the physician dismisses a backward-looking reason in favor of maximizing utility, a forward-looking reason.

## HAU Is Too Narrow

The second general criticism of HAU, the "narrowness" objection, has two aspects. On the one hand, there are some actions that maximize physical pleasure but seem to fall short of establishing the best possible scenario. Despite their physical benefits, they are deficient in a broader sense. For instance, suppose a very talented painter loses both of his hands in a car accident. Nonetheless, once recovered, he finds that collecting disability payments while watching Netflix all day, every day elicits exactly as much pleasure as his painting did. This example is comparable to Nozick's famous thought-experiment of the "experience machine." If one were plugged into an artificial device that allowed for the perpetual experience of pleasure for the duration of one's existence, such a state of being would seem hardly to maximize utility but more to constitute a waste of one's life. On the other hand, there are some actions that seem to produce no physical pain but are still objectionable. For instance, if an acquaintance who pretends to be your friend verbally sabotages you without your knowledge, you experience no physical displeasure, but the actions of your acquaintance are still wrong. It seems, thus, that pleasure and pain are not the sole determinants of morality.

Bentham's successor and protégé, John Stuart Mill, offered an alternative interpretation of HAU, suggesting that there are different kinds of pleasure, some of which are higher or more sophisticated than others. Surely, there is a difference between the pleasure experienced by a pig rolling in the mud and the pleasure experienced by a mathematician who after several tries finally proves a difficult theorem. According to Mill, the higher pleasures are those that should be maximized, as opposed to the pleasure of pigs. Nonetheless, there are at least two problems with Mill's alternative. First, he claims that to distinguish the superior pleasures from the inferior, we must rely on a poll from "competent judges." Such a poll, however, may easily collapse into a form of relativism based on the personal tastes of a few. Second, if there is truly a distinction between the higher and lower pleasures, then there must be some independent standard by which the distinction is made. Such a standard, however, may imply that pleasure and pain are not the only relevant factors in making moral decisions.

The narrowness objection, thus, seems quite damaging to HAU. At its core, HAU is a *monistic* theory, meaning that its proponents recognize that there is only one property that is intrinsically good—pleasure—and only one property that is intrinsically bad—pain. Other versions of utilitarianism recognize additional intrinsically good properties—such as truth, beauty, and justice—that should be maximized as well. This doctrine may be called *pluralistic utilitarianism*. Even though pluralistic versions of utilitarianism are more expansive, several problems remain. First, *how* exactly can properties such as truth, beauty, and justice be maximized? Truth, it seems, may be achieved simply by being as honest as possible. However, honesty can lead to very disastrous consequences. For instance, if my lady friend asks me if I like her new hairstyle and I answer honestly, telling her that I hate it, my friendship is damaged. Imagine such a consequence magnified on a larger scale, such as if a government leader were totally honest about some of the horrific actions that a nation must undertake to keep its constituents safe from harm. Moreover, maximizing a complex property such as justice first demands that moral philosophers agree to a universal definition of justice. But to avoid circularity or collapse into a hedonistic form of utilitarianism, a universal definition of justice must not be stated in purely consequential terms. Justice, thus, transcends consequentialism. Moreover, recognizing an object as beautiful seems to rely too heavily on personal taste and subjectivity. But even if a group of aestheticians designates universal criteria that constitute beauty, why maximize beauty over justice? That is a *second* problem with pluralistic utilitarianism: *How does one choose which goods to maximize?* The simple solution seems to be that one should maximize the good that produces the greatest amount of pleasure and least amount of pain, but such a prescription collapses back into HAU. The attempt to expand utilitarianism into a pluralistic form may only be an admission of its limits.

## HAU Is Too Demanding

A third common objection to HAU is that it is *too demanding*, in other words, it makes *supererogatory* actions obligatory. The term "supererogatory" literally means "beyond what is asked." For example, if I have a spare $20 that I do not intend to spend on anything I want or need, I choose to donate that money to a local charity. My donation is supererogatory. I had no obligation to donate the money, and by going above and beyond the call of my duty, I acted in an exemplary way and should be praised. If one assumes the principle of utility, however, one must always act to maximize the greatest possible good, in which case *there can be no such thing as a supererogatory action.* Consider the following scenario:

> Sam goes to a hospital to visit a friend who recently survived a car accident. At the same hospital are five patients awaiting organ transplants. One needs a heart, one a kidney, one a liver, one a spleen, and the last needs lungs. While visiting your friend, a nurse enters the room, and you tell her that if your friend needs a blood transfusion, you will volunteer. You tell the nurse your blood type: $AB^{+}$. She says that your friend's blood type is O−, so you cannot donate to him. However, she knows that each of the five patients has the same blood type as you. Unbeknownst to you, however, the nurse is a utilitarian! She plans to give you an untraceable drug that induces a heart attack and give your organs to the five patients. Five lives outweigh one, after all.

This scenario seems horrific, but for an HA utilitarian, Sam's "donation" is merely par for the course. It is what any agent who accepts HAU is expected to do. But even by the American Medical Association standards, such a practice is not only immoral but *illegal*!

There are comparably mundane examples of the supererogation problem. For instance, imagine that you have tickets to a Goo Goo Dolls concert. Imagine also that said band is not one of your favorites and you are not overly enthusiastic about the concert, but you plan to attend anyway. However, you have a colleague at work who loves the Goo Goo Dolls and would be ecstatic if he had those tickets. According to HAU, you are *obligated* to give your tickets to your friend, as doing so maximizes utility. Should you really be under such an obligation, or should you find a moral theory that prescribes a more plausible and lenient resolution? Many ethicists prefer the latter route.

### HAU Forces People to Violate Special Obligations to Others

Finally, critics of HAU contend that the theory forces agents to violate their *special obligations* to others. In other words, if one fully commits oneself to HAU, then one cannot be a full-fledged friend, lover, or family member. For instance, suppose that two people are drowning and you cannot save both—your mother and a famous musician. According to HAU, since the musician is famous, saving the musician will likely make more people happy than saving your mother. But you have an inherent obligation to protect those closest to you, those within your inner circle, before helping others. It seems, thus, that what you ought to do is save your mother, even though doing so does not adhere to the principle of utility. Similar criticisms can be made with a modified version of the trolley example. For instance, imagine that the sole individual on the first track is your mother and the five people on the second track are strangers to you. In such a case, it seems that *your* obligation is to divert the trolley to the second track, even though HAU would oblige you to do the opposite.

### Rule-Utilitarianism

An alternative to HAU is **rule-utilitarianism:**

- **Rule-utilitarianism** is the idea that an action, x, is right for person S if and only if x conforms to rules whose universal adoption maximizes pleasure and minimizes pain for all affected by x.

In other words, the principle that all agents ought to act to maximize pleasure and minimize pain should be treated as a guide for choosing rules rather than individual actions. Proponents of rule-utilitarianism insist that some rules, if adopted by everyone, would in the long-term maximize utility. The main problem with rule-utilitarianism, however, is that any rule will have exceptions, cases in which breaking the rule is necessary to maximize utility. For instance, suppose that it is a general rule that people ought to keep their promises because doing so maximizes utility. If I promise to meet someone at noon, but on the way to that meeting I must stop and help a person who is severely injured, then I had to break my promise for what I perceived to be the greater good. In that case, I reverted to HAU. So why not simply embrace HAU fully, despite its flaws? Perhaps HAU is justified by its own primary principle, in that its benefits far outweigh its deficiencies.[6]

## Social Contract Theories

Once again, the general meaning of the theory is built into its title:

- **Social Contract Theories** assert that morality consists of a set of agreements between people translating into various rights and protections that dictate behavior.

These supposed "agreements" may be either implicit or explicit. For instance, living in a modern civil society runs parallel to playing a game. If an individual agrees to play a game, then that individual must adhere to the rules of the

6 For an excellent, classic treatment of the debate on utilitarianism see *Utilitarianism: For and Against*. J.J.C. Smart provides a defense of HAU, while Bernard Williams provides a unique critique of it.

game and accept the penalties if he or she breaks the rules, regardless of whether the rules were made explicit or not. Living in society demands that everyone follow specific rules. By participating in society, one implicitly agrees to its rules and is thus afforded the same privileges and protections as other participating members. The most general rule of civil society is that everyone must refrain from harming other people unless doing so is necessary to defend oneself. The two major social contract theories addressed in this section are the following:

- **Hobbesian Contract Theory**
- **Rawlsian Ideal Contract Theory**

## Hobbesian Contract Theory

**Hobbesian contract theory** derives from the writings of the sixteenth-century English philosopher and scientist Thomas Hobbes, more specifically from his book *Leviathan*. Hobbes argued that people must agree to a social contract to escape and avoid falling into the condition he famously coined the **state of nature**. There are at least two ways to understand the **state of nature**:

1) **Pre-Social State of Affairs:** A state of nature in this sense refers to the primordial, original condition of human beings prior to the emergence of complex social arrangements, governments, or civil society. It is characterized as a state in which people scavenge for resources necessary for their survival. Given that such resources are scarce and that there are no laws or central governing authorities to hold people accountable for their actions, anyone can do whatever is necessary to meet their needs. If a bigger, stronger person steals from you, you may sharpen a stick and use it as a weapon to defend yourself and reclaim your property. Or, if you can find others to assist you, mobilize with them and mount a retaliation. Just know that people will only help you if you can help them in return. Such conditions are like those imagined by contemporary evolutionary biologists when describing the lives of very early human beings.

3) **Post-Civil State of Affairs:** A state of nature in this sense is like the first but only comes to exist when a government, central ruling authority, or civilization collapses, leaving people to attempt to survive under the same conditions as the first.

Which of the two states of existence is worse is debatable but a post-civil state of nature would leave humans with access to more powerful and destructive weapons in addition to arguably more aggressive and voracious appetites than those of humans in a pre-social state of nature. Nonetheless, Hobbes argued that both would constitute a state of existence that is "solitary, poor, nasty, brutish, and short." The absence of any central ruling authority leaves people in a constant state of war, "a war of all against all."

Ultimately, Hobbes insists that escape from the state of nature requires that people formulate a set of agreements and principles, the most important being that they will not harm each other. Abiding by this rule requires that everybody exercise some self-control for the greater good. In addition, there must be a way to guarantee that people abide by this social contract. Hence, an individual with absolute power must enforce it, a sovereign, or a king. Hobbes compares this individual to the image of the Leviathan in his book by the same name. The Leviathan is a monstrous sea creature referenced in the Hebrew Bible. Prior to the discoveries of modern scientists and the famous voyages of Magellan and Columbus, many people feared travel by sea because of the possibility that such a creature may be lurking. Hobbes would insist that the sovereign who makes possible the social contract must be cloaked in the same mystique as this mythological creature, in which people are far too afraid that the Leviathan will know if they violate the contract and dispense retribution. Allegedly, people believed in the existence of such a creature because from the shore, the activity of dolphins diving in and out of the water appeared to be a giant serpent or dragon. Just as dolphins are far less threatening than the Leviathan, familiarity with the sovereign diminishes his power by diminishing the extent to which people fear him, which, in turn, diminishes his capacity to enforce the contract. And if the contract breaks, humanity descends into the perpetual state of war that characterizes the state of nature. The following, thus, constitutes a plausible formal criterion of rightness based on Hobbesian contract theory:

- **Hobbesian contract theory** states that act x is right for person S if and only if x conforms to a contract, either explicit or implicit, whose rules prevent the collapse of civil society into a state of nature.

As the idea of a "social contract" in the modern world may not refer to any document to which contemporary people explicitly agreed, Hobbesian contract theory generally refers to the implicit acceptance of criminal and civil laws in addition to implicit codes of conduct that are necessary to prevent harm to others.

Hobbesian presuppositions about human motivation parallel those of Machiavelli, who famously asserted that it is safer for a ruler, a prince, to be feared rather than loved. Both thinkers agree, thus, that given the human capacities for selfishness and deception, people must be coerced if they are to behave. People, generally, will not help others or act for the greater good unless they stand to gain something. For Hobbes, what people stand to gain by agreeing to a social contract is protection from the state of nature and the continued enjoyment of a civil society that promises security and the fulfillment of basic needs. Moreover, both Hobbes and Machiavelli would agree that people naturally view each other as obstacles to power; hence, *we are natural enemies*.

The primary flaw of Hobbes's contract is that someone clever enough might violate the contract without getting caught. If so, then the sovereign literally has no power to punish the perpetrator. In that case, it seems to follow that the culprit did nothing wrong since the contract is enforceable only if the sovereign has the power to punish the individual. Equally problematic is that power is relative. If this clever culprit also risks rebelling against the sovereign, this will potentially usher in a new regime. Hence, Hobbesian principles can yield no absolute contract. The power of the sovereign depends largely on perception, and whether his subjects believe him to be truly insuperable.

Additional problems emerge from the idea of the "state of nature," given that it can be interpreted in at least two ways. On the one hand, any description of the primordial living conditions of early humans is bound to be speculative to *some* extent, despite the evidence that contemporary evolutionary biology affords us. On the other hand, the values and tendencies obtained through socialization will inevitably emerge even after the collapse of that society, in which case, the behavior of people in the state of nature that follows may be the result of nurture, rather than nature. But perhaps humans are not as aggressive and hostile as Hobbes imagined. Rousseau, for instance, suggested that people are born good but that society corrupts them. Maybe society can be structured to produce the best possible human beings.

## Rawlsian Ideal Contract Theory

Ideal contract theory derives from the writings and thoughts of the twentieth-century philosopher John Rawls, specifically from his magnum opus *A Theory of Justice*. He did not necessarily agree with Rousseau, but he had a more optimistic outlook than that Hobbes. Rawls is often characterized as an **egalitarian**, meaning that he valued equality above all else. Hence, he defined justice as a kind of *fairness*. In this case, "fairness" refers to the most equal distribution of rights and resources possible. For Rawls, those who are born privileged, either economically or gifted with natural talents, are fortunate but did nothing to earn or deserve their privileges. Hence, everyone should benefit from the privileges and gifts enjoyed by the few. Rawls provides a procedure by which to derive rules and policies that are just by situating people in a hypothetical **original position** behind a **veil of ignorance**:

- **The Original Position:** People are allowed to choose principles of justice prior to any existing political or social arrangement.
- **The Veil of Ignorance:** One knows nothing of his or her position in society, economic background, talents, or privileges.

The original position is comparable to Hobbes's state of nature but without his assumptions about human nature. Given that everyone is situated behind a veil of ignorance with respect to their economic status, background, talents, privileges, and gender, people will likely choose to adopt only rules that are fair for everyone, as rules biased in one's favor may adversely affect the individual.

For example, consider the following scenario. William must determine the range of salaries for his firm. He does not know what position he holds in the firm. He may be the CEO, a high-ranking executive, an administrative assistant, a receptionist, a janitor, or may fulfill some other unspecified role. Given his situation, William will likely choose a salary range in which the employees at the very bottom of the firm make a fair salary comparable to those at the very top, since William may be one of the lower-ranking employees. Suppose that William considers the following options:

**Option A:** Highest Salary = $1,000,000.00 per year

Lowest Salary = $30,000.00 per year

**Option B:** Highest Salary = $750,000.000 per year

Lowest Salary = $50,000.00 per year

**Option C:** Highest Salary = $500,000.00 per year

Lowest Salary = $75,000.00 per year

Option C is the best, as it narrows the gap between the highest and lowest salaries. If William happens to be a high-ranking employee, he makes a very lucrative salary. But even if he is a low-ranking employee, he still makes a decent salary so he can make a comfortable living. This scenario illustrates what Rawls called **maximin thinking**, maximizing the minimum outcome. In other words, Rawls believes that situated behind a veil of ignorance, people will act to make the best of the worst possible scenario.

The Rawlsian conception of justice can be generalized to many situations, especially those in which one must make a moral decision. Using the concepts of the original position and the veil of ignorance, one can construct the following criterion of rightness:

- **Rawlsian ideal contract theory** suggests that act x is right for person S if and only if x would be chosen by any rational, self-interested agent in a hypothetical original position situated behind a veil of ignorance.

For example, suppose that Joe is considering a rule by which to make donations to charity. Imagine that he considers the rule, "I will never give any money to charity." Now, imagine that a person situated behind a veil of ignorance considers this rule. It is not likely a rule that one would adopt since once the veil is lifted the agent making the decision may need charity.

Given the wording of the criterion of rightness for Rawlsian contract theory, one flaw is it seems to exclude nonrational agents, not only nonhuman animals but also human beings who cannot make rational decisions, such as severely mentally impaired adults or infantile children. Moreover, no one is capable of fully divesting oneself entirely of prejudices, given that unless one lived in an actual original position, as opposed to the hypothetical one proposed by Rawls, one's education will inevitably influence their conception of "fairness." It is entirely possible that no two people completely agree on what constitutes a fair rule, principle, or policy. Furthermore, Rawls did not seem to consider the possibility that anyone in an original position behind a veil of ignorance would take a risk to benefit oneself, although such a possibility seems unlikely.

While the aforementioned problems may be written off as mere "nitpicking," a major problem applies both to Rawlsian and Hobbesian contract theory: What if the rules chosen by people are all *utilitarian* policies? Hobbesian contract theory seems to be a version of rule-utilitarianism with the assumptions of psychological egoism built into it. Perhaps it could be called "rule-egoism." In either case, it seems to be a consequential theory and, if so, it is subject to the same problems. But even if it is not a consequential theory, Hobbes suggests that the conditions of the state of nature are bad, implying that moral judgments can be made prior to the emergence of any social contract. With respect to Rawls, it is entirely possible that from behind the veil of ignorance, people simply employ the principle of utility, simply embracing the principle that everyone ought to maximize pleasure and minimize pain and rely on rules of thumb that do so. Nonetheless, it is helpful to have rules of thumb specified by a contract, and to maximize the minimum distribution of resources seems reasonable. But neither seems to form a solid foundation for morality.

## Kantian Ethics

Kantian ethics derive from the writings of the eighteenth-century German philosopher Immanuel Kant. Kant argued that reason is the basis of morality. Recall the principle "ought implies can," the idea that if one is *obligated* to perform some action, one at least *must be able* to perform the action in question. In other words, for morality to be possible, it must be possible to hold people responsible for their actions. But unless people have free will, then no one can be held responsible for their actions. Morality, thus, rests on free will. Freedom, however, entails that one can act without either *external* constraints (such as an individual putting a gun to your head or chaining you to a wall) or *internal* constraints. Internal constraints would include psychological compulsions and passions. To be free of one's passions, however, requires the faculty of reason to counterbalance them. Thus, free will requires reason since without reason one would merely be a slave to one's passions. If free will requires reason and morality requires free will, then morality requires reason.

Through reason, Kant maintained that we can discover the one thing that is good without qualification in addition to several moral absolutes. For Kant, the one thing good without qualification is the **goodwill:**

- The **goodwill** is a person who does one's duty because it is one's duty and for no other reason.

According to Kant, the goodwill is the only thing that can be added to any situation without making that situation morally worse. There are many things *intrinsically good* but not *good without qualification*. For instance, pleasure is intrinsically good, but reprehensible things can be done for the sake of pleasure. Intelligence is intrinsically good, but intelligence can be used to harm other people. Bodily health is intrinsically good, but healthy people can also be morally unsavory. Kant insists that even happiness cannot be the basis of morality since many individuals might be content to forgo ultimate happiness if doing so requires too much effort. Moreover, people can act in bad ways for the sake of their happiness.

Connected with Kant's concept of the goodwill is the notion of *moral worth.* Ultimately, Kant insists that only those actions done *for the sake of duty*, or *from duty*, have moral worth. For instance, if an individual returns a lost wallet merely because it is the right thing to do, then one's action has moral worth, as one acted from the motive of duty. However, if one returned the lost wallet only because one desired a reward, then one did the right thing, but one's action lacks moral worth. In the second scenario, one acted *merely in accordance with duty.*

For Kant, morality consists of a set of **categorical imperatives**, which must be distinguished from **hypothetical imperatives**:

- A **categorical imperative** is a universal, exceptionless command.
- **Hypothetical imperatives**, by contrast, are "if ..., then ..." imperatives.

Just as morality demands free will and reason, it demands that right and wrong are *absolute*. Through the categorical imperative, moral absolutes can be ascertained. Kant offers several formulations of the categorical imperative, the two most famous of which are the following:

- **The Universal Law Formula:** Act only on that maxim that you can will to be a universal law.
- **The End-in-Itself Formula:** Act only in such a way that you always treat humanity, either in your own person or that of another, as an end-in-itself and never as a means merely.

Each formula deserves further consideration.

## The Universal Law Formula

The universal law formula, in less technical terminology, basically states that one should not act on a "maxim," a rule of intent, unless everyone universally could follow such a rule. For example, suppose that Harold O. is thinking of acting on the maxim "I will lie to the loan officers at the bank whenever I need money." Before acting on this maxim, Harold should ask himself, "Can I live in a world where everyone follows this rule?" If everyone acted on such a maxim, then it would result in a world in which everyone went to their local bank to lie about repaying a loan but a world, thus, in which banks would not exist, since all banks would go bankrupt! Hence, not everyone can act on Harold's maxim to lie about repaying a loan. Thus, the maxim should be rejected. Kant maintained that reason ultimately justifies the decision to reject the maxim in question, as attempting to universalize it resulted in a contradiction. Prima facie, the universal law formula seems like a version of the Golden Rule, which holds, "Do unto others as you would them do unto you." The difference between the two formulas, however, is that the latter emphasizes *preference*. According to the Golden Rule, if an individual happens to be a sadomasochist, then such an individual may torture people! The universal law formula, however, emphasizes universality, permitting people to act only in ways that *everyone else* can.

## The End-in-Itself Formula

Kant insists that rational agents are ends-in-themselves since they both give value to objects that otherwise would lack value and have free will, thus, can choose their own goals, their own ends. For example, a tool, such as an ax would not have any purpose if a human being did not exist to use it. The same may be said about other everyday items, such as pencils, pens, paper, markers, or brooms. Humans, thus, are a *source of value*. Moreover, freedom not only makes morality possible but also makes possible the pursuit of distinctly human goals, as the quality of free will distinguishes humans from other animals. Our actions, thus, must respect the freedom and value of humanity. Thus, when formulating a maxim, one must make sure that the maxim does not permit the use of any person as a *means merely.* The term "merely" is important. Kant would permit the use of a person as a means. People are used as means quite frequently. If a friend helps you move furniture, you use your friend as a means. If a clerk at a store helps you to locate an item, you use the clerk as a means. But neither of these cases nor most others constitute the use of persons as *mere means.* To treat a person as a mere means is to treat a person as one would an inanimate object, with no respect for the person's value or freedom. For instance, imagine that a student needs assistance with math homework, and they acquire the help by kidnapping a mathematician and keeping the person in a cage until the tutelage provided can yield the student a grade of A. Such a situation treats a person as a *mere* means. In fact, any time one wills a maxim that cannot be universalized, the maxim in question likely fails to respect people as ends-in-themselves since the maxim conflicts with rationality.

## Perfect and Imperfect Duties

Kant distinguished between **perfect** and **imperfect duties.** Succinctly, they can be distinguished in the following way:

- The opposite of a **perfect duty** is not even conceivable as a law of nature.
- The opposite of an **imperfect duty** is conceivable as a law of nature, but one that cannot be consistently willed.

For example, recall the example of Harold O. considering whether to lie to loan officers. If everyone acted on his maxim, it would result in a world where banks exist but also where banks do not exist, a blatant contradiction. Such a contradiction is not even conceivable as a law of nature. Thus, we have a *perfect duty not to lie.* Kant also insists that we have a perfect duty *not to commit suicide* since universalizing a maxim to end one's life results in a world that is not even conceivable. That is, even if you can imagine such a world, you still must imagine yourself alive as an observer!

As for imperfect duties, Kant lists the duty to *develop one's talents* and the duty to *help those in dire need.* For example, imagine a world where all people with the talent to become physicians never developed such a talent. It is possible that such a world can exist, but if anyone were to become sick, one would not want to live in such a world. One would want and need the services of a physician. The same conclusion applies to the duty to help those in dire need. Suppose an individual decides to never help anyone, whether it be donating money to charity, saving a life, etc. Whatever the situation, he refuses to help. However, he might need help one day, in which case he would depend on receiving aid from others.

## Assessing Kant

Whereas religious moral theories claim that religion is the ground of morality, Kant insisted that morality serves as the ground for religion, for rational faith. Not only does morality imply free will, but it implies immortality and the existence of God as well. For Kant, morality demands that one act from duty, doing the right thing solely because it is the right thing. However, people are motivated by many different factors, so much so that no one can ever truly be certain that one acts purely from the motive of duty. Doing so, thus, would require an infinite amount of time during which one can achieve perfect virtue. Morality, hence, implies immortality. Moreover, perfect justice implies that the good are rewarded and the wicked punished. Otherwise, morality is arbitrary and one's actions are in vain. Thus, morality demands the existence of a God to reward the good and punish the wicked.

Despite how thoroughly Kant crafted his moral philosophy, many thinkers still found flaws in his system, two of which are most troublesome. First, Kant's theory seems *unable to resolve conflicts of duty.* For example, suppose that a murderer shows up at your house asking for the whereabouts of your friend. Suppose also that your friend, in fact, is in your kitchen. What should you do? You have a perfect duty to tell the truth and an imperfect duty to help those in dire need. Since the former is a perfect duty, it seems to take priority over the latter, which is highly counterintuitive. To resolve this dilemma, it seems necessary to invoke consequential reasoning, lying because it is necessary to save a life.[7]

Second, Kant's theory *does not seem to apply in all situations*, such as a crowded lifeboat. On a crowded lifeboat, if someone is not ejected, everyone dies. I cannot throw anyone off the boat since doing so treats the person as a mere means. But I cannot jump off the boat either since doing so commits suicide. Once again, it seems as though consequential reasoning is the only way to justify saving lives.

Before writing off Kant completely, it may be stated in his defense that in a later writing, *The Metaphysics of Morals*, he specified that if there is any conflict of duties created by one's situation, the agent may *simply choose* which duty to fulfill, even though there seems to be no basis for such a choice in his moral philosophy except that moral agents are ends-in-themselves and, hence, sources of value. Moreover, Kant also contends that even though we can never be sure that any pure act of goodwill ever occurred, such actions must be possible and the fact that people occasionally are willing to give their lives to save another demonstrates the possibility that one can act for the good of another when one stands to gain nothing in return. Hence, if one willingly sacrifices oneself in the "lifeboat scenario," one does not merely treat oneself as a means but perhaps achieves the perfect virtue of goodwill Kant idolized. Perhaps a deeper understanding of virtue ethics can aid in the understanding of Kant.[8]

## Virtue Ethics

The theories previously addressed emphasized the process of deciding how one ought to act in various situations in addition to the formulation of general principles and rules to guide actions attempting to answer the question, "What should I do?" Proponents of **Virtue Ethics**, on the other hand, take as their focus the question, "What kind of person should I be?" Such thinkers insist that people should concern themselves with developing the necessary character traits that make one a "good person." If one is a good person, then one will always act in the best possible way. More specifically, the famous ethicist, James Rachels claims that a virtue theory of ethics attempts to accomplish four goals:

1) Define "virtue" in general.
2) Provide a list of virtues.
3) Explain each virtue on the list.
4) Explain why it is good to have each virtue.[9]

---

7 For Kant's treatment of this specific problem, see his "On the Supposed Right to Lie from Philanthropic Concerns." Kant's central argument is that one should be honest with the murderer because if one is honest, does one's duty, one cannot be held responsible for the consequences. Kant often seemed willing to bite the proverbial bullet when his theories came under attack!

8 Students interested in pursuing Kant further should begin with his *Groundwork for the Metaphysics of Morals.* The Paton translation has a very helpful commentary. There is also a very valuable anthology of essays on Kant moral theory.

9 See Rachels, *Elements,* 169–80.

Defining "virtue" is comparably easy since Aristotle did it for us! The English word "virtue" derives from the Latin term "virtus," meaning "excellence." This term has its parallel in ancient Greek, "arete," hence the reason the ethical systems of Greek philosophers such as Aristotle and his mentor, Plato, are called *Aretaic Ethics*. As the term is understood today, "virtue" generally refers to a character trait representative of an excellent individual, in other words, an attribute that makes one a good person. Aristotle's more precise definition is the following:

- A **virtue** is a character trait developed through practice over a long period of time and constitutes *a mean between extremes* of action, one of *excess* and one of *deficiency*.

Based on this definition, possessing any one specific virtue demands much time, effort, experience, and exposure to situations that avail an agent the opportunity to develop the trait in question. Moreover, like most activities in life, to develop any one virtue requires that one find the "Goldilocks" position between opposing extremes. Virtue ethics in general is best understood by using concrete examples of the specific virtues.

## What Are the Virtues, and Why Is It Good to Have Them?

Dozens of character traits may be listed as virtues, and many societies and organizations provide their own list of virtues as part of a code of conduct. Often, people will say, "Patience is a virtue," meaning that it is good to possess the trait of patience. In the East, the Samurai operated according to the *Bushido Code*—honor, loyalty, justice, courage, veracity, and benevolence. Recall also that Confucius and his followers specified desirable traits that all people should strive to achieve, such as the attributes to which the seeds of the heart listed by Mengzi give rise. Aristotle, in fact, listed 11 virtues that are necessary to achieve happiness. In the interest of saving space, this section will address the four cardinal virtues: **justice, courage, moderation**, and **prudence**. The English word "cardinal" derives from the Latin "cardo," meaning "hinge." The cardinal virtues are so called, thus, because they are the traits on which one's character *hinges*.

Since Aristotle specifies that a virtue is a mean between extremes of action, **moderation** (also known as **temperance**) is a central virtue. Basically, *moderation* means *self-control*, the ability to *avoid self-indulgence on the one hand and asceticism on the other*. In other words, one has moderation if one avoids doing too much or too little of some activity. For example, if one is supposed to be on a diet but is invited to a holiday barbecue, one should see the event as an opportunity to "cheat" on one's diet but not as an opportunity to gorge oneself with junk food and alcohol. This example implies the answer to the question of why anyone should strive to achieve moderation: *because lack of self-control will make one unhappy*. If one eats none of the delicacies at the barbecue, one misses out on the benefits of the celebration. But if one takes too much, not only does one fail at one's diet but also potentially becomes sick and/or inebriated, leading to potential health and legal problems.

A similar analysis can be made of the virtue of **courage**. Often, when asked to define this virtue a student answers, "Courage is the absence of fear," or "Courage is not being afraid." While such a definition certainly applies to scenarios in which one inevitably encounters fear, it is still erroneous. Recall that all virtues are means between extremes. *Courage* may be understood as the mean between *rashness*, the vice of excess, and *cowardice*, the vice of deficiency. For example, suppose that Anthony A. spent the previous three months of his life training at an MMA gym, not only learning how to win fights in competition but also learning some practical self-defense techniques. Suppose that Anthony gets a new haircut, a mohawk, and that an acquaintance, Jeffry B., makes a wisecrack about it. If Anthony hauls off and delivers a right cross to Jeff's face, breaking his nose, his response to Jeff does not constitute courage but *rashness*. Jeff's actions posed no true threat to Anthony, giving him no good reason to fight. However, suppose that while Anthony exits a grocery store late one night, he witnesses an older woman being accosted by an armed assailant. Not wanting to risk injury before one of his MMA fights, Anthony simply ignores the scenario and walks away. This second scenario demonstrates the opposite extreme, *cowardice*.

How could Anthony demonstrate *courage*? Essentially, if he switched his behavior in each scenario, he would more closely approximate courage. In the first scenario, simply ignoring Jeff's heckling would be the courageous act. In the second, intervening in some way would be courageous. Perhaps Anthony could approach the two subjects and get the attention of the assailant to calm the woman, fighting only if it is necessary to protect her and himself. Moreover, in the second scenario, and those like it, fighting is *not even necessary* to demonstrate courage. Even if Anthony had no fighting ability whatsoever, simply calling the police and trying to help the woman would be courageous. Just as it is good to possess moderation, it is good to possess courage, too, since in life one will likely face several dangerous situations and one must know how to act in those situations. One must not be rash and needlessly injure oneself and/or others but one should not live as a coward either, as that can be worse than death. As Shakespeare wrote in *Julius Cesar*, "Cowards die many times before their deaths. The valiant never taste of death but once."

The virtue of courage demands moderation, self-control, but also *knowledge* of how to act in specific situations. Courage, thus, demands the virtue of **prudence**. *Prudence* may be defined as *wisdom*, more specifically, as knowledge of what is best for oneself and how to achieve it. Aristotle places prudence at the midpoint between *deviousness* (excess) and *gullibility* (deficiency). Deviousness, hence, may be described as prudence unrestrained by moderation, using one's intelligence to manipulate and harm others for one's benefit. Such a vice seems to imply intellectual hubris, given the willingness of a devious individual to use others. Gullibility, on the other hand, implies not only a lack of intelligence but vulnerability to the machinations of those who are devious, con artists, schemers. Prudence, thus, implies that one knows how to use one's knowledge both for one's own good and the good of others. Prudence also consists in the ability to recognize a greater good and makes sacrifices to achieve it. Courage and moderation both seem to demand prudence, implying a unity of these three virtues. One cannot have moderation without understanding and knowing one's limits—hence, without prudence. One cannot have courage without recognizing limits and knowing when and how to act—hence, without prudence. Moreover, even prudence seems to demand courage and moderation, since prudence demands self-control and be willing to accept one's limitations.

The only virtue left to address is **justice**. While Aristotle classified justice as an economic virtue, his mentor, Plato, considered justice to be *the goal of human life*, the *chief function of the human soul*. Just as it is the function of the eye to see, the ear to hear, and the body to be healthy, the soul's function is to achieve *justice*. For Plato, justice emerges *holistically* once the soul has the other three cardinal virtues. Hence, justice is the condition of having a completely balanced and healthy *soul*, analogous to the physical health achieved by the body through homeostasis.

As stated previously, many other character traits may be listed as virtues. However, the challenge of *incompleteness* deserves to be addressed before closing the present chapter.

## The Problem of Incompleteness[10]

Remember that virtue ethics aims to establish why virtues are good, why possessing such character traits makes one a better person, improving one's own life and the lives of others. However, *explaining why the virtues are good requires more than virtue theory alone*. For instance, the answer to "Why is courage good?" is "Life can be dangerous but possessing courage helps one to overcome the danger, thereby making one's life better and improving the world overall." Such an answer uses both egoism and utilitarianism to justify the pursuit of courage. Similar problems arise for the virtues of moderation and prudence as well, in that their justification seems to demand some form of consequential reasoning.

10 See Rachels, *Elements*, 182–84, for treatment of this problem. See Wolff, *An Introduction*, 292–96, for additional challenges to virtue ethics.

Proponents of other theories might invoke social contract theories, suggesting that one should strive to develop courage, moderation, and prudence because one agreed to improve oneself continually and progressively as part of the social contract. But remember that the social contract, too, exists to serve the greater good, which makes its very justification consequential in nature, at least in part. One might also appeal to religious moral theories, suggesting that God rewards those who are courageous, wise, and tempered, an appeal that also cloaks a consequential warrant. Lastly, one might appeal to Kant's moral philosophy, suggesting that all rational agents have a duty to pursue virtues such as courage, moderation, and prudence, striving to make oneself into the elusive goodwill. But even Kant's moral philosophy flirts with consequentialism, given that the procedure for evaluating maxims and general rules emphasizes the hypothetical results in the possible world that would ensue if everyone followed such rules.

In addition, *virtue ethics struggles to resolve moral conflicts*. For example, consider two potential virtues not defined thus far: loyalty and honesty. Suppose my childhood friends, Shaun and Seth, rob a bank. I know about their crime because they asked me to aid in the robbery, but I refused. As a known associate of the two, the police question me. What should I do? On the one hand, I should be loyal to my friends, but I also have the duty to be honest, especially since I may be charged as an accessory if I withhold information. Suppose I choose to be loyal to my friends and my reason for doing so is that the police have no concrete evidence or witnesses to make an arrest, and I want to maintain my friendships. Once again, I employed consequential reasoning to decide how to act.

One final way critics argue that virtue ethics is incomplete is that *there is no specific virtue that corresponds to every good reason* that can be marshaled to justify some actions. For instance, if I wish to donate money to charity, I have multiple options. I can give the money to Oxfam, to the Salvation Army, to a local pediatric hospital, to organizations that sponsor homeless shelters, and/or several others. Suppose I decide that donating the money to Oxfam will produce the greatest good. What specific virtue did I employ? It seems that once again I simply employed good ole' consequential reasoning! Hence, for all its benefits and lofty aspirations, virtue ethics along with the other moral theories addressed in this chapter seems to collapse into consequentialism. Or *does* it?

## Virtue Ethics: The Basis for Morality?

While pursuing an MA in philosophy at Northern Illinois University, one of my teachers, Professor James Hudson, once remarked, "Everyone, *at bottom*, is a consequentialist." Professor Hudson himself seemed to embrace a form of hedonistic utilitarianism with some modifications. Nonetheless, the results of this chapter seem to confirm Prof. Hudson's suspicion about the basis for morality. However, virtue ethics deserves a closer examination before dismissing it. Recall that the early Greeks, specifically Plato, often argued for the *unity of the virtues*. That is, no one can possess one virtue without possessing the others. Plato specifically seemed to have the four cardinal virtues in mind. Recall that one of the virtues is prudence, of which the most succinct definition is wisdom. In the examples in which consequential reasoning is employed, one may also be described as employing *prudence*, in which case, one may just as easily argue that *prudence is the basis for consequential reasoning*. Moreover, the ability to produce the greater good despite one's own personal, subjective preference demonstrates *moderation*, self-control. Furthermore, the process of thinking before committing to a final decision requires that one not act rashly. And when one addresses a problem that causes others to struggle and attempts to alleviate that problem, one certainly demonstrates *courage*. Collectively, one achieves justice by employing these virtues and one may easily argue that they are the basis for pursuing the greatest possible good. Hence, perhaps being a just person, having a just character is necessary to employ consequential reasoning effectively when a situation demands it.

In addition, recall that the different versions of consequentialism, too, are limited and seem to point to a deeper more rudimentary foundation for morality beyond the quantity of pleasure and pain produced by an action, hence why moral philosophers such as Kant suggested that morality demands the postulates of both immortality and God. Plato suggested that the pursuit of justice constitutes participation in the Form of the Good itself, a transcendent and eternal absolute. And the belief in a higher power can enhance one's life even if it cannot by itself produce a suitable foundation for morality. Why? Because it seems that a being like a God is necessary to ensure that justice is done! While the author will not suggest that any ONE of these theories is the best, he can suggest a pattern by which consequentialism, Kant's ethics, virtue ethics, and religion can collaborate to aid in living a moral life and making moral decisions:

1) Strive to develop the cardinal virtues—prudence, moderation, courage, and justice. How can one achieve these virtues? Emulate those who have them and expose oneself to situations that demand them.
2) Before acting, always ask yourself two questions:
   a. Can I live in a world where everyone acted on the same principle? If the answer is no, then DO NOT act in such a way.
   b. Will my actions treat anyone as a means merely? If the answer is yes, then DO NOT act in such a way.
3) In a situation where any course of action you take may yield negative results, simply do what you can to produce the best possible outcome.
4) Have FAITH! Believe that your actions are not in vain and work to produce a world that achieves the greatest justice possible.

No person is perfect and, thus, no situation will be totally perfect. Following this pattern will allow you to account for the finite wisdom of humanity and strive for its improvement.[11]

## Chapter Summary and Key Points to Remember

This chapter provided an overview of the most common moral theories and assessed their advantages and flaws.

- **Relativistic moral theories** suggest that there are no *universal* moral absolutes. They include the following:
  - **Individual relativism**, by which actions are right if an agent simply thinks they are right.
  - **Ethical relativism**, by which actions are right if an agent's social group says they are right.
  - **Cultural relativism**, an anthropological theory holding all cultures have different values and moral standards.
  - The main problems with relativistic theories are that they permit certain obviously wrong actions, make morality arbitrary, imply that all individuals and/or their social groups are infallible, and undermine moral progress. Also, there is evidence that all societies share some values, such as honesty, loyalty, courage, and respect for persons.

11 For further information on virtue ethics, consult Plato's *Republic*, specifically Books I–IV; Aristotle's *Nicomachean Ethics*, Books I–III; Elizabeth Anscombe's article, "Modern Moral Philosophy"; and Alasdair McIntyre's *After Virtue*.

- The following often either collapse into a form of moral relativism or are embraced *because* of it:
    - **Moral nihilism**, by which there are no moral absolutes.
    - **Moral skepticism**, by which there may be moral absolutes, but they cannot be known with any certainty.
    - **Moral dogmatism**, which is the uncritical, unreflective acceptance of moral principles perpetuated by one's authorities.
    - **Emotivism**, the idea that morality reduces to emotions, i.e., those actions that elicit positive emotions are good, while those that elicit negative emotions are bad.
        - An additional school of thought maintains that moral assertions merely are expressions of emotion. For instance, the claim "Donating to charity is good" translates into "Donating to charity makes me happy."
- In contrast to moral relativism, **moral objectivism**, by which there are universal, objective moral absolutes that can be discerned through reason.
- **Religious moral theories** suggest that religious beliefs are the basis for moral absolutes. They include the following:
    - **Divine command theory (DCT)**, by which actions are right simply *because* God commands them.
        - The main problem with this theory is that it makes morality arbitrary since it would depend entirely on God's will. God may command a morally reprehensible action. However, if one objects that God would command obviously wrong actions, then one admits to a standard beyond God's will.
    - **Infallible guide theory (IGT)**, by which God commands actions *because* they are right.
        - The main problem with this theory, which also applies to DCT, is that there are problems figuring out what God commands. Even if one strictly follows a religious text, there are many different religious texts to choose, each of which has principles that conflict with those of other religions. And if one alleges that they communicate with God directly, such a claim cannot truly be verified.
    - **Natural law theory (NLT)**, which asserts that God designed everything such that everything in nature has a specific goal and/or purpose. Human beings, moreover, possess the "natural light" of reason to know their purpose, and to deviate from it is immoral.
        - The main problems with NLT are that there are several actions that do not seem to be natural but are not in themselves morally wrong, such as walking on one's hands, and NLT privileges the notion of natural teleology which most contemporary scientists reject.
    - Despite the flaws of religious moral theories, religious beliefs can enhance one's moral life since all religions perpetuate the notion of cosmic justice and the ultimate conquest of good over evil.
- **Consequential moral theories** suggest that the value of an action depends on its *results*. Positive results equal a good action, negative results equal a bad action. The most popular consequential moral theories are the following:
    - **Ethical egoism** maintains that everyone ought to act to produce what is best for oneself.
        - The main problems with ethical egoism are that it permits certain obviously wrong actions, fails to address how one's actions affect others, and is rooted in psychological egoism, the idea that people are incapable of acting contrary to their own self-interest, which seems false.

- **Utilitarianism** has many forms but the two most common are:
    - **Hedonistic act-utilitarianism (HAU),** which holds that everyone ought to attempt to maximize pleasure and minimize pain for all affected by one's actions.
        - The primary traditional objections to HAU are that it permits certain obviously wrong actions–mainly through its failure to accommodate individual rights, justice, or backward-looking reasons, is too narrow since pleasure and pain do not seem to be the only standards for right and wrong, is too demanding, and forces people to violate their special obligations to others.
    - **Rule-utilitarianism (RU)**, which holds that everyone ought to act in accordance with rules whose universal adoption would maximize pleasure and minimize pain for all affected by them.
        - The main problem with RU is that all rules have exceptions, in which case one must default to HAU consequential reasoning.

- **Social contract theories** suggest that morality emerges from agreements between people. Two popular forms of social contract theory are the following:
    - **Hobbesian contract theory,** based on the writings of the sixteenth-century English civil philosopher and scientist, Thomas Hobbes. Hobbes argued that without a set of agreements that can be enforced by a central ruling authority, people would descend into an undesirable and chaotic "state of nature." It is, thus, in the best interest of everyone to sacrifice some of their instinctive but selfish desires for the greater good.
    - **Rawlsian ideal contract theory**, based on the writings of the twentieth-century Harvard professor John Rawls. As an egalitarian, Rawls felt that resources should be distributed as equally as possible but without failing to account for individual needs and abilities. Such equality may be achieved if people place themselves in a hypothetical original position prior to any social arrangement situated behind a veil of ignorance, by which one knows nothing of one's status or privileges. Rawls believed that in such a situation, people will adopt rules and economic means of distribution that are fair for everyone, especially those least advantaged.
    - The main problem with both theories is that they seem to collapse into a form of RU. Both also seem to assume psychological egoism.

- **Kantian ethics** is rooted in the moral writings of the eighteenth-century German philosopher Immanuel Kant. His theory is often called *deontological* since it emphasizes the universality of moral duty. Themes in his moral philosophy include the following:
    - **Goodwill:** The only thing good without qualification, a person who does one's duty because it is one's duty and for no other reason.
    - **The Categorical Imperative:** A universal, exceptionless command. Kant gives several formulations of which the following are the most popular:
        - **The Universal Law Formula:** Act only on that maxim which you could will to be a universal law.
        - **The End-in-Itself Formula:** Act always so that you treat humanity, either in your own person or that of another, as an end-in-itself and never as a means merely.
    - **Perfect Duties:** Duties the opposite of which cannot even be conceived as universal laws (honesty, repaying a loan, not committing suicide).

- **Imperfect Duties:** Duties the opposite of which may be conceived as universal laws but cannot be consistently willed (developing one's talents, helping those in dire need).
- **The Postulates of Morality:** Kant insisted that the existence of God, the immortal soul, and free will must be assumed for the possibility of morality.
- The main problems with Kant's moral philosophy are that he provides no obvious procedure for resolving conflicts of duty, and thus that situations may arise in which one must defer to a more flexible moral theory such as utilitarianism.

- **Virtue ethics** emphasizes character development, urging its proponents to achieve character traits called virtues. By becoming a good person, one will always know how to act. This chapter emphasized the following aspects of virtue ethics:
    - **Aristotle's Definition of Virtue:** A character trait acquired through habitual practice that is a mean between two extremes of activity or feeling, one of excess and the other of deficiency.
    - **The Four Cardinal Virtues: Prudence**, wisdom, forethought, and/or practical intelligence; **moderation**, self-control; **courage**, strength of character, the ability to persevere despite fear or temptation; and **justice**, a holistic virtue that emerges when one possesses the previous three (a "just soul" is comparable to a "healthy body").
    - The main problem with virtue ethics is that it seems incomplete, given that explaining why the virtues are good, the resolution of moral conflict, and the ability to justify some actions require more than merely the virtues themselves. Typically, consequentialism seems necessary in such cases.
    - However, the idea of the **unity of virtue**—the idea that cannot possess one virtue without possessing all others as well—seems to indicate that virtue is a basis for being able to engage in moral reasoning in addition to more general kinds of reasoning, such as consequentialism. Virtue ethics should not be dismissed merely because of the challenge of incompleteness.

## Exercises for Application and Reflection

**Instructions:** Use what you learned in this chapter to help you respond to the following questions.

1. In Book II of Plato's *Republic*, Socrates's primary interlocutor, Glaucon, presents the fable of the ring of Gyges. In summary, the fable concerns a shepherd in Lydia, Gyges, who finds a ring that can make him invisible. He ultimately uses the ring to seduce his Queen, kill his King, and usurp the throne of his kingdom. The dilemma posed by this fable is simple: *Why should anyone be moral if they can get away with crime for their own benefit?*
    a. First, try to answer this question without making a direct reference to any of the moral theories presented in this chapter.
    b. Next, answer the question by appealing to utilitarianism, Kant's ethics, and virtue ethics.
2. Choose any theory presented in this chapter and explain how it is possible for one of its proponents to commit all four of Bacon's idols of the mind.
3. Choose any theory presented in this chapter and explain how it is possible for one of its proponents to display any four cognitive biases in maintaining that theory.

4. Choose your favorite theory presented in this chapter and explain at least three reasons why it is better than any other theory. Then, state at least one problem with your theory and explain how that problem can be resolved.
5. Choose your least favorite theory presented in this chapter and explain at least three reasons why it is worse than any other theory. Then, present an argument in favor of this theory.
6. Explain a moral dilemma that you experienced in your life. Then, explain how you resolved that dilemma and how the knowledge of moral theories you learned in this chapter could have helped you.
7. Choose one of the following moral issues and write a brief position essay on it (that is, defend a position on it, arguing whether it is morally justified or not): the death penalty, global poverty and famine relief, affirmative action and reverse discrimination, gun control, cloning, biomedical enhancement therapies, cosmetic surgeries, gender reassignment, in vitro fertilization, abortion, euthanasia, or homosexuality.
8. A moral argument can be criticized in one of three ways: (a) one can challenge the structure of the argument (whether the argument is valid or invalid, whether the argument's terms are clear, and/or whether the argument's premises are stated clearly); (b) one can challenge the facts on which the argument is based (usually, that would mean challenging the factual premise(s) of the argument); or (c) one can challenge the moral theory on which the argument is based (usually, that would mean challenging the moral premise(s) of the argument). For example, consider the following argument:

   (P1) Murder is wrong.
   (P2) The death penalty is murder.
   (C) Therefore, the death penalty is wrong.

   In this argument, (P1) is the moral premise, a normative, prescriptive statement about what is right or wrong, whereas (P2) constitutes the factual premise, a descriptive statement about reality. Keeping this information in mind, do the following:

   a) Assess the previous argument on the death penalty. Is it valid? Are its terms clear? Are its premises clearly stated? Is its factual premise correct? Is its moral premise correct? Which moral theory is the argument based on, and does it interpret that theory correctly?
   b) Create a simple moral argument using any other issue listed in question (7) except for the death penalty or the issue you chose for your essay and complete the same assessment as in (a).
   c) Go back to the argument you developed in question (7) and reconstruct it in the simplest way possible. Try to narrow your argument down to two concise premises and the conclusion. Then, conduct the same assessment as in (a) and (b).

# Conclusion

Journeys usually come full circle, and our journey is no exception. In the introduction to this book, the author contended that critical thinking is not only inevitable but *necessary*. It *was* necessary for humanity to emerge and develop into its current form as the rulers of a planet despite their inherent flaws and weaknesses and the remarkably low probability of succeeding. It *is* necessary for humanity to sustain its existence and correct those of its errors that had a deleterious effect on that planet and those within it. And critical thinking *always will be* necessary if humanity is to remain *human*. Just as a journey of 1,000 miles begins with a single step, the quest for meaning in life begins with critical thinking. After reading this text, you should possess a set of skills that will not only enable you to analyze and address a wide variety of problems in many diverse contexts that resist easy solutions but you should also have a deeper and renewed commitment to your own life and the lives of others. In short, your skills ultimately come down to abiding by one simple and concise but difficult maxim: ***know thyself!*** This text provided the tools by which to do so in the following ways:

- The chief proponent of "knowing thyself" is Socrates, a viable and reputable role model who lived a just and modest life and died to set a standard of integrity and courage that few have ever matched. Hopefully, none of us will ever be in a situation like that of Socrates. The late, great Bertrand Russell once remarked that he would never die for his beliefs since his beliefs may be wrong! At the very least, Russell emulated the intellectual humility of Socrates! Nonetheless, if there are critical thinkers in the world with a forum to voice their educated opinions, no one will ever be forced to choose between death and freedom of thought.
- In keeping with the Socratic admonition to "know thyself," such self-knowledge should now include awareness of general obstacles to critical thinking, specifically the idols of the mind and cognitive biases, flaws and habits within human nature that not only make us susceptible to errors but in fact predestine humanity to make egregious errors in both reasoning and judgments that can drastically affect the world and the lives of those within it. Awareness of a problem usually makes it easier to avoid. Hopefully, going forward, you will see the pit before you fall into it!
- The possession of knowledge in any form, including "knowing thyself," will inevitably include an understanding of what precisely constitutes knowledge in general in addition to an understanding of truth and how it differs from belief and opinion. Certainly, one must know how one's beliefs and ideas are acquired, formed, and justified and how to distinguish the subjective contents of one's mind from the objectively real, external world.
- Knowing oneself implies consistency in thought and action, *coherence*. The ability to recognize coherence and eliminate inconsistencies requires an understanding of logic and the basic forms of reasoning.
- Separating one's passions and arbitrary preferences from issues that deserve objective consideration and evaluation requires an understanding of arguments and the ability to distinguish valid from invalid arguments, sound from unsound arguments, strong from weak arguments, and cogent from uncogent arguments.

- The ability to avoid informal fallacies usually will require one to put one's personal feelings and preferences aside and carefully consider the claims and opinions of others objectively. "Knowing thyself" means knowing when one is wrong and others are right, having both the humility and courage to admit so.
- Finally, one must have a strong grasp of morality and how to discern right from wrong. One must at least be able to carefully consider how to act in a wide variety of situations, specifically those in which one's decisions affect the well-being of others. Every moral theory considered in this text required the individual to consider their own point of view but not to act with bias toward it. Nonetheless, one must always work to develop and train one's character not only to do the right thing but to *desire to do the right thing.*

Unquestionably, applying the skills afforded by this text will involve much trial and error, but with time, habitual effort, and experience, one will, to paraphrase Kierkegaard, "become that self—one truly is," a moral animal with a rational soul refined by the use and cultivation of reason.

## Selective Bibliography


Aaronson, Eliot. *The Social Animal.* 12th ed. New York: Worth Publishers, 2018.

Aristotle. *The Politics.* 2nd ed. Translated by Carnes Lord. Chicago: University of Chicago Press, 2013.

Arthur, John. "Morality, Religion, and Conscience." In *Morality and Moral Controversies: Readings in Moral, Social, and Political Philosophy*, edited by John Arthur and Steven Scalet, 25–32. New York: Routledge, 2016.

Baggini, Julian, and Peter S. Fosl. *The Philosopher's Toolkit.* 3rd ed. Hoboken, NJ: Wiley-Blackwell, 2020.

Baronet, Stan. *Logic.* 4th ed. New York: Oxford University Press, 2018.

Berkeley, George. "An Idealist Theory of Knowledge." In *The Theory of Knowledge: Classical and Contemporary Readings.* 2nd ed., edited by Louis P. Pojman, 89–96. Boston: Cengage, 2003.

Chaffee, John. *Thinking Critically.* 12th ed. Boston: Cengage, 2019.

Copi, Irving, Carl Cohen, and Victor Rodych. *Introduction to Logic.* 15th ed. New York: Routledge–Taylor & Francis Group, 2019.

Durant, Will. *The Story of Philosophy.* New York: Pocket Books/Simon & Schuster, 2006.

Gettier, Edmund. "Is Justified True Belief Knowledge?" In *The Theory of Knowledge: Classical and Contemporary Readings.* 2nd ed., edited by Louis P. Pojman, 121–23. Boston: Cengage, 2003.

Heick, Terry. "The Cognitive Bias Codex: A Complete List of 180+ Cognitive Biases." Teach Thought, October 19, 2020, https://www.teachthought.com/critical-thinking/the-cognitive-bias-codex-a-visual-of-180-cognitive-biases/.

Herrick, Paul. *Think with Socrates: An Introduction to Critical Thinking.* New York: Oxford University Press, 2015.

Hurley, Patrick, and Lori Watson. *A Concise Introduction to Logic.* 13th ed. Boston: Cengage, 2017.

Kant, Immanuel. *Groundwork for the Metaphysics of Morals.* Translated by H. J. Paton. New York: HarperCollins Publishers, 2009.

Kelly, David, and Debbie Hutchins. *The Art of Reasoning.* New York: Norton & Norton, 2020.

Kuhn, Thomas. *The Structure of Scientific Revolutions.* 4th ed. Chicago: University of Chicago Press, 2012.

Locke, John. *Essay Concerning Human Understanding.* Rev. ed. New York: Oxford University Press, 1979.

McInerny, D.Q. *Being Logical: A Guide to Good Thinking.* New York: Random House, 2005.

Morris, Tom. *Philosophy for Dummies.* New York: Wiley Publishing, Inc., 1999.

Morrow, David. *Giving Reasons: An Extremely Short Introduction to Critical Thinking.* Indianapolis, IN: Hackett Publishing, Inc., 2017.

Nagel, Thomas. *The View from Nowhere.* New York: Oxford University Press, 1989.

Pojman, Louis. *Who Are We? Theories of Human Nature.* New York: Oxford University Press, 2005.

Rachels, James. *The Elements of Moral Philosophy.* 9th ed. New York: McGraw-Hill, 2019.

Reid, Thomas. "A Common-Sense Defense of Direct Realism." In *The Theory of Knowledge: Classical and Contemporary Readings.* 2nd ed., edited by Louise P. Pojman, 108–14. Boston: Cengage, 2003.

Rosenberg, Jay. *The Practice of Philosophy: A Handbook for Beginners.* London: Pearson, 1995.

Roth, Michael. *Beyond the University: Why Liberal Education Matters.* New Haven, CT: Yale University Press, 2014.

Russell, Bertrand. "A Defense of Representationalism." In *The Theory of Knowledge: Classical and Contemporary Readings.* 2nd ed., edited by Louise P. Pojman, 115–20. Boston: Cengage, 2003.

Ryle, Gilbert. *The Concept of Mind.* Chicago: University of Chicago Press, 1949.

Stace, Walter. "Science and the Physical World: A Defense of Phenomenalism." In *The Theory of Knowledge: Classical and Contemporary Readings.* 2nd ed., edited by Louise P. Pojman, 96–100. Boston: Cengage, 2003.

Stevenson, Leslie, David L. Haberman, and Peter Matthews Right. *Twelve Theories of Human Nature.* 6th ed. New York: Oxford University Press, 2013.

Thomson, Garret. *Bacon to Kant: An Introduction to Modern Philosophy.* 2nd ed. Long Grove, IL: Waveland Press Inc., 2012.

Whitley, C. J. "Phenomenalism: Its Grounds and Difficulties." In *The Theory of Knowledge: Classical and Contemporary Readings.* 2nd ed., edited by Louise P. Pojman, 100–7. Boston: Cengage, 2003.

Wolff, Jonathan. *An Introduction to Moral Philosophy.* New York: Norton & Norton, 2020.

Zakaria, Fareed. *In Defense of a Liberal Education.* New York: W. W. Norton & Company, 2015.

Printed in the USA
CPSIA information can be obtained
at www.ICGtesting.com
LVHW081520170824
788501LV00018B/47

9 781793 542045